Spa Vacations

Your Guide to Healing Centers and Retreats

Annalisa Cunningham

AVALON
TRAVEL

Spa Vacations:
Your Guide to Healing Centers and Retreats
First Edition

By Annalisa Cunningham

Published by
Avalon Travel Publishing
5855 Beaudry St.
Emeryville, CA 94608, USA

ISBN: 1-56691-316-0
ISSN: 1534-6684

Editor: Angelique S. Clarke
Series Manager: Angelique S. Clarke
Copy Editor: Ginjer Clarke
Index: Jeff Lupo
Graphics Coordinators: Melissa Sherowski, Erika Howsare
Design and Production: Amber Pirker

Front cover photo: © Ben Simmons/the Stock Market
Illustrations on pages 1, 31, 61, 101, 151, and 187: Barrett Cox

Distributed by Publishers Group West

Printed in China through Colorcraft Ltd., Hong Kong

Please send all comments, corrections, additions, amendments, and critiques to:

Spa Vacations:
Your Guide to Healing Centers and Retreats
Avalon Travel Publishing
5855 Beaudry St.
Emeryville, CA 94608, USA
email: info@travelmatters.com
www.travelmatters.com

Printing History
1st edition—September 2001
5 4 3 2 1

Contents

U.S. Spas and Healing Centers

Contents

International Spas and Healing Centers

Foreword

The spas of the eighties have past and a new generation of spas and retreats have begun to pop up all over the country. No longer content with quick, impersonal massages, individuals are seeking something more—something healing.

Healing means "to restore health, or wholeness." Resorts are now incorporating this philosophy into all of their amenities from the actual treatments down to the type of cuisine featured. However, everyone seeks out spa experiences for a variety of personal reasons, and different spas and retreats may be more attune to your needs. Some may find a relaxing stay on a white sandy beach pure bliss, while others might enjoy a twelve-mile trek in the Appalachians. But the point is that no matter what your desire, you definitely can find what your body and mind are looking for.

Having had the chance to "sample" many of the spas listed in this book, I understand the complexities that encompass choosing the right spa vacation. No two spas are alike; not only due to geographical differences but philosophical and technical as well. I have frequented spas where a black tie was required in the restaurant to spas where clothing is entirely optional—but the point is that both were what my body needed at that time.

Annalisa Cunningham has extensively (and exhaustively) researched retreats, resorts, and spas, in order to provide you with the most comprehensive spa guide around—and she has succeeded.

So, in your quest to find the place of your dreams keep one thing in mind. "What is healing to me?"

—Melissa Scott, Associate Editor
Healing Retreats and Spas magazine

Preface

I have long lived with a passion for healing. At 18 years old, I studied therapeutic massage. In my early 20s, I began practicing yoga. I also have a Master's degree in Counseling. Attending retreats, going to hot spring resorts, and visiting spas has always been my choice for vacation. The value of health and taking care of myself became apparent to me at a young age when my father died from cancer. Something struck a cord in me, and my own fear of getting sick became a motivation for exploring health. Once I became acquainted with various healing modalities, which I incorporated into my lifestyle, I reaped the benefits with a strong immune system and vitality for living. It feels good to feel good.

There are many paths for relaxation, health, and healing, and finding what works best for you is a personal choice. Exploring various spas and healing centers is a wonderful adventure. Taking responsibility for our health and well-being is empowering. We can do something about our nagging symptoms and illnesses. Even if an illness isn't cured, finding relaxation and increased peace of mind is healing in itself.

I used to believe spas were primarily places for pampering, weight loss and beauty treatments but these spas offer much more. Holistic health, wellness education and appreciation of the mind/body & spirit connection is a theme many spas now embrace.

My background as a massage therapist, yoga teacher, and counselor has allowed me to witness the profound healing and transformation that is possible in people's lives. I am in awe of the remarkable resilience of human nature and the deep reservoir of strength we have within. Healing is not always convenient—you have to take the time needed, find the support, and make daily positive lifestyle choices.

Getting away to an uplifting, relaxing, and healing environment can be the catalyst needed for letting go of stress and making positive changes. There's something wonderful about placing yourself in an environment away from your daily routine where you are there to be on the receiving end. Imagine receiving energy and relaxing treatments from various healers, education about positive lifestyle choices, exploration in meditation techniques, support from caring people, guided walks in nature, relaxing soaks in hot tubs, revitalizing fitness programs, wonderful meals that are prepared especially for you, and inspiration from an uplifting, beautiful environment.

That's what this book is all about: Getting away to a place where you can relax, renew your strength and energy, learn new skills for healthy living, and have fun. Everyone benefits when you take time out for a healing vacation—you, your family, and even the world benefits because we have more to give to others when we feel revitalized.

I offer this book with respect to the healer and adventurer within you that has guided you to these pages where opportunities abound. Life is precious. I invite you to stretch your potential toward wellness and have fun exploring the spa vacations and healing centers available to you. May you benefit with renewed health, peace, and joy.

How to Use This Book

Finding a Destination

This book is divided into five geographic regions within the United States—Atlantic, Southeast, Central, Pacific, and Southwest—followed by international destinations—Canada, Caribbean, and Mexico. States are in alphabetical order within each region.

You can search for your ideal Spa Vacation in two ways:

1. If you know the name of the spa or healing center you'd like to visit, look it up in the Spa index beginning on page 238, then turn to the corresponding page.

2. If you'd like to spend your Spa Vacation participating in a specific activity or treatment, using the activity symbols below, look it up in the Activity Index beginning on page 240 then turn to the corresponding spas or healing centers offering that activity or treatment.

What the Activity Symbols Mean

Spa listings in this book feature activity and treatment symbols, or combination of symbols. These symbols are not meant to be all encompassing, but are a quick way to identify some of the major treatments and activities offered at each spa. An expanded explanation of each symbol can be found in the Introduction.

 ***Beauty/Relaxation:*** skincare, beauty salon services, massage and bodywork treatments, exercise programs, sauna, or whirlpool

 Cleansing/Nutrition: education and supervised fasting and detoxification

 Fitness/Adventure: endurance hikes, swimming, aerobic classes, and other recreation

 Meditation: mindful meditation, chanting, walking the labyrinth, using a mantra (sound meditation), or breath awareness

Mineral Hot Springs: natural hot springs and mineral baths

Yoga: varying levels of stretches, postures, breathing exercises, and meditation

Introduction

In today's world of stress and hurry, we all need pampering, healing, and relaxation. Our lives are out of balance as we run around with lists of places to go, obligations to fulfill, and accomplishments to achieve. Living with daily traffic, noise, pollution, family concerns, and the demands of technology can dissipate our energy, adding stress to our lives. We all know that stress and tension have a negative impact on our health and well-being. In fact, we frequently hear of health reports listing stress as a contributing factor in various health conditions and ailments. Taking time out for relaxation, rest, and healing rejuvenation is essential to counteract the daily toll on our minds and bodies.

Spas and healing centers offer ideal settings and support for renewing our energy and restoring our well-being. What is a spa vacation? It is a vacation from your everyday life that pampers you, restores your health, and brings balance and integrity of body, mind, and spirit back into your life. Whether you are facing a physical, emotional, or spiritual challenge, or simply looking for a place to rejuvenate in a nurturing environment, a spa vacation has much to offer. These vacations include any combination of services and programs including, but not limited to: traditional beauty, exercise, and nutritional regimens; or non-Western regimens of body treatments, emotional clearing, energy healing, exercise, relaxation, and stress management. Some spas and healing centers provide medical staff for consultations and all centers provide plenty of knowledgeable staff to support you.

Positive Lifestyle Changes

A strong element of the featured vacations in this book is that they are not just one week in paradise followed by a return to business as usual. Instead they provide a basis for a healing shift on many levels—physical, mental, emotional, and spiritual—as we learn to embrace positive lifestyle changes. Improved health and peace are available to all of us when we place ourselves in a healing environment and are given the proper skills and knowledge for developing and maintaining these two precious gifts. Healing spas and retreats are ideal places for learning the skills of self-care and relaxation, renewing our sense of wellness and wholeness.

Taking Time for Healthy Living

This book is about taking the time to learn how to live a healthier life. It's about getting away from your daily grind, resting, and recovering from whatever ails you. It's about reconnecting with your inner healer and learning valuable skills for lifelong vitality. When you choose one of the getaways in this book, you are taking the first step toward reclaiming your health and well-being. Whether you spend three days, one week, or an entire month at a spa or healing center, even if you start out physically exhausted or spiritually depleted, you'll come home energized and committed to making positive changes in your life. And you'll learn through direct experience that total health encompasses body, mind, and spirit.

Activity Symbols for Vacation Listings

This book is a compilation of more than 100 vacation opportunities that provide a healing environment. The lines between spas and wellness retreats are blurring these days, based on appreciation of the mind/body spirit connection. Many spas offer holistic treatments along with standard services, including yoga, meditation, hot stone therapy, Ayurvedic treatments, Labyrinths, and more. In other words, spas and centers are listening to the needs of their guests and adding many dimensions to the services they offer. To make it easier to browse through the book and find the spa experience you want, I have developed eight symbols to represent some of the activities and services available at each spa. Check the top of each listing to find which symbol, or combination of symbols, is listed for a particular location. These symbols are not meant to be all encompassing, but are a quick way to identify major activities.

Beauty/Relaxation these listings offer a complete menu of skincare, beauty salon services, massage and bodywork treatments, as well as exercise programs and time for relaxation in the sauna or pool. Pampering is usually part of the package because the staff is there to assist you and help coordinate your stay.

Cleansing/Nutrition these listings provide staff, and often medical, support as guests cleanse their bodies and learn to establish healthier eating habits. Gentle exercise, bodywork treatments, and relaxation sessions are usually part of the program.

Fitness/Adventure these listings offer challenging exercise and recreation programs, along with healthy cuisine to improve health, stamina, and relaxation. Programs are usually balanced with massage, hot tubs, and relaxation.

Meditation these listings enable guests to learn techniques for quieting the mind such as sitting in silence, the practice of mindful meditation, chanting, walking the labyrinth, using a mantra (sound meditation), or breath awareness and meditation.

Mineral Hot Springs these listings have natural Hot Springs and mineral baths available to guests. Guests enjoy soaking in the warm and therapeutic baths. Massage treatments are often available to compliment the relaxing benefits of the mineral baths.

Yoga these listings offer specific techniques for balancing body, mind, and spirit. During yoga classes you participate in learning and practicing yoga postures, breathing exercises, and meditation.

Opportunities for improved health, renewal, relaxation, adventure, and fulfillment are in abundance in this book. More than 100 spas and healing centers are listed. Offered throughout the United States, Canada, and Mexico, these vacations provide an energizing spark that rekindles your zest for life and awakens your innate capacity for healing. Enjoy reading through all of the vacation possibilities within these pages and finding the right one for you.

Guide Notes

As you read through this book, you will find a wide variety of spas, healing retreats, and vacation opportunities. Listings are organized alphabetically within geographic region. Some centers have accompanying photographs. All listings provide overnight accommodations of varying lengths.

Once you determine which vacations you are most drawn to, contact the spa or retreat center to ask for a current brochure. Check listed websites as well. Take time to ask specific questions you may have about the center you are considering. In addition to what you read in this guide, you may want to find out more about the following information:

ACCOMMODATIONS: Sleeping arrangements come in all shapes and sizes. Each listing gives a brief description of what you can expect. Ask specific questions about the number of people per room, bed size, closet and drawer space, convenience to bathrooms, number of showers available, noise factors, and so forth.

RATES: Because rates and costs fluctuate constantly, the prices quoted in this book may have changed. Be sure to inquire about the current rates. Rate quotes don't always include taxes, services, gratuities, or all activities and travel expenses, so be sure to ask about these extra costs.

DIET: Most of the vacation packages in this guide include meals, but some do not. Read the descriptions carefully. Many of the listings state that special diets can be accommodated. If you have special dietary needs, specify your needs when making reservations.

Some packages include fasting programs and may introduce you to a new healing diets. Again, read descriptions carefully so you know what to expect before you arrive, and don't hesitate to ask questions.

SERVICES: Bodywork treatments are often a wonderful part of a spa or healing vacation. This heading tells you the specific treatments available at each center listed. Some spa and retreat packages include treatments with the cost of overnight stays, but others do not. If you are considering this wonderful indulgence, find out the fee and the time allotted.

RECREATIONAL ACTIVITIES: Many vacation settings offer recreational activities that participants can enjoy during their free time. Be sure to ask what the costs are for additional activities such as snorkeling, bus tours, boating, and so forth. Ask if equipment can be rented or if you need to bring your own.

HEALTH CONSIDERATIONS: Many of the vacations listed in this book are designed specifically to be beneficial for improving health. If you have any health concerns or challenges, be sure to let the reservationist know about your situation ahead of time. Make sure the vacation you choose is appropriate for your specific condition. Don't hesitate to ask questions. Wheelchair accessibility is listed under the heading **Disability Access.**

SPECIAL NOTES: Added information about each place is provided under this heading.

NEARBY ATTRACTIONS: Some people enjoy seeing surrounding sights and areas of interest while they are on vacation. During the time you are at the spa or retreat, you may not want to leave the grounds. You can plan to see areas of interest before or after your stay.

GETTING THERE: It's a good idea to check out low-cost flights, airports, and road travel advice before you make travel plans. Some healing retreats and spas provide maps and specific directions, which they will gladly send to you ahead of time. Under the **Nearest Airport** heading, you will find the best airport for the spa of your choice. This could be very important if the location of your selected spa is in a remote area or borders another state or province. Find out if airport, train station, or bus station pickup is provided and if someone will greet you when you arrive.

WEATHER: Weather can be unpredictable, but it's a good idea to have some indication of temperature highs and lows when you're packing for a trip. Ask for estimated weather reports.

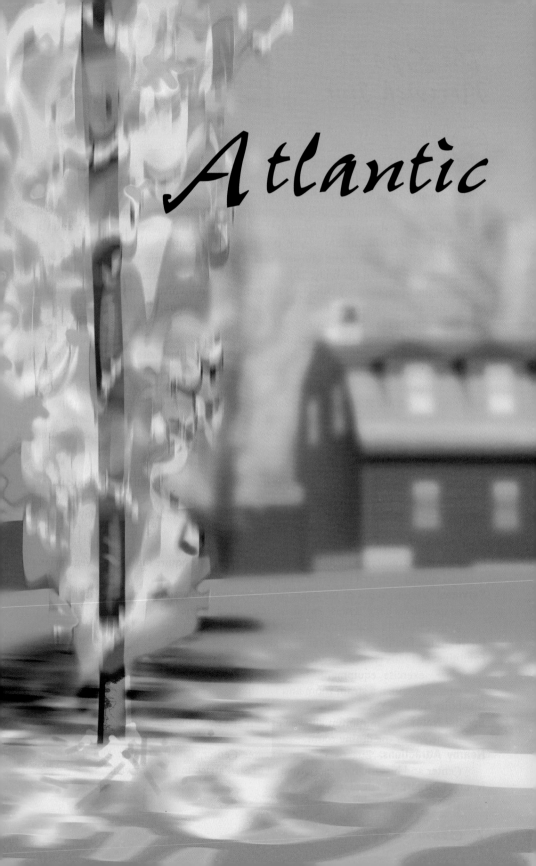

Atlantic

The Spa at Norwich Inn

607 West Thames Street, Route 32
Norwich, CT 06360
800/275-4772 or 860/886-2401; fax 860/886-9483
Website: www.thespaatnorwichinn.com

The Georgian-style Norwich Inn is located on 40 acres of New England woodlands. Graceful white columns and red brick accentuate the charm of this regal country estate. Intimate breakfast tables open up to old asters and groomed lawns bordered with brilliant flowers. The inn is a perfect getaway for busy city people who need a quiet place to de-stress.

Spa treatments, while intended to pamper, are also methods of improving the well-being of body, mind, and spirit through the initial benefits of stress reduction and the more subtle effects of ancient health practices. For example, the ancient Japanese practice of reiki is offered and consists of a practitioner placing the hands over various "energy centers" of the body. This noninvasive, gentle healing method is believed to realign the body's energy. An Ayurvedic mud wrap involves applying rejuvenating muds from India that are said to enhance circulation and pull toxins out of the body. Various hydrotherapy treatments target specific concerns; for example, the Dead Sea salt bath relieves topical skin conditions, the seaweed bath is said to stimulate the circulation, and the volcanic mud bath uses mineral-rich mud with anti-inflammatory and muscle-relaxing properties. All baths help eliminate toxins. Body treatments include an acupressure foot massage that not only relaxes but also helps balance the body's vital organs. A session in polarity therapy revives the nervous system and relaxes the mind and body. Emphasis is placed on balance and moderation rather than deprivation to allow guests to make permanent, as opposed to temporary or drastic, lifestyle changes.

Accommodations: Inn rooms, country rooms, and private villas, all with private baths. Some rooms come with a fireplace, a deck, and private access to the clubhouse.

Rates: Vary according to season, room, and spa package. High season is May through October, and low season is November through April.

Credit Cards: AE, D, MC, V

Meal Plans: All meals are included with some packages. Inquire for details. Vegetarians and special diets can be accommodated.

Services: Various types of massage, hydrotherapy, thalassotherapy, polarity therapy, acupressure, body wraps, loofah scrubs, salon services, cooking demonstrations, weight training, and fitness lectures

Recreational Facilities: Tennis, biking, golf

Facilities: A 1920s Georgian-style inn with lakeside villas, a taproom with a stone fireplace, exercise equipment, indoor and outdoor swimming pools, men's and women's sauna, a steam room and whirlpool, and a golf course

Disability Access: Yes

Special Notes: The minimum allowed age for spa guests is 18. Smoking is not allowed in the spa or the dining room.

Nearby Attractions: Eugene O'Neill Theater Center, Gillette Castle, Old Lyme Art Center and historic homes, Cathedral of St. Patrick in Old Norwich

Nearest Airport: Hartford, CT

Getting There: Car rental is available at airport. Driving from Hartford, take Route 2 East to Exit 28 South onto I-395 South. Exit 79A onto Route 2A East to Exit 1, less than .5 mile; stay left and use ramp lane to traffic light; left at light onto Route 32 North; spa is 1.5 miles on the left. (1 hour) Driving from New York, take I-95 North to Exit 76/I-395 North (left lane). Continue on I-395 to Exit 79A/Route 2A East; follow above directions to spa. (2.5 hours) Driving from Boston, take I-90 West (Mass Pike) to I-395 South. Exit 79A onto Route 2A East; follow above directions to spa. (2 hours)

Poland Spring Health Institute

32 Summit Spring Road
Poland, ME 04274-6704
207/998-2894; fax: 207/998-2164
Email: PSHI226@aol.com

A stay at Poland Spring means living in the guest room of a large New England farmhouse for 1-3 weeks, surrounded by 135 acres of woodlands and garden. Programs emphasize the center's philosophy that health is not an accident but an achievement gained by following the laws of nature. The program involves a simple lifestyle, using the elements of natural food, exercise, rest, body therapies, a supportive familylike atmosphere, clean air, and pure water. The famous Poland Spring drinking water complements a vegetarian diet, and guests drink 8-10 glasses a day directly from the springfed well. Spring water is also piped into the steam room, hydrotherapy baths, whirlpools, and showers.

Never more than 10 guests at a time participate in the programs offered at this Christian "health reconditioning facility." Prevention is emphasized during the one- to three-week stay, and a wide variety of natural remedies and alternative approaches are used to treat chronic degenerative diseases such as hypertension, decrease cholesterol levels, and manage conditions such as diabetes and arthritis. Stress management, smoking cessation, weight management, and healthy, relaxing vacations are also offered.

The program includes nutrition and health-related instruction, hydrotherapy, and exercise supervised by the institute's four registered nurses. Therapists administer hot packs, steam baths, massage, and hydrotherapy to help each guest relax, eliminate toxins, and improve muscle tone. Guests maintain a vegan diet, served either family or buffet style.

Accommodations: Five large rooms, one with a private bath, are available for single or double occupancy.

Rates: Vary according to length of stay and lodging. The seven-day Health and Healing Program is $745-950.

Credit Cards: None accepted

Meal Plans: Vegetarian meals consisting of salads and steamed, homegrown vegetables, fresh-baked bread, and seasonal fruit are served daily. Most of Poland Spring's produce is grown on the property.

Services: Hot packs, hydrotherapy, massage, steam baths, therapeutic bodywork, lectures on health-related subjects, and an exercise program

Recreational Activities: Canoeing, swimming, biking, ice-skating, sleigh rides, cross-country skiing, snow shoeing

Facilities: 135 acres with three large farmhouses, a whirlpool, walking trails, a rural lake, hay fields, gardens, and orchards

Disability Access: Yes; full access is available.

Special Notes: Alcohol is not allowed. Smoking is allowed only outdoors off the premises. Guests should remember to bring sturdy walking shoes or hiking boots, a sweater or jacket, rain gear, and personal medical records as requested.

Nearby Attractions: Shopping and sightseeing trips to Portland, Maine, and the Atlantic Ocean; Lebanon, New Hampshire; Historic Shaker Village

Nearest Airport: Portland, ME

Getting There: Complimentary shuttle service is provided to airport and Lewiston, Maine; Greyhound station. Advance reservations advised. Driving from Portland International Jetport, take I-495 North, exit at Highway 26 North/Exit 11. Continue for 13 miles; left on Schellinger Road; right on Summit Spring Road; spa entrance is on right. (1 hour)

The Sewall House

c/o Donna Sewall-Miller Davidge
P.O. Box 254
Island Falls, ME 04747
888/235-2395; fax: 888/235-2395
Email: info@sewallhouse.com
Website: www.sewallhouse.com

The Sewall House has been entered into the National Register of Historic Places. Built in 1865 for William Sewall, Island Falls' first-born citizen, it was the community's first post office. By 1870 the home served as a well-known "open house" for travelers who visited Island Falls (among them Theodore Roosevelt). Now, generations later, Sewall's great-granddaughter, Donna Sewall-Miller Davidge, continues the guest house tradition and has opened the home up as a yoga and nature retreat house. The retreat offers guests a chance to commune with nature in a peaceful environment while using Donna's expertise as a Kundalini Yoga instructor. Yoga and meditation classes are given each morning (8:30–9:45 A.M.) and afternoon (4:30–5:45 P.M.). Various massage treatments, such as polarity, healing touch, and shiatsu, are available by appointment.

Filled with antiques and reminders of a simpler time, The Sewall House provides the environment of a family home that happens to be full of history. In today's fast-paced world, visiting this 125-year-old guest house is a refreshing change of pace. Located in Northern Maine, Island Falls is close to Canada and near Mt. Katahdin. Nearby are forests, lakes, and National Parks, with wildlife such as moose and loons. The town itself is small and quiet, with an island and waterfall displayed in the middle. A tranquil fishing lake located one mile away offers opportunities for camping, hiking, canoeing, and meditation. Guests who stay at The Sewall House can relax and enjoy the solitude of nature and the small town ambience of Island Falls. Some people love to just hang out and sit on the porch watching the world go by.

Accommodations: Five private bedrooms, each with double beds. Single mattresses are available for family/friends who want to share the room. One bedroom is located on the main floor with a half bath. Four bedrooms are on the second floor, with a shared full bathroom. The third floor also has a full bathroom next to the massage room and library.

Rates: $111 per person, per day ($88 per person, double occupancy) includes overnight accommodations, two meals a day, morning yoga class, and evening meditation.

Credit Cards: None accepted

Meal Plans: Two meals are offered per day and include garden-fresh locally grown vegetables, with chicken and fish options.

Services: Yoga, meditation, and various massage and healing techniques

Recreational Activities: Hiking, biking, lake tours (including swimming, fishing, and arranged camping), canoe rentals, boating, and golfing (18-hole golf course)

Facilities: A 125-year-old guest house with five guest rooms, a living room, a library, a parlor room, a massage room, a kitchen, a dining room, a front porch, a barn, a two-person hot tub, and a sauna

Disability Access: Access is limited; please call in advance.

Special Notes: The Sewall House is open only July through Columbus Day.

Nearest Airport: Bangor, ME

Getting There: Buses and rental cars are available in Bangor. CYR Bus departs Bangor daily at 6p.m. to Sherman. Driving from all points along I-95, exit at Sherman 90 miles north of Bangor. Follow signs to Sewall House just off highway. (1.5 hours)

Canyon Ranch in the Berkshires Health Resort

165 Kemble Street
Lenox, MA 01240
800/726-9900 or 413/637-4100; fax: 413/637-0057
Email: info@canyonranch.com
Website: www.canyonranch.com

Sloping lawns and a symmetric reflecting pool lead toward the centerpiece of Canyon Ranch in the Berkshires—the historic brick and marble Bellefontaine Mansion, built in 1897 as a copy of Louis XIV's Petit Trianon. This sister resort of the world-renowned Canyon Ranch in Tucson, Arizona, is situated on 120 acres of New England woodlands. The 150,000-square-foot spa opened in 1989 and was repeatedly named Best Spa by the readers of Condé Nast Traveler magazine.

The spa offers award-winning luxury vacations that promote healthy living through fitness, nutrition, and lifestyle education. An emphasis is placed on lifestyle, prevention, and awareness. The center offers an array of indoor and outdoor fitness activities, including hiking, biking, rowing, and skiing programs; spa and beauty services; nutritious gourmet dining; private consultations; and workshops.

Program coordinators assist guests in arranging a schedule of individualized programs. All packages include accommodations, three nutritious and balanced gourmet meals per day, use of spa and resort facilities, fitness classes and sports activities, airport and train transfers, gratuities, and a selection of services. Preventive health care assessments can also be arranged, and the on-site Health and Healing Center offers the professional services of a medical staff, exercise physiologists, behavioral health professionals, and movement therapists. Healthful cooking classes and nutrition consultations are also available.

Accommodations: 126 guest rooms and suites in a New England–style inn

Rates: Vary according to season and package; $930 for a three-night package, $1,180 for a four-night package through March. After March, rates are slightly higher. Rates do not include the 18 percent service charge and sales tax. Discounts apply for longer stays.

Credit Cards: AE, D, MC, V

Meal Plans: Three healthy, gourmet meals plus snacks are provided daily. Vegetarian and special diet options are available on request.

Services: Lifestyle programs; acupuncture; massage; therapeutic bodywork, including craniosacral therapy, reiki, energy balancing; thalassotherapy; aromatherapy; medical and behavioral health services; salon services; nutritional, movement therapy, and exercise physiology services; and health-related lectures

Recreational Activities: Hiking, biking, tennis, skiing, swimming, canoeing, snowshoeing, sculling, kayaking

Facilities: A 120-acre woodland retreat featuring the historic Bellefontaine Mansion; a reflecting pool; formal gardens; a demonstration kitchen; exercise and weight-training rooms; indoor tennis courts; racquetball and squash courts; indoor and outdoor swimming pools; an indoor jogging track; herbal and massage rooms; a beauty salon; men's and women's saunas; and steam, whirlpool, and inhalation rooms

Disability Access: Yes; all facilities provide access for people with disabilities.

Special Notes: Canyon Ranch has an almost 3-to-1 staff-to-guest ratio. The minimum allowed age of spa guests is 14. Alcoholic beverages are not permitted in public areas, and smoking is not permitted indoors or in public areas.

Nearby Attractions: Tanglewood Music Festival, Jacob's Pillow Dance Festival, Williamstown Summer Theatre, Appalachian Trail, museums, Shakespeare & Company

Nearest Airports: Hartford, CT; Albany, NY

Getting There: Complimentary shuttle service is provided from both airports and Albany Amtrak with 48-hour notice. Driving from New York, take the New York Thruway (I-87) north or the Taconic State Parkway to I-90 east. (I-90 becomes the Massachusetts Turnpike.) Take Exit 2 (Lee, Mass.) off the Massachusetts Turnpike; right at Route 20 West to Lenox; left on Route 183 South/Historic Lenox; left at Junction 7A/ Kemble Street (1 mile, and at Trinity Church); spa is .5 mile on the left. (3 hours) Driving from Boston, take Massachusetts Turnpike to Exit 2 (Lee, Massachusetts). Follow above directions to spa. (3 hours) Driving from Connecticut (Hartford, New Haven area), take I-91 North toward Springfield, Massachusetts. Take Exit 14 to I-90, (Massachusetts Turnpike); exit onto I-90 West to Exit 2 (Lee, Massachusetts); follow above directions to spa. From Bridgeport, Fairfield area, take Route 8 North to Winsted and Route 44 West. Continue on Route 44 West to Canaan and Route 7 North; follow Route 7 approximately 25 miles to Lenox; left onto Route 7A north (at traffic light); spa is .5 mile on the right. (1.5 hours)

Kripalu Center for Yoga and Health

P.O. Box 793
West St., Route 183
Lenox, MA 01240
800/741-7353 or 413/448-3152; fax: 413/448-3384
Email: reserve@kripalu.org
Website: www.kripalu.org

For more than 25 years, the Kripalu Center has served as a haven for those seeking to revitalize their bodies, open their hearts, and awaken their spirits. It is one of the largest centers for yoga and health in the country. Dedicated to self-discovery through yoga and wholistic health, the Kripalu Center is a safe setting for self-exploration, rest, and renewal. The main building that houses the Kripalu Center, which was previously a Jesuit seminary, is a sprawling, institutional-looking facility, which has 167,000 square feet of floor space covering approximately four acres. At first sight, this building can be overwhelming, but the staff is friendly and welcoming, so that the institutional feeling fades into a warm, pleasant environment. The atmosphere is clean, comfortable, and simple.

The staff facilitates instruction of yogic principles through many yoga, self-discovery, holistic health, and spiritual programs. Programs offered include yoga and biking, yoga and cross-country skiing, stress reduction through Kripalu yoga, qi gong for beginners, Kripalu three-day meditation retreat, partner massage, raw juice fast, energy balancing, and retreat and renewal. Various world-class educators serve as guest instructors to offer additional program options, classes, and services.

Accommodations: The Kripalu Center can house up to 450 guests. The modest accommodations of this former Jesuit seminary range from rooms with private baths, to semiprivate rooms with shared hall bath facility, to spacious dormitories.

Rates: Overnight prices begin at $75 per person per night in a dormitory, with a two-night minimum stay required. Rates include room, meals, full use of facilities, and access to daily activities. Program tuition is additional and varies based on the program.

Credit Cards: MC, V

Meal Plans: Three vegetarian meals (including egg- and dairy-free options) are served each day. Meals can be taken in the main cafeteria-style dining room or in smaller, silent dining areas. Breakfast is a silent meal in every room. Lunch is the major meal, and vegetarian cuisine ranges from good to incredible.

Services: Kripalu Health Services offers treatment options such as Kripalu bodywork, reflexology, shiatsu, craniosacral therapy, and energy balancing.

Recreational Activities: Walking, hiking, and swimming in the summer

Facilities: A four-story building with a reception room, guest rooms, a kitchen, a dining room, and large rooms for yoga classes, dance, lectures, conference rooms, and other programs. The Kripalu Center also offers a sunroom, a 24-hour meditation room, separate women's and men's saunas, and a whirlpool, as well as the Kripalu store and café, featuring books, CDs, videos, clothing, jewelry, snacks, and more. Kripalu guests enjoy full use of 300 acres that include forests, meadows, meditation gardens, a private beach on Lake Mahkeenac, and woodland walking trails.

Disability Access: Some rooms have handicap accessibility; please call ahead.

Special Notes: Guests and staff alike adhere to a no-smoking and no-alcohol policy.

Nearby Attractions: Located directly across the street from Tanglewood, the summer home of The Boston Symphony Orchestra and easily accessible to Jacob's Pillow, the Norman Rockwell Museum, and many other cultural attractions

Nearest Airports: Albany, NY; Boston, MA

Getting There: Airport shuttle Thursday, Friday, Sunday, only, $40 each way. Call spa for reservations and departure times. Bus service is also available, Bonanza, 800/286-3674; Peter Pan, 800/343-9999. Tobi's, 413/637-1224, provides airport taxi service. Amtrak, 800/872-7245, services Pittsfield (9 miles to spa). Metro North, 800/638-7646, services Wassaic, New York (49 miles to spa) from Manhattan daily. Driving from Albany, take I-90, exit at Route 22. Follow Route 22 South; left at Route 102 East; continue 6 miles to juncture of Routes 102 and 183; left at Route 183; spa entrance is 3.8 miles (1.25 hours) Driving from Boston, take I-93, exit onto I-90 (Massachusetts Turnpike). Take Exit 2 (Lenox, Lee, Pittsfield) off the Massachusetts Turnpike; stay right on exit ramp onto Route 20 West; continue on Route 20, it will merge with Route 7; 100 yards past the merge, turn left onto Route 183 and into Lenox; follow signs to Tanglewood; left onto Richmond Mountain Road; bear left, the entrance to Kripalu is immediately on your right. (2.5 hours)

The Option Institute

2080 South Undermountain Road
Sheffield, MA 01257-9643
800/714-2779 or 413/229-2100; fax: (413) 229-8931
Email: happiness@option.org
Website: www.option.org

Founded in 1983, the Option Institute rests on a 95-acre campus, nestled among the Berkshire Mountains of Western Massachusetts. The Option Institute helps thousands of people from around the world improve their health, career, relationships, and quality of life. Through a uniquely transformative and empowering system of self-exploration called The Option Process, program participants learn to transform their lives with conviction, boldness, and a renewed sense of purpose.

The innovative work of Option Institute co-founders, authors/teachers Barry Neil Kaufman and Samahria Lyte Kaufman, is the core of The Institute's teaching. Underlying every program is the philosophy that each person is his or her own best expert. Participants learn through highly experiential exercises and applied attitudinal technologies to uproot self-defeating beliefs and other roadblocks to happiness and replace them with new motivators that inspire confidence, clarity, empowerment, and newfound energy for a profound impact in every aspect of life.

Programs range from the three-day Happiness Option Weekend, to the weeklong Empowering Yourself, to the ultimate life experience offered in the four- and eight-week Living The Dream. Program counselors are available to discuss individual goals or challenges and to work with individuals to find the materials and programs that work best for them.

Accommodations: Participants stay in guest houses, including double rooms and triple rooms. A few single rooms are available for special needs.

Rates: Varies by program length. The weeklong program rate is $1,495.

Credit Cards: MC, V

Meal Plans: Three meals are served every day. Special dietary needs *cannot* be accommodated. A healthy, low-fat, vegetarian menu is offered. Stoves are available in the housing accommodations if guests desire to cook for themselves.

Services: One-on-one dialogue sessions with trained professional mentors is offered. These sessions are available either in person or by phone.

Facilities: Comfortable, rustic buildings, a swimming pond, seasonal activities, magnificent views, and nearby hikes and nature walks.

Disability Access: No access is available in buildings; however, arrangements can be made to accommodate special needs. Please call for details.

Nearby Attractions: Boston Symphony at Tanglewood, Jacob's Pillow Dance Festival, Shakespeare and Company Theater, museums, the Appalachian trail, skiing, artisan shops, and antique stores

Special Notes: Smoking is not allowed inside any of the Institute's buildings. Ashtrays are located outside most buildings. Volunteer opportunities available.

Nearest Airport: Hartford, CT

Getting There: Car rental is available at airport. Service from Greyhound station in nearby Lee, Mass. is provided by AA Transport, 877/528-3906 and Bonanza, 800/556-3815. Located three hours by car from Boston and New York City airports; 1.5 hours by car from Bradley International Airport in Hartford, Connecticut.

New Age Health Spa

P.O. Box 658, Route 55
Neversink, NY 12765
800/682-4348 or 845/985-7600; fax 845/985-2467
Email: office@newagehealthspa.com
Website: www.newagehealthspa.com

Rural luxury mixed with a holistic approach to wellness—this is the New Age Health Spa. The spa claims 280 acres of Catskill Mountain foothills, with a converted farm as the inviting focal point. The motivating philosophy behind all spa programs is to create an environment in which people can learn to make lasting and positive lifestyle changes.

Programs, which are tailored around each guest's individual needs, can keep guests busy for as many as 12 hours a day or allow them to lie back in a hammock for quiet reflection. The spa promotes the concept of balance in nutrition, fitness, and personal growth; therefore, many activities are available in all three areas. This might mean hiking to the stone ridge of a Catskills overlook, learning how to prepare the delicious and low-fat treat of bananas in a crepe with orange-ginger sauce, or participating in guided visualization. Guests also have the option of climbing the 50-foot Alpine Tower (weather permitting) or scaling the challenge-ropes course, which is intended to get guests in shape and boost their self-esteem.

Another ingredient on New Age's serving plate is the Cayuga Yoga and Meditation Center, a 1,500-square-foot studio space on the spa grounds, where daily hatha yoga classes are offered. Yoga is a key part of the spa program all year. There are also special monthly intensive sessions featuring guest instructors in various forms of yoga, such as Iyengar, Ashtanga, Restorative, Kripalu, and Kundalini. In addition, daily meditations at 6:30 A.M. and 5:10 P.M. are offered and can include Oriental Healing exercises, pranayama breathing, chanting, and guided visualizations. New Age also features a Wholistic Health Care Center. The center offers traditional mind-body, complementary, and alternative treatments.

Accommodations: Single, double, and triple cottages with private bath

Rates: Vary according to lodging and services. Spa services are $30–175.

Credit Cards: AE, D, MC, V

Meal Plans: Three meals are served each day, including vegetarian and nonvegetarian entrées. A salad bar is filled with organic vegetables and soups.

Services: Health planning consultations; Ayurvedic botanical therapy and body treatments; therapeutic massage; aromatherapy; reflexology; hydrocolonic therapy; hypnotherapy; loofah scrubs; mud, algae, and herbal wraps; facials; fitness consultations; aerobics; tai chi, yoga, and meditation; nutritional counseling; guided fasting; and astrological charting

Recreational Activities: Snowshoeing, cross-country skiing

Facilities: A 280-acre country estate with a two-story main house, cottages, a gym, exercise equipment, indoor and outdoor pools, men's and women's steam rooms and saunas, treatment rooms, an Alpine climbing tower and challenge-ropes course, a 1,500-square-foot yoga/meditation studio, weight and exercise rooms, tennis courts, hiking trails, and corporate meeting rooms

Disability Access: No

Special Notes: Smoking, alcohol, and nonprescription drugs are not allowed.

Nearby Attractions: Woodstock, New York; New York City; Catskills Forest Preserve

Nearest Airport: New York City, NY

Getting There: Shuttle service is provided from Madison Avenue and 72nd Street to Neversink on weekends and holidays; $40 each way, advance reservations required. (2.5 hours)

Omega Institute for Holistic Studies

150 Lake Drive
Rhinebeck, NY 12572
800/944-1001 or 845/266-4444; fax 845/266-4828
Email: registration@eomega.org
Website: www.eomega.org

Founded in 1977, Omega still holds fast to its mission to look everywhere for the most effective strategies and inspiring traditions that might help people bring more meaning and vitality into their lives. The 140-acre campus of rolling hills, vegetable and flower gardens, and woodlands is in the countryside of the Hudson Valley, an area rich in history, cultural vitality, and natural beauty. There are usually 5-10 workshops per week in subjects that include yoga, meditation, dance, world music, writing, holistic healing, painting, martial arts, and relationships. Newcomers may want to experience Introductory Weekends, offered five times from May through October.

The five-day Wellness Week, one of the institute's most popular retreats, uses a mind-body approach. Diet, nutrition, fitness, exercise, lifestyle, and attitude are all addressed during core program workshops between 9 A.M. and noon. In the afternoon, you practice muscle strengthening, creative movement, stretching, and low-impact aerobics.

Optional dawn programs of yoga, meditation, or tai chi are held by the lake. A day of learning usually ends with anything from a concert, a community gathering, or dance.

Accommodations: Double cabin rooms with a roommate and either a private bath or a shared bath with an adjoining room. Dormitory single rooms with a bath are shared by eight guests. Tent cabins and camping are also available. Rates range from $300 for a two-day workshop with campsite to $795 for a weeklong program in a shared double cabin with a private bath. A 10 percent discount applies to early registration, full-time students, and senior citizens.

Credit Cards: MC, V

Meal Plans: Three meals—mostly gourmet vegetarian with occasional servings of fresh fish—are prepared daily and are included in the housing fee.

Services: A wide variety of body therapies, including shiatsu, therapeutic massage, nutrition and stress reduction counseling, sauna, reflexology, and aromatherapy

Recreational Activities: Walking, hiking, tennis, basketball, swimming in the lake, canoeing, and row boating

Facilities: A 140-acre upstate New York campus, including dormitories, cottages, campsites, a Wellness Center, a book and gift store, a café, tennis courts, a basketball court, gardens, woods, and a lake

Disability Access: The campus is generally accessible to the disabled but is large and hilly. Contact Omega if you have a disability that affects your mobility so that the staff can best accommodate your needs.

Special Notes: Smoking is not allowed in or close to any building. An extensive children's program for preregistered children ages 4-12, scholarship, work study, and community exchange programs are available.

Nearby Attractions: Catskill Mountains, Hudson River, vineyards, "pick-your-own" farms, Vanderbilt Mansion, Montgomery Place

Nearest Airport: New York City, NY

Getting There: Ride share, airport, bus, and train service are available. Inquire during reservations. Driving from Manhattan, take I-87 (New York State Throughway) North to Taconic Parkway; exit at Bulls Head Road West; and onto Lake Drive; follow signs to entrance. (2 hours)

Vatra Natural Weight Loss Spa

Route 214, Box F
Hunter, NY 12442
800/232-2772 or 518/263-4919; fax 518/263-4994
Email: loseweight@vatraspa.com
Website: www.vatraspa.com

Health and weight-loss programs are offered at the 12-year-old Vatra Natural Weight Loss Spa. The lodge is located at the base of Hunter Mountain, just 2.5 hours north of New York City. Programs emphasize wellness as a lifelong commitment, and activities integrate the elements of mind, body, and spirit.

On arrival, guests meet with the spa director to schedule a program of diet, fitness, and spa treatments. The wellness director then meets with guests to discuss their overall health and well-being and any nutritional or herbal needs. Spa programs include three vegetarian meals a day, with the option of juice fasting; a choice of reflexology, shiatsu, aromatherapy; a personalized fitness program; use of all spa facilities; access to walking trails and tennis courts; a year-round heated indoor pool and seasonal outdoor pool; and a wide range of winter sports. Evening group discussions address topics such as herbal wellness, dealing with stress, and how to cook "lite."

An intimate lodge atmosphere pervades at Vatra. Guests dine by candle-light together in the dining room. Juice or Vegetable Happy Hour affords guests a predinner chance to socialize. During the summer, evening group discussions can take place on a deck overlooking the majestic North Range of the Catksill Mountains. In winter, attendants at evening programs gather around the lodge fire-place, surrounded by fresh-picked mountain wildflowers and festive decorations. Personal retreats can last from a weekend to a week or longer. Theme programs include a women's health care week, a singles weekend, and retreats for business and profes-sional women.

Accommodations: Private rooms with bath, television, and phones. Some rooms have balconies and skylights.

Rates: Vary by program and accommodation; the two- to three-day program is $495–695.

Credit Cards: MC, V

Meal Plans: Three vegetarian meals are offered per day. Juice fast diet is also available for detoxing and cleansing.

Services: Individualized diet, fitness, and treatment plans; therapeutic massage; aro-matherapy, yoga, and meditation; and aerobics, hiking, and dance. A winter ski clinic and cross-country lessons are available for various levels of skiers.

Recreational Activities: Guided walks, hiking, body sculpting classes, golf, horseback riding, mountain biking, tubing and canoeing nearby

Facilities: A 15-acre resort with a chalet-style main house, a fitness room, a sauna, indoor and outdoor heated swimming pools, tennis, basketball, and volleyball courts, and walking trails

Disability Access: Ramps and ground-floor rooms are accessible for people with disabilities.

Special Notes: The lodge operates as a ski resort with a limited spa program in winter.

Nearby Attractions: Woodstock, antique stores, horseback riding, golf

Nearest Airport: New York City, NY

Getting There: Bus service to Hunter is available from Port Authority, Adirondack Trailways, 800/225-6815. Driving from the south (NYC) take I-87 (New York State Throughway/Saw Mill River Parkway) North to Exit 20; left after toll; right onto Route 32N; left onto 32A; left onto 214; spa entrance one mile on right. (2.5 hours) Driving from the north (Albany), take I-87 (New York State Throughway/Saw Mill River Parkway) South to Exit 21 (Catskill); take Route 23W at end of town; follow 23A to 214; left onto 214; spa entrance one mile on right. (1.5 hours)

Deerfield Manor Spa

650 Resica Falls Road
East Stroudsburg, PA 18301
800/852-4494 or 570/223-0160; fax 570/223-8270
Email: deerspa@ptd.net
Website: www.deerfieldspa.com

Deerfield Manor is a tranquil destination spa tucked away in Pennsylvania's Poconos mountain range. Twelve acres of forest surround an elegant, rambling country house, and every day guests explore the various walking trails throughout them. Selected as one of America's best new spas by *Shape* magazine, Deerfield offers a variety of programs designed to relieve everyday stress, tone the body, and ultimately lead to a lasting healthy lifestyle. Attitude is viewed as the essential starting ingredient of health, and guests are encouraged to set and visualize their goals.

As a destination spa, Deerfield can boast that all programs are geared toward the guests' health and well-being, with no diversions. To maintain an intimate atmosphere, no more than 33 people at a time participate in programs. All programs are personalized for individual self-improvement. Fitness programs, in particular, take a holistic approach, integrating the elements of exercise, healthy nutrition, and stress management techniques. A typical day might start at 8 A.M., with a breakfast of wholegrain cereal and fresh seasonal fruit, followed by tai chi. Ambitious guests might squeeze in a neuromuscular massage and a reiki hands-on healing session before lunch, which might consist of locally grown and deliciously prepared vegetables and perhaps some chicken or fish. Afterward, guests can either board a shuttle to embark for a Poconos Mountain trailhead or attend a fitness class of African dance or aquatic exercise in the heated outdoor pool. After dinner, guests might gather in the lounge for a mind-body-spirit lecture or take part in an informal group discussion. Personal counseling and group discussions are available.

Accommodations: Double and single rooms with private baths. Rooms have wicker furniture, antique furnishings, air-conditioning, cable television, and pleasant views.

Rates: Weekends are $340–460; the weeklong rate is $799–1,190. Add 6 percent sales tax and a 15 percent service charge onto the base rate.

Credit Cards: D, MC, V

Meal Plans: Three low-calorie meals are prepared daily with locally grown produce, fresh fruit, and optional fish and chicken.

Services: Reiki, reflexology, shiatsu, Swedish and neuromuscular massage, body treatments, salon services, personal counseling, group discussions, customized fitness programs, aerobics, dance, aquatic exercise, body sculpting, circuit training, step aerobics, tai chi, yoga, and mind-body-spirit lectures

Recreational Activities: Hiking in the mountains, horseback riding

Facilities: A main country house with three informal lounges, dining rooms, a heated outdoor pool, a hot tub, a sauna, a spa, and a fully equipped gym

Disability Access: Yes; ramps and lodging are available for people with disabilities.

Special Notes: Smoking is not allowed indoors.

Nearby Attractions: Pocono Mountains, shopping in nearby Stroudsburg, summer theater

Nearest Airports: Allentown, PA; New York City, NY

Getting There: Car rentals, private car, and taxi service are available at airport. Bus service to East Stroudsburg is provided by Martz Trailways, 800/233-8604, and Greyhound 800/229-9424. Driving from New York, take I-80 West to George Washington Bridge then Delaware Water Gap Bridge. Exit I-80 at Exit 52 (Route 209/Marshall Creek); follow Route 209 for 4 miles; turn right then immediately left at firehouse; bear right onto Route 402 North; continue on Route 402 North for 2 miles to spa. (1.5 hours) Driving from Washington/Baltimore, take 495 to Route 270 North to Route 15 to I-83 (toward Harrisburg) to I-81 East to Route 18/22 East. Exit onto Route 33 North to Route 80 East; take Exit 52 (Route 209/Marshall Creek) follow above directions to spa. (2.5 hours)

Himalayan Institute Center for Health and Healing

R.R.1, Box 400
Honesdale, PA 18431
800/822-4547 or 570/253-5551; fax: 570/253-9078
Email: chh@himalayaninstitute.org
Website: www.himalayaninstitute.org

Forested hills, a spring-fed pond, and abundant wildlife surround the international headquarters for the Himalayan Institute of Yoga Science and Philosophy of the USA. The late Swami Rama founded the institute in 1971 to help people grow physically, mentally, and spiritually through programs that combine ancient Eastern teachings and modern scientific approaches. Workshop subjects change each year but usually include subjects such as holistic health, hatha yoga, meditation, psychology, and more.

The institute's Center for Health and Healing provides individualized Ayurvedic rejuvenation programs. The programs are available through a custom-designed weekend or a seven- or 10-day residential program. The program is designed to reduce the effects of stress and fatigue and restore good health after an extended chronic illness, surgery, or accident. For those who already maintain general good health, the intended effect is a state of dynamic wellness. Included in the program are holistic medical consultation, yoga therapy, therapeutic massage, biofeedback sessions, restorative Ayurvedic herbs, and cleansing therapies.

Accommodations: The main building accommodates 100 in one- and two-bedroom units with sinks. Toilets and showers are shared; bed linens and towels are provided. A few single-occupancy rooms are available; limited accommodations can be arranged for families with children.

Rates: The two-night program is $240 for Himalayan Institute members, $260 for nonmembers for a double room, meals, and seminars. Two-week advance registration is required. Weekend, three- to five-day seminars, as well as personal retreats, are offered year-round. Internships are available.

Credit Cards: MC, V

Meal Plans: Three nutritionally balanced vegetarian (organic) meals are prepared daily. Vegan options are available.

Services: Holistic medical consultations; detoxification and cleansing therapies; workshops on yoga, holistic health, and self-development; fasting; homeopathy; Ayurvedic body treatments; hatha yoga; cooking classes; and relaxation techniques

Recreational Activities: Ice-skating, tennis (bring your own equipment), basketball, and ski resorts

Facilities: A 400-acre campus with a three-story main building, vegetable and flower gardens, an orchard, exercise equipment, a bookstore, a gift shop, tennis, handball, and basketball courts, hiking trails, a springfed pond, and a nearby waterfall

Disability Access: Access depends on the disability. There are no elevators in the building, only stairs. Please call with concerns.

Special Notes: Smoking is not allowed indoors. Guests are recommended to bring soap, a bathrobe and slippers, an alarm clock, a flashlight, a yoga mat, an umbrella, and warm clothing.

Nearby Attractions: Lake Wallenpaupack, ski resorts

Nearest Airport: Scranton, PA

Getting There: Car rental available at airport. Driving from New York City, take I-495 to Route 46 West then I-80 West and exit at Route 15 North; continue through New Jersey and into Pennsylvania as it becomes Route 206 then Route 6 West; at Honesdale, right on Church Street; left on Route 670; spa is five miles on right.

Himalayan Institute Center for Health and Healing **23**

The Equinox

Historic Route 7A
Manchester Village, VT 05254
800/362-4747 or 802/362-4700; fax 802/362-4861
Email: reservations@equinoxresort.com
Website: www.equinoxresort.com

To ensure that a critical element of Vermont's heritage remains development free, the owners of the historic Equinox Hotel established a preservation trust to protect 900 acres of Equinox Mountain, the 3,800-foot peak rising behind historic Manchester Village. The trust brings the local community, as well as resort guests, closer to the natural environment.

The 2,300-acre New England resort began as the stoic, two-story wooden Marsh Tavern in 1769. Today, it is devoted to the type of luxury reminiscent of an old Bogart movie, with an amenity spa offering the European ideal of culture, nature, and rejuvenation. Guests have many reasons to visit The Equinox, including the award-winning Gleneagles Golf Course designed by the legendary Walter Travis, the first falconry school in America, and the first year-round land rover driving school.

The spa offers treatments primarily designed to relax and revitalize. The Spa Rejuvenation Package is a good prescription for anyone who is stressed, overworked, or fatigued. The package includes accommodations, with the option of upgrading to the nineteenth-century Orvis Inn; three nutritious gourmet meals per day; daily steam and sauna; daily nature walks; and a sampling of four spa treatments, which range from an exfoliation with a massage or a hot muslin wrap with a massage to aromatic oil treatment, reiki, reflexology, or an algae body mask. Fly-fishing, snowshoeing, and skiing—both downhill and cross-country—are also outdoor options during the program. Skiers will be happy to know that the spa has one of the first physiotherapy centers in New England.

Accommodations: 183 guest rooms and suites furnished with antiques and decorated with Audubon prints. Some rooms have fireplaces, kitchens, porches, and mountain views. The historic Charles Orvis Inn offers nine deluxe one- and two-bedroom suites with marble baths, cherry-paneled kitchens, and living and dining areas.

Rates: Vary according to room, season, and package. The four-day Spa Rejuvenation Package costs $934 for a triple, $983.50 for a double, and $1,252 for a single room.

Credit Cards: AE, D, MC, V

Meal Plans: Three low-fat, nutritionally balanced meals are included each day with the spa package. Vegetarian and special diets can be accommodated with advance notice.

Services: Body composition analysis, physical therapy assessment, massage, reflexology, reiki, herbal wraps, exfoliation treatments, and aromatherapy

Recreational Activities: Falconry training, canoeing, mountain biking, hiking, nature walks, horseback riding and carriage rides, and nearby fly-fishing

Facilities: A physiotherapy center, a Turkish steam bath, a Swedish sauna, whirlpools, exercise equipment, indoor and outdoor heated pools, a boardroom, a billiards room, the four-diamond Colonnade restaurant, the Gleneagles Golf Course, a cross-country ski center, and three tennis courts

Disability Access: Fully accessible

Special Notes: Smoking is allowed only outdoors and in guest rooms.

Nearby Attractions: Historic homes, antique shops, art galleries, theater in Manchester Village; Stratton Mountain ski resort; Norman Rockwell Museum; Marlboro Music Festival; Brattleboro Museum; Frog Hall crafts center

Nearest Airport: Albany, NY

Getting There: Call spa for airport transportation details. Car rental is available at airport. Driving from Albany, take Route 87 North and left onto Route 7 East (Bennington). Left at Exit 3; left onto Route 313; right onto Historic Route 7A North; continue 12 miles to spa entrance. (4 hours) Driving from Boston, take Route 2 West to I-91 North. In Brattelboro, take Exit 2/Route 30 North; continue and left onto Historic Route 7A (Manchester); continue 1 mile to spa entrance. (4.5 hours) Driving from Hartford, take Route 91 North to Exit 2/Route 30 North, and follow Boston directions listed above. (3.5 hours)

Four Seasons Healing, Inc.

340 Deeper Ruts Road
Cabot, VT 05647
802/563-3063; fax: 802/563-6061
Website: www.FourSeasonsVT.org

 Four Seasons' programs are held in Vermont on a private, secluded 1800s working homestead at the end of a dirt road, with campsites along the brook, on the edge of the hayfields, around small ponds, or in the woods. In 1997, after nearly 20 years of working with individuals, couples, and groups, Dr. Israel and Cathie Helfand were awarded a grant from the Center for Psychology and Social Change (an affiliate of the Department of Psychiatry at the Cambridge Hospital, Harvard Medical School) to help further their signature Rites of Passage Program, "Soul Awakenings: A Contemporary Vision Quest," and to develop an Ecopsychology college course.

Rites of passage programs are designed to help people in transition through back-to-nature camping retreats, which offer times of activity as well as solitude and moving slowly. The philosophy behind this program is that living close to nature, eating from the farm, creating self-directed ceremony, and having council time around the fire helps people find deeper meaning, enables them to face important transitions, and facilitates spiritual growth.

Techniques offered at Four Seasons include dreamwork, shamanic journey, meditation, psychodrama, focusing, hypnosis, journaling, self-directed ceremony, basic wilderness skills, and other spiritual self-help practices. The Soul Awakening/Vision Quest program involves participation in 1–4 days of a solo quest (being alone in nature at one of the campsites while fasting), which occurs toward the end of the week, after which the community rejoins for shared stories and acclimatizing for the return home. The programs help people who are seeking to heal personal wounds, renew a spiritual connection with nature, or break destructive habits. Group examples include father/son, couples communication, getaway weekends, corporate employee team building, and private parties.

Accommodations: The guest room and cottage are under construction. Call for availability information. Campsites are open year-round.

Rates: The eight-day August soul awakening program is $950. Private programs run about $150 per day. Scholarships are available. Barter or trade can be arranged.

Credit Cards: Not accepted

Meal Plans: A variety of food is offered, from seasonal game to farm-raised meat and vegetables. Most food is homegrown right on the farm, and breads and cakes are home-baked and sausage is homemade. Pig or lamb roasts are available for larger groups. Vegetarian meals are also available.

Services: Holistic counseling psychodrama, hypnosis training, sexploration, shamanic journey work, help with self-directed ceremony and ritual, Soul Awakening/Vision Quests, and an independent study course in ecopsychology

Facilities: A 40-acre 1800s working homestead with vegetable and herb gardens in a rustic country setting, an outdoor wood-fired hot tub, fishing, swimming holes, hiking trails, farm animals, and starry skies. Indigenous animals include deer, moose, bear, fisher cat, bobcat, coyotes, mink, squirrel, river otters, and jackrabbits.

Special Notes: Guests usually provide their own camping gear, but some gear can be rented. No smoking is allowed in the barn.

Nearby Attractions: Cabot Creamery, Catamount Arts in St. Johnsbury; Vermont's capital Montpelier has many attractions and great restaurants such as the Culinary Institute; Groton State Forest for moose viewing; and Joe's Pond for four seasons of recreation, from canoeing to ice-fishing.

Nearest Airport: Burlington, VT

Getting There: Airport transportation is provided with advance reservations and additional fee. Car rental is available at airport. Amtrak train lines services New York City to Burlington. Driving from Burlington, take I-89 South to Mount Pelier and Route 2 East. Continue on Route 2 for 20 miles; left on West Shore Road (West Danville); right on Deeper Ruts Road (2 miles); spa entrance located at end of road.

New Life Hiking Spa

c/o The Inn of the Six Mountains
P.O. Box 395
Killington, VT 05751
800/228-4676; fax: 802/422-2071
Email: info@newlifehikingspa.com
Website: newlifehikingspa.com

Although it sounds like a workout, the benefits of a New Life Fitness Vacation go deeper than skin, muscle, and bones. Guests return from a rigorous five days of hiking, exercise, meditation, and massage feeling revitalized and optimistic. For 20 years, Jimmy LeSage, a former chef turned fitness guru, has offered his down-to-earth wellness vacations to an intimate group of no more than 25. Guests breathe the fresh Vermont air and venture out over mountain streams, working farms, and sections of the Appalachian and Long trails. Hiking options accommodate all fitness levels, so beginners need not worry about being force-marched up the second-highest peak in Vermont. The advanced level has participants trekking across Pico Peak to take a spirited ride down an Alpine slide.

A typical day begins with a morning stretch and half-hour walk at 7:30 A.M. Breakfast is served at 8 A.M., followed by a stretch before the five- to seven-mile hike over various types of terrain. Each day, hikers progressively take on more challenging trails. At noon, a 20-minute post-hike stretch counteracts muscle contractions caused by exertion and allows muscles to lengthen, relax, and regain oxygen. A lunch of chicken curry salad or perhaps a sandwich with spicy tofu filling is served, and guests have a few minutes to rest before the 2 P.M. water workout. Both swimmers and nonswimmers benefit from the toning and conditioning that aquacise provides. At 3:15 P.M., a body conditioning class is scheduled, followed by afternoon yoga at 4 P.M. Stress reduction and meditation methods are taught during the 5 P.M. relaxation class. The methods are meant to allow the body and mind to rest while creating greater self-awareness. Dinner is scheduled for 6:30 P.M., followed by an evening health lecture. Guests can wind up the evening with a full-body massage before crashing into a soft pillow in preparation for the next day's hike. New Life Hiking Spa programs are offered May through October.

Accommodations: Guests stay at the Inn of the Six Mountains. The hotel is spacious and comfortable, offering 100 single and double rooms with private baths.

Rates: Vary according to lodging and package. The six-day Classic New Life Program is $1,099–1,199 per person; a long weekend sampler is $659–759 per person. Nine percent sales tax and a 15 percent service charge are added to the base rate.

Credit Cards: MC, V

Meal Plans: Three low-fat meals per day consist of food high in complex carbohydrates. Special dietary needs can be accommodated with advance notice.

Services: Stress-reduction and fitness programs, therapeutic and relaxing massage, yoga, tai chi, aerobics, aquacise, body-toning, and facials

Recreational Activities: Hiking, swimming, biking, golf, horseback riding

Facilities: The Inn at Six Mountains resort complex, complete with exercise equipment, an indoor lap pool, a steam room, a sauna, a heated outdoor pool, tennis and racquetball courts, mountain bikes, and hiking trails

Disability Access: Yes

Special Notes: Smoking is allowed only in designated areas.

Nearby Attractions: Appalachian Trail, Marlboro Music Festival, Manchester Village, the performing arts center at Woodstock, Dartmouth College Hopkins Center, antique shops, summer stock theater, concerts

Nearest Airports: Lebanon, NH; Albany, NY

Getting There: Airport service is provided by Rutland Travel, 800/228-4311. Driving from New York City, Connecticut, and all southern points, take the Connecticut Turnpike or I-95, to I-91. Continue on I-91 to North of Bellows Falls (Vermont); Exit 6 (Rutland) to Route 103; exit at Route 100 North; exit to US 4; follow to Killingham Road and spa entrance. (5 hours from NYC)

Southeast

Uchee Pines Lifestyle Center

Uchee Pines Institute
30 Uchee Pines Road
Seale, AL 36875-5702
334/855-4781; fax 334/855-4780
Email: ucheepines@msn.com
Website: www.ucheepines.com

For 30 years the Uchee Pines Institute has offered retreats to help people achieve and maintain total health in body, mind, and soul. Uchee is also known as Anvwodi, the Cherokee word for "get well place," and that is exactly what Calvin and Agatha Thrash envisioned when they founded Uchee Pines. Both Calvin and Agatha are medical doctors who have co-authored several books on natural remedies and preventive medicine. Uchee is staffed by a team of Seventh-Day Adventists who specialize in natural methods of healing and who want to help guests gain control of their health.

Retreats offer many noninvasive remedies and educational seminars on preventive medicine. Participants learn what they can do naturally for themselves and others to combat disease. They are encouraged to rediscover the natural rhythms of their bodies through rest, a healthy diet, sunlight, fresh air, and community service, such as chopping wood or tending the orchard.

The 21-day retreats begin on Mondays. After meeting the staff and settling into a room, the guests meet with a lifestyle counselor, who remains with them throughout the program. The counselor serves as both therapist and cheerleader, working closely with each guest to ensure that the natural healing can occur as quickly and as thoroughly as possible.

During the program, guests receive a complete physical examination, two blood profiles, regular consultations with a physician, hydrotherapy and thermal treatments, exercise, and massage. Participants attend lectures and take classes on health, natural remedies, gardening, and cooking. They are encouraged to get as much fresh air, sun, and water as they can tolerate. The program is intended to help guests develop more meaningful relationships with God.

Accommodations: Seven rooms have twin beds, modern furnishing, and semiprivate baths. Campsites and trailer hookups are available for seminar guests.

Rates: The 21-day program is $3,300; inquire about rates for spouses or other accompanying people. Five-day seminars are $300 per person, $525 for married couples, $85 extra per child. All rates include housing, meals, and workshops.

Credit Cards: D, MC, V

Meal Plans: Three vegetarian meals are provided daily.

Services: Massage, water therapy, physical examination, blood work, physiotherapy, health lectures, natural remedies, morning devotionals, classes

Recreational Activities: Walking and hiking

Facilities: A 200-acre wooded retreat with a farm, main lodge, walking trails, and orchard

Disability Access: Yes, but limited; please call ahead.

Special Notes: Smoking is not allowed. Staff includes four medical doctors and 10 lifestyle counselors trained in various types of therapies.

Nearby Attractions: Callaway Gardens features a butterfly house and azalea show; Roosevelt State Park; Little White House in Warm Spring, Georgia; Providence Canyon State Park

Nearest Airports: Columbus and Atlanta, GA

Getting There: Spa provides airport service with advance notice. Driving from Atlanta, take I-85 South approximately one hour to the Columbus exit. Exit onto Route 80 and continue until it ends at the junction of Routes 431 and 290; left onto Route 431 south, left again on 165; right on Route 39; left on first road (Kitetown Road); then left on Uchee Pines Road to spa entrance. (2.5 hours)

Hippocrates Health Institute

1443 Palmdale Court
West Palm Beach, FL 33411
800/842-2125 or 561/471-8876; fax: 561/471-9464
Email: hippocrates@worldnet.att.net
Website: www.hippocratesinst.com

Founded by Ann Wigmore and Viktoras Kulvinaskas more than 40 years ago, the Hippocrates Health Institute is based on the ancient Hippocratic wisdom to "Let food be your medicine." Today, directors Brian and Anna Maria Clement encourage guests to achieve personal goals using healing techniques they can employ at home. Brian Clement is also the author of *Living Foods for Optimum Health*.

This holistic health and learning center, located on a 30-acre, tropical, wooded estate, uses an enzyme-rich nutritional regimen and natural oxygenating therapies to detoxify, cleanse, and revitalize the mind, body, and spirit. The three-week Life-Change Program, in particular, integrates this approach. During the program, guests receive private consultations with the resort health team, a live-cell analysis, daily lectures, stress-free exercise, group-sharing therapy, buffet meals of live organic food, weekly massage, and electromagnetic treatments. Other activities include excursions to the beach, museums, and shopping areas. Guests also have access to the dry sauna, four ozonated outdoor pools, and the Native American–inspired Vapor Cave, which constantly emits a therapeutic warm vapor.

Food is of primary importance at Hippocrates and is defined as anything that enables one to live and grow. Consequently, meals consist of inspired combinations of fresh fruits and vegetables. A sample menu includes an almond basil loaf with red pepper coulis, stuffed avocado platters, cauliflower and mushrooms à la greque, and a broccoli salad with garlic and oregano. Guests also have 24-hour access to a self-help wheat grass juice bar and are served a daily staple Green Power drink consisting of organic vegetables and sprouts.

Accommodations: 23 rooms, on and off the premises, most of which are equipped with queen-size beds and hot tubs

Rates: $1,650–3,850 per person, per week. Includes lodging, meals, services, and use of all facilities.

Credit Cards: AE, D, MC, V

Meal Plans: Two live organic vegetarian meals are prepared every day. Wheat grass and vegetable and fruit juices are offered between meals.

Services: Colonic irrigation, Thai massage, hydrotherapy, acupuncture, reflexology, chiropractic, centropic integration, psychotherapy, yoga, shiatsu, watsu, deep-tissue massage, lymphatic drainage, polarity energy balancing, aesthetics, and H-wave treatments

Facilities: A 30-acre estate with Spanish-style haciendas, garden apartments, four ozonated outdoor pools, a sauna, a vapor cave, a meditation yurt, an electromagnetic treatment system, a jogging trail, a nature trail, and exercise equipment

Disability Access: Yes

Special Notes: Cigarettes, alcohol, and meat are not allowed on the premises.

Nearby Attractions: Palm Beach, Kravis Cultural Center, beaches, shopping, John MacArthur Park nature reserve and beach, museums, Morikame Gardens

Nearest Airports: Palm Beach, West Palm Beach, and Miami, FL

Getting There: Car rental is available at airports. Driving from Palm Beach, take Belvedere Road West; right on Skees; left on Palm Dale Road; right on Palm Dale Court to spa. (.5 hour)

PGA National Resort and Spa

400 Avenue of the Champions
Palm Beach Gardens, FL 33418-3698
800/633-9150 (resort) or 800/843-7725 (spa);
fax: 561/622-0261
Email: PGAinfo@pga-resorts.com
Website: www.pga-resorts.com

Incorporating the elements of a luxurious European spa with the latest beauty, fitness, and nutritional services, this resort and spa offers guests more than 100 treatments, from body services and aromatherapy to facials and salon services. The philosophy behind this world-class facility is to offer guests an all-encompassing approach to living well, with the combined expertise of professionals in the fields of health, nutrition, athletic performance, and lifestyle management. Spa programs are tailored to the goals of the individual and include follow-up to track the guests' progress at home. Guests can choose à la carte services or half-day, full-day, two-day, or four-day packages. The Spa's signature is the "Waters of the World," a collection of mineral pools with salts imported from the world's most renowned water sources, including the Dead Sea and Salies de Bearn.

A typical Spa Sampler Package includes deluxe accommodations with a private balcony or terrace; full breakfast daily; use of all spa facilities, including access to the resort's state-of-the-art 32,500-square-foot fitness center, lap pool, and the mineral pools; choice of one 50-minute Swedish massage, reflexology treatment, or deep cleansing facial per person; and choice of one 25-minute neck and shoulder massage, reflexology treatment, or manicure with a shampoo and style per person. The PGA resort also boasts an organic herb garden filled with a variety of healing plants, such as ajuga, sweet woodruff, and clary sage.

Accommodations: Single and double standard rooms, suites, and cottage suites. There are 339 guest rooms in the main hotel, each with a private terrace or balcony. Each unit offers panoramic views overlooking the lake, pool, or golf course. There are 60 one- and two-bedroom suites, a 2,000-square-foot Presidential Suite, and 65 cottage suites, which overlook the golf course and have two bedrooms, two complete baths, a large living room, a fully equipped kitchen, and a washer and dryer.

Rates: Vary according to room and services. The Day of Beauty spa package is $249. Room rates range from $169–389 per night single or double occupancy for deluxe accommodations.

Credit Cards: AE, D, MC, V

Meal Plans: The resort offers seven dining facilities, including a tropical poolside indoor/outdoor café serving spa cuisine.

Services: More than 140 spa services are offered, including Swedish, neuromuscular, and lymphatic massage; hydrotherapy tubs; Vichy shower; salt glow rubs; marine algae wraps; aromatherapy; nutritional consultations; facials; and salon services.

Recreational Activities: Swimming, walking, golf

Facilities: A 2,340-acre resort with guest rooms, suites, and cottages; state-of-the-art exercise equipment; a spa building with 25 coeducational treatment rooms; hydrotherapy tubs and a Vichy shower; eight restaurants; a health and racquet club; a five-lane lap pool; five golf courses; 19 outdoor tennis courts; five croquet lawns; and three indoor racquetball courts

Disability Access: Yes, specially equipped rooms are designed for people with disabilities.

Special Notes: Child care is available; golf and tennis lessons are included, and private instruction is available at certain times during the summer.

Nearby Attractions: The Gardens of the Palm Beaches; The Kravis Center; Norton Museum of Art; Worth Avenue; the Flagler Museum

Nearest Airport: West Palm Beach

Getting There: Airport transportation is provided by the spa. Call for details and advance reservations. Driving from West Palm Beach and all points along I-95, take Exit 57B onto PGA Boulevard. Continue on PGA Boulevard past Florida Turnpike; left on Avenue of Champions; spa entrance is at end of road.

Regency House Natural Health Spa

2000 South Ocean Drive
Hallandale, FL 33009
800/454-0003 or 954/454-2220; fax 954/454-4637
Email: regencyspa@usa.net
Website: www.regencyhealthspa.com

Bright blue beach chairs complement the cream-colored stucco and red tile of the Regency House Natural Health Spa. The spa is only a short walk from the beach, and guests can smell the crisp ocean air by breathing deeply. Throughout its 13 years, the spa has had an exceptionally successful history of helping people lose weight and body fat. It also strives to be a comprehensive body-mind health spa. Lifestyle awareness, detoxification, and rejuvenation programs are offered in addition to weight-loss and physical fitness programs.

An average eight-day program begins with each guest personally consulting with director Dr. Frank Sabatino on arrival. A nutrition and exercise program is established at this meeting. Guests then settle into a regimen of three gourmet vegetarian meals a day, early morning walks on a white-sand beach, daily health and nutrition lectures, vegetarian cooking demonstrations, psychology seminars, exercise classes, yoga, and meditation. Two free massages come with the seven-night package and include a deep sport, aromatherapy, Swedish, neuromuscular therapy, shiatsu, reflexology, or dry skin brush massage. For an additional fee, guests can schedule reiki, hypnotherapy, chiropractic care, bone density testing, lymphatic drainage, psychic astrology, and more. Guided organic juice and water fasting is also available and is supervised by Dr. Sabatino.

An informal atmosphere pervades the spa, and guests are advised not to pack a large wardrobe or bring expensive jewelry. Casual clothes are par for the course, and guests are advised to supply their own suntan lotion, hair dryers, alarm clocks, personal toiletries, and bathrobes.

Accommodations: Standard rooms have two double beds, cable television, and a private bath. Studio rooms have ocean views.

Rates: Vary according to room, season, and package. Winter rates for the eight-night package are $1,095–1,195 per person, double occupancy. Special summer rates are available after April 30.

Credit Cards: AE, D, MC, V

Meal Plans: Three gourmet vegetarian meals are served daily. Optional juice and water fasting is available.

Services: Massage, reflexology, facials, body wraps, sea-salt scrubs, hypnotherapy, reiki, yoga, meditation, stress-reduction techniques, wellness counseling, psychic astrology, progressive relaxation/hypnosis, chiropractic, in-depth nutritional profile, and health lectures

Recreational Activities: Swimming, walking

Facilities: An oceanside resort with Spanish-style guest and dining rooms, a gym, a heated outdoor pool, a hot tub, a sauna, and a sundeck

Disability Access: No access

Special Notes: Pets are not allowed on the premises. The minimum allowed age for spa guests is 16. Smoking is not allowed in rooms or on the grounds. Anyone found smoking is asked to leave without a refund.

Nearby Attractions: Broward Performing Arts Culture Center, Pro Players baseball stadium, Gulfstream Park, Miami Convention Center, Golden Isle Tennis Center, shopping, cinema, boating, jet skis, golf

Nearest Airport: Ft. Lauderdale, FL

Getting There: Airport transportation is available through Grayline (954/561-8888), Super Shuttle (800/BLUEVAN), taxis, and car rental. Driving from Ft. Lauderdale and all points along Highway 1, take Highway 1 South to Sheridan Street East; right on South Ocean Drive; continue 4–5 miles; spa entrance is on left.

Spa Atlantis Health and Fitness

1460 South Ocean Boulevard
Pompano Beach, FL 33062
800/583-3500 (reservations only) or 954/941-6688; fax: 954/943-1219
Email: reservations@spa-atlantis.com
Website: www.spa-atlantis.com

"Fit for Life: Health & Lifestyle Enhancement" is the basic program at Spa Atlantis. It is founded on the belief that the body has the natural ability to heal itself and to maintain good health when given proper nutritional and psychological support, as well as an adequate exercise regime. The goal behind this philosophy—and all programs at Spa Atlantis—is to teach people how to make better choices for a healthier mind, body, and spirit. Vacation packages are geared toward pampering, fitness, lifestyle enhancement, stress management, and emotional health. A personalized, structured program is also offered for weight management.

The 70-room resort is situated just footsteps from the shore of Florida's Gold Coast, where guests enjoy walks on the beach. The resort is designed to promote easy access for all guests, with the Cybex fitness center, lecture hall, dining room, lobby, and kitchen all adjacent to one another.

A typical eight-day, seven-night package includes accommodations, three nutritious meals daily, access to all exercise classes and health lectures on the weekly schedule, and three complimentary one-hour services of your choice. From La Stone therapy to reiki to reflexology, the full-service Aveda spa and salon caters to a large variety of body treatment needs. The minimum stay is three nights, but seven nights are recommended to fully benefit from the diet and lifestyle change. A free information video is available to anyone considering the program.

Accommodations: 70 poolside or oceanview rooms with single or double occupancy and private baths. Most rooms have private patios or balconies.

Rates: Vary according to length of stay, season package, and room type. A seven-night package starts at $999 per person for double occupancy.

Credit Cards: AE, CB, D, DC, MC, V

Meal Plans: Three healthy meals are served each day, with the option of vegetarian, fish, or free-range chicken.

Services: Nutritional consultations, acupuncture, personal training, a full-service spa and salon, yoga, tai chi, meditation, aqua aerobics, step aerobics, spinning, kick boxing, Pilates, and wellness lectures

Recreational Activities: Swimming, walking

Facilities: An oceanside resort with eight private treatment rooms, an outdoor heated and ozonated pool, a poolside dining room, a fully equipped gym, a sauna, and a hot tub

Disability Access: All facilities are wheelchair accessible.

Special Notes: The minimum allowed age for spa guests is 18. No dairy products, caffeine, smoking, or alcohol are allowed on the premises.

Nearby Attractions: The spa is close to the trendy Las Olas Boulevard and the award-winning Misner Park. The area offers stylish boutiques and art galleries. Miles of shopping are available at the Riverfront, Town Center, Galleria, and Sawgrass Mill malls.

Nearest Airports: Pompano Beach Airport and Ft. Lauderdale, FL

Getting There: Call spa for details on airport transportation. Car rental is available at Ft. Lauderdale airport. Taxi Service is available at Pompano Beach Airpark (11 minutes to spa). Driving from Ft. Lauderdale and all points along I-95, take I-95 North to Commercial Boulevard East. Exit to A1A North; spa entrance is 1.25 miles on right. (35 minutes)

The Spa at Chateau Elan

Haven Harbour Drive
Braselton, GA 30517
678/425-6064; fax: 678/425-6069
Email: chateau@chateauelan.com
Website: www.chateauelan.com

Taking in a healthy retreat at Chateau Elan is like ordering the three-layered tiramisu and learning that it is not only fat-free but also good for you. The health benefits come in a pleasant disguise known as the "Luxury Vacation." The resort itself looks like it was imported directly from the French country-side, along with sprawling grape fields for the on-site winery. The building is actually a reproduction of a 16th-century French manor house, and within its confines lies a 20-room, world-class spa.

Chateau Elan will never be singularly thought of as a health retreat because it offers too many spectacular activities, from wine tasting to golf tourna-ments; however, for those interested in promoting their well-being through a holistic approach, the Luxury Vacation is the best bet. The program lasts six days, with guests arriving on Sunday. Guests can expect three gourmet meals per day, a compre-hensive fitness assessment, a deep cleansing facial, a manicure, a pedicure, two Swedish massages, a hydrotherapy massage, a hot stone massage, a salt glow/body polish with Vichy shower, an anti-stress wrap, an aromatherapy massage, a hydrotherapy bath, foot reflexology, salon services, access to the steam room, sauna, whirlpool, and indoor resistance pool, afternoon tea, and more. A smaller version of the Luxury Vacation is the "Mini Vacation," which has many similar elements. The benefits of the package are primarily to reduce stress through a healthy diet and personalized care, yet many of the treatments—such as underwater massage, which has been known to relieve arthritis—promote physical well-being.

Accommodations: 14 deluxe rooms with queen-size beds; two loft suites available. A 274-room French-style inn is also on the property, and 18 villas border the golf course.

Rates: Vary according to room, season, and package. The three-day "Spa Getaway" is $889–1,489, including two breakfasts, two lunches, two dinners, lodging, and spa services.

Credit Cards: AE, D, DC, MC, V

Meal Plans: Meals are included with some packages, and vegetarian options are available.

Services: Various types of massage, reflexology, aromatherapy, thalassotherapy, body wraps and scrubs, facials, salon services, yoga, relaxation techniques, exercise equipment, nutritional assessments, fitness evaluations, and a heated outdoor pool

Recreational Activities: Bicycling, horseback riding, concerts, golf

Facilities: A 3,400-acre private resort community with a reproduction 16th-century French manor chateau, a conference center, a library, six restaurants, shops, a spa with 26 treatment rooms, exercise equipment, a Vichy shower, a sauna, a steam bath, a coeducational whirlpool, a hydrotherapy bath, an outdoor heated pool, a health club, seven tennis courts, four golf courses, bicycles, vineyards, a winery, an equestrian center, woodland trails, and a private lake

Disability Access: Yes; full access is available.

Special Notes: The minimum allowed age for spa guests is 18.

Nearby Attractions: Downtown Atlanta's dining, shops, museums, and theater

Nearest Airport: Atlanta, GA

Getting There: Airport transportation provided by spa. Call for reservations and details. Driving from Atlanta, take I-85 to Exit 126; bear left and continue over bridge; spa entrance is on left. (45 minutes)

Wildwood Lifestyle Center and Hospital

P.O. Box 129
Wildwood, GA 30757-0129
800/634-9355 or 706/820-1493; fax 706/820-1474
Website: www.tagnet.org/wildwood

Since 1941, people have come to Wildwood's 600 acres of forested Georgia mountainsides to take part in a residential health program. Over the course of 10 or 17 days, guests learn simple methods of attaining the highest possible condition of wellness. Prevention is stressed at Wildwood, and diet is an important element of that goal. Many serious and chronic conditions are treated at the center—from hypoglycemia to ulcerative colitis—but you don't have to be chronically ill to participate in a program. Wildwood is for anyone who wants to improve his or her health, whether that means learning a healthier way to eat or handle stress or applying lifestyle-changing techniques for preventing heart disease.

The center is run by a staff of Seventh-Day Adventists, but all programs are nondenominational, except for stress-handling methods, which are approached from a Christian perspective. Each program includes the basic elements of a complete medical history, a physical examination, a blood chemistry, periodic physician consultations, a whirlpool, a sauna, massage, hydrotherapy treatments, herbal therapy, guided walks, lectures on health and nutrition, vegetarian cooking classes, meals, and lodging. A typical day starts with a 7 A.M. breakfast, followed by a short walk through the 25 miles of trails. A health lecture begins at 9 A.M., followed by warm-up exercises. A hydrotherapy session is squeezed in before lunch, and another short walk is scheduled afterward. The afternoon consists of a health lecture and cooking class. Dinner is at 6 P.M., after which is a lecture on spiritual or health-related topics.

Accommodations: 26 rooms, double and single occupancy, with private and shared baths

Rates: The 10-day program is $1,740, with a required $150 deposit; the 17-day program is $2,675, with a required $250 deposit. Prices are subject to change without notice. A "Get Acquainted" offer allows you to experience Wildwood at a greatly reduced rate. For only $60 per night, guests can attend health lectures, take guided walks, relax with a massage, and enjoy a delicious vegan buffet.

Credit Cards: AE, MC, V

Meal Plans: Three vegan meals are prepared daily.

Services: Seminars on nutrition, stress management, and addiction recovery; massage; hydrotherapy; health lectures; nutrition classes; cooking demonstrations; physical examinations; medical treatments, including surgical procedures and physical therapy; and spiritual counseling

Recreational Activities: Hiking, boating

Facilities: A 600-acre retreat center with a medical and dental clinic, a lodge with a fireplace, a chaplain's department, a sauna, a whirlpool, hydrotherapy showers, exercise equipment, walking trails, and a lake

Disability Access: Yes; full access is available.

Special Notes: Smoking is not allowed indoors. Phones are available only on request and require a $25 deposit.

Nearby Attractions: North Georgia forests, Chattanooga train museums, Point Park Civil War sites

Nearest Airports: Chattanooga, TN; Atlanta, GA

Getting There: Free transportation from Chattanooga airport or Greyhound with advance reservations. Driving from Knoxville or Atlanta, take I-75 to I-24 West. Continue 15 miles to Exit 169; right at first road; spa entrance is almost 1 mile ahead on left. (2 hours). Driving from Nashville or Birmingham, take I-24 East to Exit 169; right at first road; spa entrance is almost 1 mile ahead on left. (2 hours)

Foxhollow Life Enrichment and Healing Center

8909 Highway 329
Crestwood, KY 40014
800/624-7080 or 502/241-8621; fax: 502/241-3935
Website: www.foxhollow.com

The Foxhollow Life Enrichment and Wellness Center is a place of healing and regeneration that is founded on the principles of European biological medicine. The central purpose of biological medicine is to support people in their processes of healing and renewal by helping to reestablish a right relationship with the natural rhythms of life. Through a synthesis of approaches, including therapeutic spas, creative arts, movement studios, and state-of-the-art clinic facilities, Foxhollow offers people of all ages an environment in which to develop new lifestyle patterns that promote healing.

Foxhollow is located on 1,300 acres of lush Kentucky farmland. Guests can stay in the lovely 150-year-old manor house or in several smaller cottages on the property. The Foxhollow Clinic of Integrative Biological Medicine offers comprehensive assessment, therapeutic, and educational services by a group of highly trained physicians and other medical professionals. The clinic's mission is to support people of all ages in developing new lifestyle patterns that promote healing for body, mind, and spirit.

Also located on the property, the Wetlands Wellness Spa at Foxhollow offers therapeutic services in an artfully attractive redecorated farmhouse, surrounded by fields in which Kentucky thoroughbred horses roam and frolic. Therapies offered include regular massage, lymphatic massage, hydrotherapy, reflexology, Vichy shower treatments, body wraps, Ayurvedic treatments, facials, and more. A sister spa facility, Foxhollow by the River, is located about 20 minutes away in downtown Louisville, Kentucky.

Accommodations: 19 rooms in six guest houses
Rates: $55–80 per night, single occupancy; a nominal extra fee is charged for an additional person. Clinic and spa services are priced separately.
Credit Cards: AE, MC, V
Meal Plans: Gourmet meals, primarily vegetarian, are served daily.
Services: The clinic offers comprehensive health services based on biological medicine. The spas offer a wide range of spa services. Foxhollow also offers various yoga classes, Pilates, and other fitness programs, as well as creative art therapies. Meditation and nature trails are also available to guests.
Facilities: A 1,300-acre country estate with a 150-year-old manor house, a medical clinic, a therapeutic spa with an outdoor swimming pool, a fitness facility, a tennis court, a meditation garden, and walking trails
Disability Access: Yes
Special Notes: Smoking is not allowed indoors.
Nearby Attractions: Churchill Downs, Louisville Slugger Museum, Speed Art Museum, Actors' Theater of Louisville, Louisville Orchestra, Louisville Zoo, horseback riding, and more

Nearest Airports: Louisville, KY; Cincinnati, OH

Getting There: Spa provides airport transportation from Louisville with advance reservations, $40 each way. Car rental is available from airports. Driving from Louisville, take I-264 East to I-71 North; take Exit 14/Crestwood; left onto Highway 329; continue for about 2.5 miles to spa entrance on right. (.5 hour). Driving from Cincinnati, take I-71 South to Exit 14 and follow Louisville directions above. (1–1.5 hours minutes)

Westglow Spa

2845 Highway 221 South
Blowing Rock, NC 28605
800/562-0807 or 828/295-4463; fax: 828/295-5115
Email: request@westglow.com
Website: www.westglow.com

Serenely nestled in the shadow of Grandfather Mountain in North Carolina's Blue Ridge Mountains lies Westglow Spa, a European-style destination spa offering leisure, recreation, and rejuvenation for the mind, body, and soul. The primary foci at this spa include relaxation, nutrition, fitness, and stress management.

Westglow is situated on a historic 20-acre estate, which was once the summer home of artist and author Elliot Dangerfield, who named the estate "Westglow" because "the sunsets are always glowing, never glaring." The spa, which looks like a stately plantation from the past, sits on a knoll with a 360-degree view of Grandfather Mountain, the Blue Ridge Parkway, and vistas beyond. The Colonial-style mansion on the estate, known as the Manor House, was built in 1916 and is listed in the National Register of Historic Places. The house includes seven elegantly restored bedroom suites furnished with period antiques. The grand entraceway with its sweeping staircase is the registration and reception area.

Westglow divides its programs and services into four main concentrations: relaxation and beauty, cardiovascular conditioning, weight management, and total health and image. Specialized services include fitness assessment and exercise prescription, massages, facials, body scrubs, craniosacral work, touch for health, stress management counseling, cooking classes, and more. Another important feature available to guests is the hiking and outdoor activity program. The Blue Ridge Mountains of western North Carolina contain miles of scenic hiking trails and ancient rivers for explorers and nature lovers of all fitness levels. Guests may choose from several planned hikes varying in distance and difficulty. Personal trainers ensure the correct exercise program for each guest and motivate the implementation of a regular exercise program.

Accommodations: Seven rooms in the main house and two cottages with one or two bedrooms

Rates: Packages range from one night at $356 per person for standard double occupancy to seven nights at $2,722 per person for deluxe single occupancy.

Credit Cards: MC, V

Meal Plans: Three meals daily are included in the two- to seven-night packages.

Services: Massage, body scrub, herbal wrap, facials, hair and nail salon, personal trainer, aqua aerobics, yoga, dancercise, kickboxing, step aerobics, circuit training, and cooking

Recreational Activities: Walking, daily supervised hikes in the Blue Ridge Mountains, horseback riding, tennis, and croquet

Facilities: The Life Enhancement Center contains a 15-station Cybex weight training area, a cardiovascular center, an indoor pool, two hot tubs, two wet/dry saunas, an aerobics floor, treatment rooms, a sun deck, a hair and nail salon, private showers, and dressing areas

Disability Access: Yes; full access is available.

Special Notes: The staff-to-guest ratio is 3 to 1. Smoking is not permitted inside the facilities, only outdoors. Children younger than age 16 are not permitted in the facilities.

Nearby Attractions: Miles of mountain trails, whitewater rafting, canoeing, trout fishing, horseback riding, skiing, and unique shops in Blowing Rock

Nearest Airport: Charlotte, NC

Getting There: Car rental is available at airport. Driving from Charlotte, take I-77 North, then I-40 west to Exit 321. Continue on Highway 321 North to Blowing Rock; exit at Sunset Boulevard; take Main Street to Highway 221 south and continue to spa entrance. (2.5 hours)

Tennessee Fitness Spa

299 Natural Bridge Rd.
Waynesboro, TN 38485
800/235-8365 or 931/722-5589; fax: 931/722-9113
Email: shaw@netease.net
Website: www.tfspa.com

The Tennessee Fitness Spa is located at the beautiful and historic Natural Bridge. The bridge was formed over millions of years by nature and is the only known double-span, naturally formed bridge formation in the world. The site is bordered by Forty-Eight Creek, which contains crystal-clear cool water. Many species of fish can be seen from the banks. In addition to this natural setting, the spa has added beautiful landscaping and flower gardens. There is a clear-water stream on the property, trout ponds, and lovely walking trails.

A typical day begins with a healthy breakfast. The daily exercise program starts with a warmup and a walk. The length of your walk depends on your ability and fitness. Your group leader guides you through walks varying from 2–12 miles of scenic beauty. Next is an aerobics class, followed by lunch. The afternoon often starts with a nutrition/fitness lecture, followed by an aerobic step class, weight training, walking, and aquacise. After dinner, you enjoy an evening lecture and cross-training exercises, such as volleyball or pool games, and cooking classes or movies. These activities are provided so that you receive the maximum benefit from your fitness vacation; however, you are also free to just relax at any time.

Accommodations: Quads, doubles, deluxe doubles, private rooms, and a penthouse are available. All units are carpeted and have heat and air-conditioning. All units have either twin beds, a twin and a double, or two double beds. They have either a full bath or a bath with shower only. Each chalet-type building has a large front deck, complete with swings and hanging baskets and an excellent view of the pond and creek.

Rates: $550 quad; $700 double; $770 deluxe double; private from $1,025

Credit Cards: AE, D, MC, V

Meal Plans: The foods served are low in calories and fat and highly nutritious. Both standard and vegan meal plans are available. All meals are low in sodium and sugar and have no artificial sweeteners. Natural sweeteners are used as needed. Medical dietary restrictions can be accommodated with timely notifications.

Services: Massages, facials, manicures, and a full-service salon. Cooking lectures are given so that you may follow the healthy cooking philosophy in your home.

Recreational Activities: Horseback riding, canoeing, hiking, golf, and tennis

Facilities: A large indoor heated pool, a 500-square-foot gym, a racquetball court, a dining room, a pro shop, massage rooms, a beauty salon, a recreation room, a hot tub, a sauna, trout ponds on site, and streams

Disability Access: No access

Special Notes: Smoking is allowed in designated outside areas and on chalet porches only. The spa is closed from December 17 through February 20 each year.

Nearby Attractions: Helen Keller's home, a Jack Daniels' distillery, the Shiloh National Civil War Battleground, Amish communities, and the Grand Ole Opry are all within a two-hour drive.

Nearest Airport: Nashville, TN

Getting There: Spa provides airport service with advance reservations, $60 round trip. Driving from Nashville and northern points, take I-65 to Route 412 (Columbia/ Exit 46). Continue on Route 412 West to Hohenwald; left on Route 20; 1 mile to Route 99 W; follow Route 99 W for 20 miles to spa entrance. Driving from southern points, take I-65 to Exit 1 (Highway 31) after crossing Tennessee state line. Continue North on Highway 31 to Pulaski; left on Highway 64 for 50 miles; 1 mile east of Waynesboro, right onto Highway 99 E; continue 9 miles to spa entrance.

Hartland Wellness Center

P.O. Box 1
Rapidan, VA 22733
800/763-9355 or 540/672-3100; fax: 540-672-2484
Email: wellness@hartland.edu
Website: www.hartland.edu/nuhealth

The Hartland Wellness Center, founded in 1983, is situated on 760 acres in the picturesque Piedmont Valley, just 75 miles south of Washington, D.C. This health retreat is operated by Seventh-Day Adventists to meet the needs of people of all religious persuasions. Residential programs approach health from the perspective of prevention and lifestyle management.

Hartland's guests include those who may already be healthy and simply want a refreshing tune-up, as well as others who may have chronic ailments such as diabetes, arthritis, cancer, and heart disease. Smoking cessation programs are also available. The programs are designed as therapeutic reconditioning and health education experiences for people wanting to establish lasting good health. The sessions start with an initial health evaluation, which includes blood profiles followed by medical consultations with a resident physician, health lectures, nutritional counseling, massage and hydrotherapy treatments, gentle exercise, and recreational outings.

Lodging is in a modern, two-story Colonial-style building with private accommodations. Meals consist of low-fat vegan cuisine. The program includes scheduled weekend outings to natural areas and historic sites. During free time, guests can enjoy the indoor swimming pool, exercise room, sauna, sundeck, and garden. For those who want to learn more about Hartland before committing to a residential retreat, the center opens its doors to the public for a complimentary low-fat vegan lunch. Anyone interested can call to make arrangements.

Accommodations: Up to 15 in a two-story Colonial-style building with queen-size beds and private baths

Rates: A 10-day session is $1,995; an 18-day session is $2,995; both packages include lodging, meals, and services.

Credit Cards: None accepted

Meal Plans: Three low-fat vegan meals are included in the program.

Services: Personal consultations and evaluations with a resident physician, nurse, and therapists; blood profiles, health lectures, stress-management presentations, and nutritional instruction; massage, hydrotherapy, and calisthenics; Christian-based spiritual guidance; and recreational outings

Recreational Activities: Hiking, walking, swimming

Facilities: A 760-acre estate with a two-story residential and treatment building, exercise equipment, a sundeck, a sauna, a steam bath, an indoor pool, and a garden

Disability Access: Yes

Special Notes: Smoking is not allowed.

Nearby Attractions: Monticello, home to Thomas Jefferson; Montpelier, home to James Madison; George Washington's birthplace; Skyline Drive in Shenandoah National Park; the Appalachian Trail; Civil War sites

Nearest Airport: Charlottesville, VA

Getting There: Airport transportation is provided with advance reservations, $30 each way. Driving from Charlottesville, take Highway 29 North to Route 230.

Continue on Route 230 East to Highway 15 North; exit onto Route 614 East (Locust Dale); spa entrance is 1.25 miles east on Route 614. (45 minutes). Driving from all northern or southern points along I-95, take I-95 to US-64 to Charlottesville. Follow Charlottesville directions listed above.

Yogaville

Route 1, Box 1720
Buckingham, VA 23921
800/858-9642 or 804/969-3121; fax: 804/969-1303
Email: iyi@yogaville.org
Website: www.yogaville.org

Yogaville (also known as the Satchidananda Ashram) is a spiritual center and community in which people of diverse faiths come together to practice the principles of integral yoga as taught by Sri Swami Satchidananda. It is situated on 750 acres of woodland along the James River at the foothills of the Blue Ridge Mountains. One of the unique landmarks of Yogaville is the Light of Truth Universal Shrine (LOTUS), which serves as a central gathering place for people of all backgrounds and beliefs to silently worship, meditate, or sit in contemplation, according to their individual traditions, all under one roof. Inside there are 12 altars, representing each known religion of the world. The shrine is built in the shape of a lotus flower and set amid the peace and calm of a 16-acre lake, with the Blue Ridge Mountains in the background. The interfaith center contains pools, waterfalls, and a grand cupola topped with a golden spire. There are two Peace Poles on which is inscribed "May Peace Prevail on Earth" in eight different languages.

The programs at Yogaville include retreats, meditation, hatha yoga workshops, and health-oriented weekend workshops, such as "Menopause: A Yogic Approach to the Change of Life," "Ayurveda and Yoga for Health," "Transcending Fear, Anger, and Depression," "Health Enhancement Lifestyle Program," "Fasting and Detoxification," "Wellness Retreat," and a "Health Symposium." Each summer, a two-week residential program is available for children ages 8–16. Activities include hatha yoga, swimming, sports, arts and crafts, drama, hiking, and campfires.

Accommodations: Two dormitories with rooms that sleep 2–8 people. Semiprivate rooms are also available for singles, married couples, and families. Each dormitory has a shared bathroom, shower, and laundry facility nearby. The Lotus Inn, consisting of six units, is adjacent to the dormitories and offers private rooms. Tenting is also an option.

Meals: Three nutritious lactovegetarian meals are served each day, including whole grains, protein sources such as tofu and legumes, fresh fruit, and vegetables. No meat, poultry, fish, or eggs are permitted at the retreat. No personal food items are allowed in dorm rooms.

Rates: Vary depending on length of stay and choice of accommodations. A weekend stay runs approximately $220 per person, which includes the program, dorm accommodations, and three meals daily. Midweek rates are slightly lower.

Credit Cards: MC, V

Facilities: More than 1,000 acres with Ashram dorms, an inn, an ecumenical shrine, a yoga/meditation hall, a sauna, and a hot tub

Services: Daily group meditations and hatha yoga classes, a Saturday Ashram and LOTUS Tour, massage therapy, chiropractic, and a resident physician

Recreational Activities: 1,000 acres of wooded land, with many paths for walking and hiking; swimming in the lake and nearby river in the summer

Disability Access: Yes; facilities are fully accessible.

Nearby Attractions: Monticello, the home of Thomas Jefferson, and Montpelier, the home of James Madison, are located in nearby Charlottesville, Virginia.

Nearest Airports: Charlottesville, Norfolk, and Richmond, VA

Getting There: Transportation is provided from Charlottesville with advance reservation, $25 each way. Driving from Charlottesville, take I-64 West toward Lynchburg. Exit to 29 South Bypass to I-64 East toward Richmond; after 3 miles take Exit 121A onto Route 20 South through Scottsville; right onto Route 655; bear right as Route 655 becomes Route 601; continue along winding hill to intersection with Route 604; left onto Route 604; right at sign for "Satchidananda Ashram-Yogaville." Driving from Boston and New England, take Massachusetts Turnpike West to Sturbridge and 1-84 West. Follow 1-84 to Scranton, PA; exit to 1-81 South towards Staunton, VA; exit to I-64 East and continue to Charlottesville (about 30 mi.); exit at Route 20 South (Scottsville) and follow directions from Charlottesville listed above.

Coolfont Resort, Conference Center, and Health Spa

1777 Cold Run Valley Road
Berkeley Springs, WV 25411
800/888-8768 or 304/258-4500; fax: 304/258-5499
Email: steve@coolfont.com
Website: www.coolfont.com

Some people attribute the founding of Coolfont Resort and Spa to a snow-storm. In 1961, Sam Ashelman drove to the eastern panhandle of West Virginia for an Easter vacation with his young son. A heavy snowfall forced him to spend the night in nearby Berkeley Springs, where Ashelman saw a "For Sale" sign on a 1,200-acre estate. Today, the stately Manor House, lakes, streams, cabins, and hiking trails provide guests with an idyllic escape for rejuvenation, renewal, and relaxation.

Spa programs at Coolfont are designed to achieve and maintain a balance of the wellness spectrum, including fitness, nutrition, and stress reduction. A typical package includes lodging and three low-fat, high-fiber spa meals per day; walking and hiking programs; stress-management sessions; yoga, tai chi, and relaxation techniques; and access to the spa dining room, indoor solar-heated swimming pool, sauna, whirlpool tub, and Cybex exercise equipment. Throughout the year, Coolfont offers Spectrum of Learning courses covering various health-related topics. Courses average 3–5 days, and room and board are included in tuition. Some topics include the five-day "Introduction to the World of Herbs" and the three-day "Touch for Health Kinesiology: Balance the Energy Flow."

Coolfont also takes an active role in protecting the environment. Since 1965, owners Sam and Martha Ashelman have been committed to providing a demonstration center for environmental preservation. The resort has hosted a panel discussion on Earth's deteriorating condition, based on astronaut Mary Cleave's observation of how much worse Earth looks from space now than it did years ago. Cleave and Nature Conservancy author Bruce Rich hosted the discussion.

Accommodations: Single and double rooms with private baths in lodge rooms and chalets with wood-burning stoves and whirlpools. Private vacation homes are also available.

Rates: Vary according to room, program, and season. Two-night spa packages start at $250.

Credit Cards: AE, D, MC, V

Meal Plans: Three low-fat, high-fiber meals are prepared daily with lots of fresh fruit, vegetables, and whole grains. Fish, poultry, and vegetarian entrées are available.

Services: Workshops on natural foods, stress reduction, and problem solving; team-building programs sponsored by Outward Bound; nutritional consultations; massage; craniosacral therapy; herbal wraps; facials; meditation, yoga, tai chi; relaxation techniques; salon services; aquacise; body sculpting; weight training; fitness classes; walking and hiking programs

Recreational Activities: Horseshoes, horseback riding, snow-tubing in the park

Facilities: A 1,350-acre estate with lodges, chalets, log cabins, an indoor solar-heated pool, a sauna, a whirlpool tub, exercise equipment, basketball and volleyball courts, and a beach on a private lake

Disability Access: Yes; full access is available.

Special Notes: Smoking is allowed only in designated areas.

Nearby Attractions: Championship golf at Cacapon State Park, White Tail Ski Resort, Berkeley Springs State Park

Nearest Airport: Washington Dulles, DC/VA area

Getting There: Airport transportation is available from AES Limo, 800/832-6561. Advance reservations are recommended. Driving from Berkeley Springs, take Route 522 to Route 9 West. After going over crest of hill (.75 miles), turn left onto Cold Run Valley Road; spa entrance is 4 miles on left. (15 minutes) Driving from Washington, D.C. and Maryland suburbs, take I-270 North to I-70 West. Take Exit 1B, which becomes Route 522 South; continue on Route 522 to Berkeley Springs, Virginia and follow directions listed above. (2 hours) Driving from Baltimore, take I-70 West to Exit 1B, which becomes Route 522 South; continue on Route 522 to Berkeley Springs, Virginia and follow directions listed above. (3 hours)

The Greenbrier

What look like slender White House columns protrude from the regal façade of the Greenbrier, a AAA Five-Diamond resort. The Greenbrier began as a cottage community more than 200 years ago and now claims 6,500 acres of an Allegheny Mountain valley. The community evolved around the famed mineral baths, which were first discovered in 1778. When word got out that a woman's rheumatism was "cured" minutes after immersion in the sulphur water, the migration began.

The spa has changed face since 1912, with a $7 million renovation. Today, the 25,000-square-foot wing contains an indoor pool and a Rhododendron Terrace Lounge, along with the historic baths. "We offered hydrotherapy in 1912 and still offer it today," says Greenbrier president Ted Kleisner. Fresh, natural mineral waters fill private walk-in whirlpool baths. Treatments are patterned after European spas, which emphasize water therapy, massage, body wraps, and skincare.

A unique facet of this luxury resort is the Greenbrier Clinic. Based on the reasoning that healthy people make healthy corporations, the clinic was founded in 1948 to offer prevention-oriented health care in a luxury setting to the nation's top executives. The staff includes eight medical doctors, a cardiologist, two radiologists, and a nutritionist. The spa works in conjunction with the clinic to offer a five-day Spa and Clinic Program. Guests receive lodging for five nights, daily breakfast and dinner, a complete diagnostic evaluation, a fitness evaluation with a follow-up consultation, two full-body massages, a mineral bath and soak in White Sulphur Springs' waters, a Swiss shower and Scotch spray, a European pressure-point facial, a manicure with paraffin, a haircut and blow dry, an exfoliation treatment, and unlimited use of the exercise facilities.

Accommodations: 637 guest rooms, including 71 guest houses and cottages and 46 suites

Rates: Vary according to room, services, and season. Children stay and eat free when sharing a room with their parents.

Credit Cards: AE, D, MC, V

Meal Plans: The Modified American Plan includes breakfast in the main dining room and dinner either in the main dining room or at Sam Snead's at the golf club. The main dining room breakfast offers low-calorie and standard eggs-and-bacon choices; Sam Snead's offers gourmet entrées, with meat, poultry, fish, and vegetable options.

Services: Swedish and aromatherapy massage, herbal body wraps, hydrotherapy, facials, salon services, aerobics, body composition assessments, weight training, internal medicine, radiology, cardiology, nursing, mammography, ultrasound, lab work, nutritional and psychological counseling, kids' programs

Recreational Activities: Fly-fishing, skeet- and trapshooting, croquet, carriage rides, horseback riding, hiking, nature walks, golf, and a land rover driving school

Facilities: Scotch spray; steam, sauna, and therapy rooms; private walk-in mineral baths; indoor and outdoor swimming pools; exercise equipment; a health clinic; a lounge; six dining rooms; a game room with billiards and a bowling alley; three 18-hole golf courses; 20 indoor and outdoor tennis courts; and shops

Disability Access: Yes; full access is available.

Special Notes: Smoking is not allowed in the spa.

Nearby Attractions: Shopping in White Sulphur Springs, Presidents' Cottage Museum

Nearest Airport: Washington Dulles, DC/VA area

Getting There: Greenbrier Travel Service, 800/624-6070, assists guests with travel arrangements and makes all necessary reservations. Driving from Washington, D.C. and suburban Maryland, take I-66 West to I-81 South (Lexington, VA). Continue on I-64 to Sulphur Springs exit; spa entrance is 1.5 miles from exit. (4.5 hours)

Central

Eden Valley Lifestyle Center

6263 North County Road 29
Loveland, CO 80538
800/637-WELL or 970/669-7730; fax 970/667-1742
Email: edenvalleyls@juno.com
Website: www.tagnet.org/edenvalley

The Eden Valley Lifestyle Center is situated on 550 acres of fields, woods, lakes, and streams in Colorado's Rocky Mountains. The center offers seven- to 24-day lifestyle programs providing therapy, nutrition, and exercise for people suffering from chronic conditions such as allergies, high blood pressure, and arthritis. The program began in 1987 as an extension to services offered at the nearby Eden Valley senior citizens' home. The home can still be found on the grounds, as can a Seventh-Day Adventist medical missionary school.

Natural remedies and a holistic approach are essential elements of the lifestyle programs. A comprehensive physical examination, including a blood chemistry analysis, starts off the program. Guests can also expect to receive nutritional counseling, daily exercise, paraffin baths for arthritis, health lectures, cooking classes, and herbal remedies. Hydrotherapy, therapeutic massage treatments, and optional guided fasting are also a part of the program. Meals consist of fresh vegan cuisine made with fruit and vegetables from the center's organic garden. During free time, guests can walk along quiet mountain trails or visit nearby antique shops and ghost towns.

Eden Valley's staff strives to send guests home with improved physical, mental, and social well-being, as well as a renewed sense of vitality, strength, and stamina. Because disease is viewed as a result of an unhealthy lifestyle, staff members work to help guests understand the cause of their disease in order to correct it. Guests then learn health-promoting principles to continue their lifelong journey to wellness. A healthy lifestyle consisting of no smoking or alcohol, a high-fiber, low-fat vegetarian diet, and normal weight maintenance is emphasized to prevent illness.

The center has had successful results in treating chronic illnesses, including heart disease, digestive problems, chronic fatigue, high blood pressure, and arthritis. The center's New Start Program is designed, in particular, to combat the effects of stress, obesity, and addiction. The acronym NEWSTART summarizes the program's basic elements: Nutrition, Exercise, Water, Sunlight, Temperance, Air, Rest, and Trust in God.

Accommodations: Five rooms are in private homes and five are in a new guest house, three of which have private baths.

Rates: One-week program $600; two-week program $1,100; three-week program $1,500

Credit Cards: MC, V

Meal Plans: Three vegan meals are prepared daily for Lifestyle participants.

Services: Lifestyle programs, hydrotherapy/massage treatments, colonics, health lectures, medical examinations, and cooking classes

Recreational Activities: Nearby swimming, horseback riding, hiking, downhill and cross-country skiing, fishing, boating, tennis, golf

Facilities: A 550-acre retreat center with exercise equipment, a sundeck, a sauna, a hot tub, walking trails, a garden, lakes, a solarium, and greenhouses

Special Notes: Smoking is not allowed. All staff members are Seventh-Day Adventists.

Nearby Attractions: Outdoor recreations, rodeos, the county fair, trail rides, ghost towns, balloon rides

Nearest Airport: Denver, CO

Getting There: Car rental is available at airport. Driving from Denver, take I-25 North to Loveland. Exit on County Road 27 and continue to County Road 29 to spa entrance. (1.5 hours) Driving from Boulder, take Canyon Boulevard and turn right onto 28th street. Exit onto I-25 North towards Ft. Collins; exit I-25 at US-34 West (Exit 257B); right onto US-34 West/Eisenhower Boulevard; right onto Route 56; left onto Country Road 29 and spa entrance. (1.5–2 hours)

Gold Lake Mountain Resort and Spa

3371 Gold Lake Road
Ward, CO 80481
800/450-3544 or 303/459-3544; fax: 303/459-3541
Email: reservations@goldlake.com
Website: www.goldlake.com

Located in the Rocky Mountains, Gold Lake Mountain Resort is an early-19th-century fishing resort and girls' camp that has been renovated into a charming lodge and spa. This resort offers a natural, peaceful ambience derived from its rustic architecture and its sense of solitude. The focus is on relaxation and pleasure. None of the accommodations has telephones, televisions, or other modern distractions. Instead, a variety of mountain recreational activities is available for guests, including hiking, canoeing, kayaking, sailing, ice-skating, swimming, horseshoes, croquet, billiards, board games, snowshoeing, and cross-country skiing. And then there is the spa. With a full menu of treatment options, visitors can indulge, relax, and rejuvenate with various massage therapies and signature spa treatments. Guests also enjoy soaking in four hot pools built into the rocks above the lake, which view the Continental Divide.

The "All-Inclusive Weekend Getaway" includes two night's lodging in the accommodation of your choice, daily Swiss-style Continental breakfast, Saturday lunch, one pampering spa service per participant, two participatory class sessions with Executive Chef Eric Skokan (in the Lake House using a homestyle kitchen), an intimate seven-course dinner on Saturday featuring menu selections from cooking class sessions with wine pairings, and free time to relax, recreate, and enjoy the resort amenities.

Guests at the resort experience a taste of old-fashioned Colorado living without sacrificing elegance and comfort. The historic resort cabins, scenic outdoor hot pools, and signature spa treatments make one think paradoxically of both romance and personal time. Gold Mountain Resort is an ideal getaway for couples or solo escape.

Accommodations: Standard, deluxe, and private cabin lodging. If you need a phone, please request one at the time of your reservation.

Rates: Vary depending on season and accommodations. Range from $195–515 per night. Cost for the All-Inclusive Weekend Getaway is $450–600 per person depending on choice of lodging accommodation.

Meal Plans: A complimentary Swiss Continental breakfast is included with an overnight stay. Food and beverage costs for lunches and dinners are extra. Alice's Restaurant in the historic lodge features a "from-scratch" kitchen using organically grown produce and whole foods whenever possible, as well as free-range, hormone-free animal products.

Services: Massages, facials, hot rock treatments, craniosacral work, reiki treatments, salt glow, thalassotherapy, and more

Recreational Activities: Hiking, canoeing, kayaking, sailing, ice-skating, swimming, horseback riding, snowshoeing, croquet, billiards, board games, and horseshoes. For those bringing their own gear, the resort also offers fly fishing, mountain biking, and backcountry skiing. All activities are not available in all seasons; please inquire in advance.

Facilities: The main lodge, 18 restored cabin lodgings, a restaurant, a tepee, a billiards room, a sauna, and lakeside hot pools

Disability Access: No access

Special Notes: Gold Lake is primarily an adult-centered resort and does not offer children's programs or child-sitting services. None of the accommodations have telephones, televisions, or other modern distractions. If you need a phone, you can request one at the time of your reservation. No alcohol, pets, or radios are allowed on the premises.

Nearest Airport: Boulder, CO

Getting There: Car rental is available at airport. Driving from Boulder, take Canyon Boulevard (Highway 119) to Nederland. Exit at Highway 72 and continue 12 miles northwest toward Estes Park; right on County Road 100; right onto Gold Lake Road; spa entrance 2.5 miles on road. (25 minutes)

HealthQuarters Lodge

955 Garden of the Gods Road, Suite C
Colorado Springs, CO 80907
719/593-8694; fax 719/531-7884
Email: healthqu@healthquarters.org
Website: www.healthquarters.org

The HealthQuarters 11-day lifestyle program is one aspect of the larger Health Quarters Ministries. The purpose behind the program is to promote physical and spiritual wellness through nutrition, natural health care practices, and instruction on how to renew one's connection with Jesus through prayer and devotional life. All HealthQuarters programs are based on Christian philosophies.

Guests begin with a seven-day intensive detoxification fast-and-cleansing process. Organically grown juice drinks are consumed daily, along with nutritional support. Guests receive water or coffee enemas three times per day and one liver/gallbladder flush. Daily dry brushing and two scheduled therapeutic massage sessions help remove dead skin, revive the cells, and improve circulation. A total of eight instructional classes provide nutritional information, and three classes teach guests how to meet their spiritual and emotional needs. The program winds down with a vegetarian banquet, and guests are given access to follow-up with HealthQuarters' staff and resources.

Don't expect nursing care, drugs, or medications. The lodge is not a hospital or clinic, and it does not claim to treat specific diseases. Rather, guests learn the principles of nutrition and how to detoxify their bodies and rebuild impaired immune systems. They then get a chance to apply their newly learned habits during the 11-day sessions, which are offered once a month year-round.

Accommodations: Nine bedrooms in a B&B-style lodge, each with a private bath. Only 10–15 participants are allowed at a time to preserve the unique group dynamics.

Rates: HealthQuarters recommends that you call ahead for details.

Credit Cards: MC, V

Meal Plans: Seven of the 11 program days are juice fasting. The remaining meals are organic and vegetarian.

Services: Guided fasting, detoxification programs, enema cleanses, spiritual counseling, massages, herbal supplements, dry brushing, light exercise, nutritional seminars, and networking assistance

Recreational Activities: Walking

Facilities: A lodge with a large dining area and instructional room

Disability Access: Some facilities are accessible for people with disabilities.

Special Notes: Smoking is not allowed.

Nearby Attractions: Garden of the Gods, Seven Falls, Cave of the Winds, Cheyenne Mountain Zoo, Will Rodgers Shrine, Pro Rodeo Hall of Fame, Mining Museum, Cliff Dwellings

Nearest Airport: Denver and Colorado Springs, CO

Getting There: Spa provides complimentary transportation from Colorado Springs Airport. Driving from Denver, take I-70 West to I-225 South. Continue to Colorado Springs; exit at Highway 24 West; follow up mountain pass; left on Pikes Peak Highway; bear left at fork in the road continuing on Pikes Peak Highway; after Santa's Workshop, immediately turn left at "Black Barrian" sign; spa entrance is on the left. Driving from Colorado Springs, take S. Powers Boulevard, left onto E. Fountain Boulevard; continue as it becomes US-24; continue along US-24; go up ramp; keep right at fork in ramp and enter I-25N; exit at Exit 146/Garden of the Gods Road; keep left at fork and merge onto W. Garden of the Gods Road, spa entrance .5 mile. (.5 hour)

Hot Sulphur Springs Resort and Spa

P.O. Box 275
Hot Sulphur Springs, CO 80451
800/510-6235 or 970/725-3306
Email: reservations@hotsulphursprings.com
Website: www.hotsulphursprings.com

Hot Sulphur Springs is Colorado's oldest spa, established 130 years ago, and was discovered hundreds of years before that by the area's original inhabitants. The Ute Indians considered these waters to be sacred and referred to them as "big medicine." In 1996 the local Ute Indians were invited to the rededication of the spa as a healing facility after new owner Charles Nash gave the resort a $1 million renovation.

Nestled within 80 acres of lush riverside land, the mineral-rich waters are maintained at temperatures of 95–112°F. The pools and baths do not contain abrasive minerals or chemicals, are not filtered, and are not re-circulated. Naturally occurring minerals include sodium, sulfate, chloride, silica, potassium, calcium, floride, and magnesium.

The entrance to the resort is through a winding, beautifully landscaped road that crosses the Colorado River. The resort rests at the foot of a hill, with 21 hot pools, private hot baths, and a summer swimming pool. Lodging is available in the motel building and a renovated cabin built in 1840. Free pool use is included with either lodging option.

Time moves at a leisurely pace at Hot Sulphur Springs, so be prepared to be pampered, picnic, and enjoy all that nature offers.

Accommodations: Seventeen rooms have Western/modern décor and a double bed, queen bed, or two twin beds. Rooms have views of the Colorado River or the mountains.

Rates: Lodging prices range from $78 for one person to $128 for two people, which includes use of all outdoor pools and the solarium pool.

Meal Plans: A summer snack bar at the motel serves sandwiches, salads, and fresh fruit smoothies from May to September. Several restaurants are located nearby.

Services: Massages, facials, hot stone therapy, salt glow, and body wraps

Recreational Activities: Hiking, rafting, snowshoeing, skiing, snow mobiles, sleigh rides, and dog sleds

Facilities: The main lodge with a fireplace lounge, solarium, and snack bar; massage rooms; a conference room; 20 outdoor pools and private baths; a swimming pool; and bathrooms

Disability Access: Access is available to the lodge and pools, but not to the sleeping rooms. Please call for accommodation suggestions.

Nearby Attractions: Winter Park Ski Area (Colorado's busiest ski area); 10 minutes from Silver Creek Ski Area; 60 minutes from Summit County which has major skiing and sailing, and just over an hour to Vail and Steamboat Springs; 20 minutes from Grand Lake, Shadow Mountain Lake and Lake Granby for sailing and fishing.

Special Notes: No televisions or telephones are provided in the rooms. No smoking is allowed in the rooms or on the premises. The Colorado River runs through the property, as does the Amtrak railroad.

Nearest Airport: Denver, CO

Getting There: Airport transportation is available through Home James 800/451-4844. Driving from Denver, take I-70 to Highway 40 and city of Hot Sulphur Springs. (2 hours)

The Lodge and Spa at Cordillera

P.O. Box 1110, 2205 Cordillera Way
Edwards, CO 81632
800/87-RELAX (877-3529) or 970/926-2200;
fax: 970/926-2714
Website: www.cordillera-vail.com

The many reasons to visit The Lodge and Spa at Cordillera include spectacular hiking and skiing, the glamour of Vail, gourmet dining, in-room fireplaces, and the luxury of a dry brush massage. But wellness? The new "Wellness Weekend" now provides yet another reason to visit the plush surroundings and state-of-the-art spa tucked away in Colorado's Rocky Mountains. The weekend is not intended to be a quick cure but to teach the practice of a healthy lifestyle.

Six rooms are held for the event, which takes place in September. The weekend begins on Thursday, when—after checking in and unpacking—guests attend a reception and an introduction to stress-release techniques. The following morning begins with yogic breathing and stretching, followed by a gourmet vegetarian breakfast. A hike follows, and the nearby White River National Forest, is a beautiful and healthy exercise option. Aromatherapy follows, with guests learning about the benefits of flower oils and essences. After lunch, guests have free time for spa services, a golf or tennis clinic, or some shopping in nearby Vail. Dinner is combined with a cooking class led and prepared by a spa chef. Saturday starts with an early breakfast, and the routine is similar to the previous day, except for the addition of an aquatics class and a Pilates session. Guests check out at noon on Sunday.

Accommodations: 56 deluxe rooms and suites, some with a fireplace, sundeck, and balcony

Rates: Vary according to season and choice of lodging. The Wellness Weekend package is $710–1,180.

Credit Cards: AE, D, MC, V

Meal Plans: A breakfast buffet is included with the room rate. Three restaurants are located on the property. Some packages include meals; inquire for details.

Services: Massage, hydrotherapy, aromatherapy, watsu exercise equipment, sauna, steam room, lap pool, salon services, yoga, Pilates

Recreational Activities: Golf, tennis, hiking, mountain biking, fishing, skiing, snowshoeing, snowmobiling, dogsled rides, ski tours, croquet, volleyball, badminton, gourmet picnic lunches

Facilities: A 5,000-acre resort with a three-story lodge, a lobby with a large limestone fireplace, a restaurant, a coeducational exercise room, an aerobics studio, an indoor lap pool, an outdoor heated pool, men's and women's saunas, private hiking, biking, and cross-country skiing trails, and three world-class golf courses

Disability Access: Yes; full access is available.

Special Notes: The spa has regularly been voted among one of the top 10 spas in North American by notable travel magazines.

Nearby Attractions: White River National Forest, Beaver Creek, El Mirador Peak, shopping and dining in downtown Vail

Nearest Airport: Denver, CO

Getting There: Colorado Shuttle, 970/476-5544, provides transportation to spa. Call ahead for rates and reservations. Driving from Denver, take I-70 to Exit 163/Edwards. Exit onto Route 6; continue to Squaw Creek Road then Cordillera Way; follow signs to main lodge.

Shoshoni Yoga Retreat

P.O. Box 410
Rollinsville, CO 80474
303/642-0116; fax: 303/642-0116
Email: kailasa@shoshoni.org
Website: www.shoshoni.org

Named after nearby Shoshoni Mountain, Shoshoni Yoga Retreat was founded by Sri Shambhavananda, who believes that when people are allowed to rest and recharge in a nurturing environment, they naturally discover the beauty and love within themselves.

The retreat sits on 210 acres, with lush aspen groves, tall ponderosa pines, hidden valleys, and springfed streams. Bright prayer flags and large Buddhas painted on rock walls adorn the valley. Visitors are welcomed to log cabins nestled in the forest and the smell of sweet pine.

Originally a children's summer camp, the property has six rustic duplex guest cabins, a lodge, a meditation building, a shrine, and a temple. A large variety of wild flowers, including lavender columbines and Indian paintbrush, blossom abundantly in spring and summer.

In addition to yoga and meditation, Shoshoni offers Ayurvedic cleansing and renewal programs. Consultations focus on lifestyle, health, and diet concerns. Spa facilities include five treatment rooms, two showers, a sauna, and a hot tub. Treatments include traditional massages, hot oil purification treatments, herbal facials, body scrubs, herbal wraps, and raindrop therapy.

Accommodations: Guests sleep in small, rustic cabins, which offer the basics and a few extras, such as all-natural toiletries. Each cabin has 2–4 beds, carpeting, and a bathroom with shower. There is also a men's and women's dorm, which houses four or more people. Campsites are available for those who bring tents.

Rates: Prices include three vegetarian meals per day, daily yoga, meditation classes, and overnight accommodations. A private cabin with bath is $130 per person, per night; a double cabin with private bath is $80 per person per night; the dorm is $65 per person per night. A retreat cabin (rustic) with a bathhouse nearby is $55 per person per night; and tent camping (bring your own tent) is $45 per person per night.

Credit Cards: MC, V

Meal Plans: Three low-fat, nondairy, vegetarian meals are provided. Food is made with organically grown ingredients as much as possible. Ayurveda meals are featured as well.

Services: Massage, aromatherapy facials, herbal body scrubs, Ayurvedic consultations, and private yoga classes

Recreational Activities: Wonderful hiking trails; swimming or canoeing in a nearby lake in the summer; skiing in the winter

Facilities: A 210-acre retreat with outdoor and indoor shrines for meditation, a temple, the main lodge, six log cabins, five treatment rooms, a sauna, and a hot tub

Disability Access: No access

Special Notes: Shoshoni is a residential Ashram and spiritual retreat center. The resident yogis open their homes to visitors, giving them personal experience of the yoga lifestyle. They practice chanting and meditation daily and believe that the shakti (meditative energy) that permeates their environment is healing, cleansing, and restorative.

Nearby Attractions: The Continental Divide is a 45-minute walk; El Doran ski resort is 20 minutes away.

Nearest Airport: Boulder and Denver, CO

Getting There: Airport transportation is available through Super Shuttle, 800/BLUE-VAN, $18 each way or $36 round trip; SkyRide, 303/299-6000, $8 one way; or local bus service (RTD) to Nederland, 303/299-6000. Spa provides van service from Nederland Visitor's Center on First Street, $7.50 single person, $10 full car. Car rental is available at airport. Driving from Boulder, take Canyon Boulevard west to Nederland. At Nederland take Route 119 South approximately 5 miles; left after Kelly-Dahl campground; follow signs to spa. (1 hour) Driving from Denver Airport, exit onto Pen Boulevard. Take I-270 West to I-70 West; exit at I-25 North; exit at Highway 36/Boulder; in Boulder turn left on Canyon Boulevard; follow above directions to spa. (2 hours) Driving from Ft. Collins and points North, take I-25 South to Highway 119 to Longmont. Continue south to Boulder; Highway 119 becomes Iris Street; left onto Broadway; right onto Canyon Boulevard; follow directions from Boulder above. (2.5 hours)

Wyndham Peaks Resort and Golden Door Spa

136 Country Club Drive, Box 2702
Telluride, CO 81435
800/789-2220 or 970/728-6800; fax 970/728-6567
Email: dbessera@wyndham.com
Website: thepeaksresort.com

This spa features a wide expanse of slender aspen, regal velvet-green foothills, and carved and solemn rock outcrops topped with pure white. It's no wonder then that this world-class destination resort and spa is known as The Peaks.

For those interested in wellness, the newly launched Next Level Spa offers several "quests" that can be tailored to each guest's individual needs. Rejuvenation of the mind, body, and spirit is the spa's philosophy, with the goal that each guest can transcend the traditional spa experience and achieve the "next level" of his or her well-being. Next Level offers a comprehensive guest instructor program, which is included in the price. Thirteen rooms connect directly to the spa by way of a private enclave within the hotel.

The quest begins with a phone call to the spa. Guests are assigned a personal spa concierge, who assists them in creating a customized program. Five quests are offered, each exploring various avenues of improved health: rejuvenation, vigor, tranquillity, adventure, and change. A typical day of rejuvenation starts with a 7 A.M. wake-to-oneness ceremony, inspired by the Southern Utes. A breakfast of energy-boosting, low-fat spa cuisine follows. Afterward, guests participate in a mind-body-spirit workshop. Lunch is served at noon, and then guests receive a private consultation with a health counselor. Free time is followed by a 4 P.M. body treatment. The Alpine Strawberry Rejuvenator sounds heavenly. Guests can expect local produce and regional specialties for dinner at 7 P.M. If it's your first time visiting a spa, be sure to request the brochure "How to Spa like a Pro." The four- and seven-night Next Level Spa packages are offered from late May through November. Other specialized spa packages, such as Ski & Spa and Spa Sampler, are available during the ski season.

Accommodations: 174 rooms in a 10-story mountain resort, including 25 luxury suites

Rates: Vary according to season, package, and choice of room. The Next Level Spa package (four-night minimum) is $1,390–1,910 for single occupancy and $2,200–2,720 for double occupancy.

Credit Cards: AE, D, MC, V

Meal Plans: Spa packages include three gourmet spa meals plus healthy snacks per day. Meals are very low in fat and use little butter, oil, or cream.

Services: Workshops on astrology, breath work, chakra clearing, homeopathy, therapeutic touch, and Tibetan healing sounds; various types of massage, including shiatsu, shirodhara, and targeted massage with parafango; aromatherapy, hydrotherapy, reiki, reflexology, and stress management techniques using biofeedback; body wraps and scrubs; facials; salon services; cooking demonstrations; health lectures; and journaling workshops

Recreational Activities: Racquetball, squash, mountain biking, hiking, wall climbing, skiing, fly fishing, gondola rides

Facilities: A luxury mountain resort with a 42,000-square-foot spa, two restaurants, a kiva with purification bath, exercise equipment, a weight room, a cardiovascular deck, squash and racquetball courts, an indoor lap pool connected by a water slide to a lower indoor/outdoor pool, a sauna, steam rooms, whirlpools, an indoor climbing wall, five tennis courts, a golf course, and a television lounge

Disability Access: All areas are wheelchair accessible.

Special Notes: Day care is available. Smoking is not allowed.

Nearby Attractions: Anasazi cliff dwellings, Ouray and Pagosa hot springs, Million Dollar Highway, Black Canyon National Monument

Nearest Airport: Telluride, Montrose and Denver, CO

Getting There: Spa provides complimentary shuttle from Telluride Regional Airport with advance reservations. Driving from Montrose, take Route 550 to Main Street/CO-62. Continue on CO-62 as it becomes CO-145; left on Mountain Village Boulevard; left on Country Club Drive. (2 hours)

Heartland Health Spa

Kam Lake Estate
1237 East 1600 North Road
Gilman, IL 60938
800/545-HTLD (545-4853) or 815/683-2182; fax:
815/683-2144
Website: www.heartlandspa.com

On the 31-acre Kam Lake Estate in the heart of rural Iroquois County lies the Heartland Health Spa, one of the Midwest's most recognized spas. Heartland was recently included in *Condé Nast Traveler* magazine's "25 of the Best" spas throughout the world. Helping guests achieve lasting wellness is emphasized at this secluded health retreat, which is situated just 80 miles south of Chicago. Programs are designed to provide guests with the knowledge and skills to utilize the current wealth of information regarding health, nutrition, and stress management to improve their lives. Guests leave Heartland revitalized and inspired to make positive lifestyle changes.

Heartland's programs can be divided into four basic categories: general lifestyle, nutrition, stress management, and beauty. General lifestyle programs start with a detailed questionnaire, after which guests receive individual counseling on the most effective ways to make the desired healthy changes. During the stress management program, guests receive therapeutic massage; learn yoga, tai chi, relaxation, and meditation techniques; and participate in gentle movement exercises. The nutritional program emphasizes a sound diet as the first step toward living a full life with the health and stamina required to achieve personal goals. Guests learn about nutrition, food preparation, and behavior modification techniques for weight loss. Beauty programs spoil guests with many personal services, including loofah scrubs, manicures, pedicures, massage, and aromatherapy relaxation treatments.

Because of the voluminous offering of daily classes and activities, guests are encouraged to participate only in those activities that address their personal goals. The weekend and five- and seven-day program rates include taxes and lodging, meals, classes, use of the spa and sport and exercise facilities, lectures, massages, facials, complementary exercise, and clothing.

Accommodations: 14 rooms, single or double occupancy, with antique furnishings, twin beds, and private baths

Rates: Vary according to lodging, program, and season. Winter rates for a five-night, all-inclusive program are $1,200–1,700.

Credit Cards: AE, D, DC, MC, V

Meal Plans: Three gourmet, low-fat meals and snacks are served daily.

Services: Massage, reflexology, facials, body wraps, sea-salt scrubs, salon services, tai chi, yoga, nutrition evaluation and counseling, resistance conditioning, boxercise, manicures, pedicures, group discussion on health-related topics, and lectures on stress management, life enhancement, and fitness assessment

Recreational Activities: Country line dancing, aerobics, racewalking, horseback riding, fishing

Facilities: A 32-acre estate with a challenge course, exercise equipment, an indoor pool, a three-acre lake, a steam room, a whirlpool, tennis, hiking, a par course, a quarter-mile track, a high-ropes course, water bikes, cross-country skiing, and paddle boats

Disability Access: Limited access is available with assistance.

Special Notes: Smoking is not allowed indoors.

Nearby Attractions: Tall Grass Farms, Frank Lloyd Wright's architecture in Oak Park, and the home and tomb of Abraham Lincoln in nearby Springfield

Nearest Airport: Chicago, IL

Getting There: Car rental is available at airport. Spa provides transportation from Gilman's Amtrak Station with one week advance notice. Driving from Chicago, take Dan Ryan Expressway South to I-57 South. Continue for 77 miles to Exit 283 (Gilman/Chasworth); left at top of ramp to Route 24; right at "Camp Wahanaha" sign (6 miles) onto RR#1220E; left at spa sign (2 miles); entrance is on immediate right. (2 hours)

Lomax Retreat Community

Lomax Station, Inc.
3153 South 900 West
San Pierre, IN 46374
219/896-2600
Email: manthony@lomaxretreat.com
Website: lomaxretreat.com

In 1853, the Junction Railway Company installed tracks, switches, lights, and crossings throughout the town of Lomax, Indiana. As the central railroad access to outlying towns, Lomax witnessed a burst of economic growth. During the 1930s, however, electricity replaced steam power, and the town's progress slowed to a halt. Today, this historic railroad and pipeline town has transformed into Lomax Station, a holistic residential community offering health and rejuvenation programs for the mind and body. Some interesting new takes on old functions include the historic Telegraph Office, now a center for transcendental meditation and creative visualization.

Lomax is also on the migratory path for sandhill cranes, which fly past in the fall and return in April. Along with the three wildlife preserves that border the center, Lomax works to protect and restore the surrounding natural environment, which is home to a wide variety of medicinal plants and herbs. Each year, 300–350 trees are planted around the center.

Wellness retreats and programs at Lomax emphasize disease prevention and anti-aging, although stress management, weight reduction, and chronic ailments are also addressed. Programs are individualized, and most begin with a comprehensive medical examination. Then a nutritionist makes dietary recommendations and, in some cases, prescribes nutritional supplements. Biofeedback, yoga, meditation, massage, and exercise may all be a part of the daily routine. A psychotherapist specializing in the use of flower essences is also available. Lomax, however, does not promise to cure all. "We try to educate people along their path," says Chief Business Consultant Michael Anthony. "They may be here for just one week, but the program is the rest of their lives."

Accommodations: Single- or double-occupancy cottages with a fireplace, wood floors, a screened porch, a sleeping loft, a small galley kitchen, and whirlpools; log cabins and dormitories are also available.

Rates: Vary according to lodging and services. Accommodations are $40–125 per night. Holistic treatments are $50 for an initial colonic therapy session and $240 for an initial medical examination.

Credit Cards: MC, V

Meal Plans: Three meals are served daily; vegetarian meals are optional.

Services: Nutritional medicine, traditional Chinese medicine, herbology, colonic therapy, massage, reflexology, aromatherapy, chiropractic, acupuncture, acupressure, homeopathy, biofeedback, emotional release therapy, and transcendental meditation

Recreational Activities: Hiking, cross-country skiing, canoeing, fishing, boating

Facilities: 29.5 acres bordering the southern shore of the Kankakee River, 27 homes with whirlpools and fireplaces serving as B&Bs, an educational facility, a wellness center, a restaurant, a woodworking company, and trails

Disability Access: Yes

Special Notes: The staff includes Dr. Steven Novil, an internationally recognized authority on metabolic and eating disorders, who now specializes in anti-aging treatments; medical doctors specializing in mind-body medicine, acupuncture, and traditional Chinese medicine; a psychotherapist; a certified biofeedback specialist; and a transcendental meditation specialist. Many wellness programs are reimbursable by insurance.

Nearby Attractions: Kankakee Fish and Wildlife Wetland Preserve, Jasper-Pulaski State Fish and Wildlife Nursery Area, Tippecanoe River State Park, historic Knox

Nearest Airport: South Bend, IN; and Chicago, IL; Lomax airstrip (FAA-approved)

Getting There: Car rental is available at all airports. Driving from South Bend, take Highway 30 West and turn left onto Highway 421. Continue through towns of Wanatah and Lacrosse; cross Kankakee River; after crossing bridge, left onto Route 400 South (1 mile); left onto Route 900 West; spa entrance on left. (2 hours) Driving from Chicago, take Skyway East to I-65 South or take 294 East to 80/90 to I-65 South. From I-65 South, continue to Route 231; exit at Crown Point; right at exit and follow road into town of Hebron; left onto Highway 8, second stop; continue through town of Kouts and into Lacrosse; right onto Highway 421 at the first stop sign in Lacrosse; follow directions from South Bend listed above. (2 hours)

The Raj

1754 Jasmine Avenue
Fairfield, IA 52556-9005
800/248-9050 or 641/472-9580; fax 641/472-2496
Email: theraj@lisco.com
Website: www.theraj.com

The Raj is a Maharishi Ayurveda Health Center that invites guests to experience perfect health. All programs are designed to restore balance throughout the mind and body. Although many different programs are available, each one is based on a comprehensive system of health care. Consequently, whether it's aroma and sound therapy or learning how to work out to relieve stress, each step supports every other to accelerate the process of increasing vitality and well-being.

The Maharishi Rejuvenation Program is offered for a minimum of three days, although one week is recommended for first-time guests. Because Ayurveda has been known to be particularly helpful with chronic disease, the program begins with an in-depth health evaluation and includes the ancient pulse diagnostic technique to determine an individual's mind-body balance and to detect any preillness imbalances. After specific recommendations are made regarding diet, daily routine, exercise, and behavior, guests receive detoxification treatments. Two and a half hours each day are spent receiving shirodhara oil massages, herbalized steam baths, aromatherapy, and gentle oil enemas, after which the effects of stress, fatigue, and environmental toxins are eliminated. The program also includes a gourmet vegetarian diet, health education courses, yoga, and lectures from visiting experts. The program is meant to be a foundation for lasting well-being, guests are given a home program to continue working toward a health-promoting lifestyle. The Raj can refer departing guests to an Ayurvedic physician in their area.

Accommodations: Capacity for about 30 guests in 20 deluxe rooms and various two-story villas. All villas have three guest suites.

Rates: Vary according to room and services. The Maharishi Rejuvenation Program is $1,626 for three days, $2,710 for five days, and $3,795 for seven days.

Credit Cards: AE, MC, V

Meal Plans: Three organic vegetarian meals per day are included.

Services: Ayurvedic purification therapies, consultations with medical doctors and Ayurvedic experts, yoga classes, transcendental meditation classes, Royal Skin Rejuvenation programs, nutrition and diet counseling, and lectures on health-related topics

Recreational Activities: Tennis, golf, and horseback riding are located nearby, although these activities are not encouraged during the actual treatment program.

Facilities: A 100-acre wooded estate with a three-story, French country–style main building, including a health center, a private guest living room, 18 bedrooms, an herb and gift shop, medical offices, an exercise room, conference and meeting rooms, the Raj Restaurant, five private villas, an 18-room hotel, a reflecting pond, and an Osage orange grove

Disability Access: Yes

Special Notes: The Raj has 50 staff members, with a 2-to-1 staff-to-guest ratio. Smoking is not allowed.

Nearby Attractions: Dutch historic settlement, southeast Iowa woodlands and meadows, Amish communities

Nearest Airport: Cedar Rapids, IA

Getting There: Airport transportation is available from Harris Limos, 319/396-5981, $75 one way. Driving from Cedar Rapids, take I-380 South. Continue towards Iowa City as I-380 merges with Highway 218; exit at Highway 1 South towards Fairfield; right on Airport Road; right on Jasmine Avenue; entrance is .5 mile on left. (1.25 hours)

Creative Health Institute

112 W. Union City Road
Union City, MI 49094
517/278-6260; fax: 517/278-5837
Website: www.creativehealthusa.com

In rural Michigan, the Coldwater River runs past the Creative Health Institute, a 300-acre health and lifestyle institute and home to abundant natural wildlife. The center is dedicated to the "living foods" principles of the Ann Wigmore Center in Boston, which operated for more than 20 years. Creative Health offers an unpretentious and simple approach to wellness education and practice, with the ultimate goal of teaching people to heal themselves in mind, body, and spirit.

The institute was founded in 1982 by Don Haughey. After Haughey was treated with more than 116 different medications for a chronic illness, he was told that nothing more could be done. Haughey tried the "living-foods" lifestyle and has been healthy for more than 21 years. The lifestyle encompasses not only a diet of organic living foods but also methods for colonic cleansing and developing a positive outlook. It is presented as an alternative to the high cost of medicine and unhealthy processed foods. A typical diet consists of organic produce and greens, fermented foods, "Energy Soup," Rejuvelac, enzyme-rich foods, and sprouts. The program has had proven success for people suffering from heart disease, diabetes, arthritis, cancer, asthma, and other chronic diseases.

A one-week intensive session starts on Sunday and ends Saturday. An emphasis is placed on hands-on, experiential learning. The program includes a diet of wheat grass and living foods, learning about living-foods theory, sprouting, indoor gardening and composting, raising and using wheat grass, colonic health and elimination, lymphatic circulation, exercise and breathing, living-foods preparation, alternative healing methods, food combining, videotapes and audiotapes on health, and ways to continue the program at home.

Accommodations: 20 standard dormitories, with semiprivate and private rooms available

Rates: Vary according to room and length of stay. The one-week program is $600 for a semiprivate room or $800 for a private room per person; the two-week program is $1,200 for a semiprivate room or $1,000 for a private room per person. Guests can also stay in the dormitory for the two-week program for $900 per person. Additional weeks are $400 per week. Rates include lodging, meals, videos, class instruction, and educational material.

Credit Cards: MC, V

Meal Plans: Three live, organic, vegan meals are served each day.

Services: Hands-on experience in vegetable and herb sprouting, growing greens indoors, and living-food preparation, massage, hydrotherapy, daily exercise classes, stress reduction techniques, nutritional and lifestyle counseling, colonics, educational videos, courses on various aspects of health and cleansing, and wheat grass juice therapy, consisting of wheat grass implants, skin poultices, and mouth, eye, nose, and ear washes

Facilities: A nine-acre estate bordering two rivers, with an informal community lodge, lodging for guests, classrooms, and walking trails

Disability Access: Access is limited; please call in advance.

Special Notes: The center cannot accept guests who are unable to care for themselves. Smoking and alcohol are not allowed.

Nearby Attractions: Coldwater Lake, golf, horseback riding

Nearest Airport: Kalamazoo, MI

Getting There: Car rental is available at airport. Driving from Kalamazoo, take I-94E to Exit 98A (MI-66 South). Continue on MI-66 South; left on MI-60; right on 8 Mile Road; continue as it becomes Adolph Road; left onto Union City Road and spa entrance. (1 hour)

Birdwing Spa

21398 575th Avenue
Litchfield, MN 55355
320/693-6064; fax 320/693-7026
Email: birdwing@hutehtel.net
Website: www.birdwingspa.com

The area surrounding Birdwing Spa is so pristine that it was once the sight of a Disney nature movie. Located on a former bird sanctuary, this upper Midwest spa is the perfect getaway for those who want to ignore phones, traffic, or 9-to-5 drudgery for a few days. And they do it with style—*McCall's* magazine recently featured Birdwing as one of the "Ten Best Spas." Says owner Richard Carlson, "We provide an island where people can get away from stress and bad habits, and we get them started on a better course of life."

Only 18 guests are allowed at a time on this 300-acre estate. Although Birdwing will never claim to be a health center, the Extended Life Enhancement package provides enough healthy air, food, exercise, education, and spa services to give guests the jump start they need toward a healthier lifestyle. The package includes a detailed lifestyle assessment and a consultation with a dietitian. Nutritious gourmet food is combined with the pampering pleasures of full-body massage, herbal wraps, and body polishes. Guests also get the chance to explore the rich natural scenery through bicycling, skiing, hiking, or canoeing. If it's too cold to get outdoors, they can work out in the fitness building or relax in the spa's sauna and whirlpool. Activities include guest speakers on stress control, nutrition, and cardiac health; cooking classes; and feature films.

Birdwing's philosophy is to offer "a balance of pampering, relaxation time, fitness activities, and a nutritionally balanced cuisine." In its fourteenth year of operation, Birdwing's philosophy is serving its guests well. Owner Carlson relates a story of how in 1993 a sheik from Saudi Arabia visited the spa. No one knew he was a sheik until he had left, and staff members were nervous about whether his expectations had been met. After a few weeks, a formal invitation arrived for Carlson to attend the wedding of the sheik's son.

Accommodations: Standard single, standard double, barn hot tub suite, master suite

Rates: Vary according to length of stay and lodging. Five-day packages are $1,050–1,350. Rates include meals, accommodations, and all services. Discounts are available for extended stays.

Credit Cards: MC, V

Meals: Three healthy, low-calorie meals are provided daily.

Services: Facials, massage, paraffin treatments, manicures, pedicures, herbal wrap, body polish, and nutritional counseling

Recreational Activities: 12 miles of trails for hiking, biking, cross-country skiing, and snowshoeing

Facilities: A 300-acre wooded estate with a renovated barn, an outdoor swimming pool, an aerobics room, saunas, a coeducational whirlpool, a massage room, bicycling, canoeing, cross-country skiing, and bird-watching

Disability Access: No access

Special Notes: Smoking is not allowed indoors in public areas. Guests must be at least 16 years of age.

Nearby Attractions: Sioux uprising historic sites, Civil War museum, Mall of America, tennis, golf

Nearest Airport: Minneapolis, MN

Getting There: Car rental is available at airport. Driving from Minneapolis, take Highway 12 West into Litchfield. Turn left at second light; right on Ripley Street; left at second stop sign (Country Road #1, has no sign); left on 575th Avenue; spa entrance 2 miles on left. (1.5 hours)

The Marsh, A Center for Balance and Fitness

15000 Minnetonka Blvd.
Minnetonka, MN 55345
952/935-2202; fax: 952/935-9685
Email: info@themarsh.com
Website: www.themarsh.com

Situated literally in a marsh surrounded by natural wetlands, The Marsh, A Center for Balance and Fitness, was built on the philosophy that health goes beyond a physically fit body. The mind, spirit, and emotions are seen as integral aspects of total health, and the center offers an eclectic menu of activities, programs, and services designed to promote it. Inspired by the meditation and movement therapies she used to overcome a debilitating case of lupus, founder Ruth Stricker opened the center in 1985.

The center takes a traditional Western approach to health, combined with complementary Eastern practices. The center houses a health education department, a therapy pool, and a meditation tower with a view of natural Minnesota wetlands. Guests can work out on an underwater treadmill, practice their backstroke in the 75-foot lap pool, or learn the Pilates method. The training center is stocked with state-of-the-art aerobic and resistance equipment.

Memberships, rather than programs, are the modus operandi at The Marsh. Member privileges include a fitness assessment, a health history review, a total blood cholesterol level test, a body composition analysis, an electrocardiogram, and a personalized exercise program. Members also receive discounts on health and nutrition consultations, spa therapies, sleep fitness screening, cooking and nutrition classes, and workshops and special events. Overnight guests have full use of all facilities and classes.

The Marsh 24-Hour Getaway is designed as a personal mini-retreat for mind and body and begins with an aroma steam shower, followed by a full body wrap or Moor mud therapy. A 12-jet Swiss shower is next, followed by a one-hour deep-tissue massage and a one-hour custom facial. Plenty of time is allowed for classes and meditation. Dinner is taken on the Moon Terrace. The next morning begins with a spa breakfast before a pedicure, manicure, and scalp massage; a shampoo and style finish off the program.

Accommodations: Six overnight guest rooms, with double and single occupancy
Rates: Single $100 per night; double $115
Credit Cards: AE, MC, V
Meal Plans: Continental breakfast is included with a night's stay. The on-site restaurant provides a variety of fresh, healthful menu items served in both informal and fine-dining settings.
Services: Tai chi, qi gong, yoga, meditation, acupuncture, acupressure, therapeutic massage, shiatsu, watsu, craniosacral therapy, trigger-point therapy, Feldenkrais, Alexander technique, Core method (based on Pilates), body wraps, herbal wraps, and salon services
Recreational Activities: Hiking, biking, cross-country skiing, snowshoeing
Facilities: A 67,000-square-foot structure built on a marsh, with a wraparound deck, a 75-foot lap pool, exercise equipment, a warm-water therapy pool, indoor and out-

door tracks, a four-level silo with a meditation tower and mental gym, an underwater treadmill, a hydrotherapy tub, physiogymnastic balls, a training center, and a gift shop

Disability Access: All facilities, pools, and some guest rooms are handicapped accessible.

Special Notes: The Marsh is smoke free and discourages cell phone use in the building.

Nearby Attractions: Minneapolis Art Institute, Mall of America

Nearest Airport: Minneapolis, MN

Getting There: Car rental is available at airport. Driving from Minneapolis, take Highway 494; exit onto Minnetonka Boulevard; go west .5 mile to the spa entrance on right. (20 minutes)

Wholistic Life Center

RR 11, Box 1783
Washburn, MO 65772
417/435-2212; fax 417/435-2211
Email: wlc@ipa.net
Website: www.wholisticlifecenter.org

Located on 900 acres of Ozark countryside, the Wholistic Life Center offers year-round residential cleansing and rejuvenation workshops. The Center, which was originally designed as a martial arts training camp, now offers programs individually tailored to meet the specific health needs of each guest.

The health and lifestyle programs are based on the belief that "dis-ease" is a state of imbalance within the body and that true healing comes from within.

The underlying philosophy of the center's programs is that in order to be truly happy, healthy, and fulfilled in life, one must work toward a state of physical, emotional, mental, and spiritual balance, thus the name Wholistic Life Center. Fruit and vegetable juicing is also a vital element of the center's programs. Raw and cooked whole food is prepared with an emphasis on the importance of eating "live" foods to promote health and healing.

A typical day at the center starts with morning light movement and stretching classes, which might be followed by a workshop on the mind-body connection. Throughout the week, guests experience classes in colonic cleansing, food combining, nutrition, juicing, stress management, and more. After a lunch of natural whole foods, light exercise prepares guests for an afternoon class in boosting your immune system naturally, maintaining a healthy heart, or creating your ideal body weight, followed by juicing and hydrotherapy. Throughout the day, guests may schedule themselves for a chiropractic treatment, colonic irrigation, therapeutic massage, or reflexology treatment. The evening might include a group discussion on the universal concepts of life or a group or private session with counselors aimed at dealing with any personal problems of an emotional or spiritual nature. The Center's staff work to create a supportive and nurturing atmosphere to facilitate a profound level of healing.

Accommodations: Guest lodging is a renovated three-story historic stone house, which accommodates up to 18 guests. Both private and semiprivate rooms have shared bathrooms. The house is situated on a rock bluff overlooking the lake.

Rates: The three-day package is $395, one week is $850, two weeks is $1,600, and four weeks is $3,000. Private rooms are available at an additional rate. All rates are based on a suggested donation basis. The Wholistic Life Center is a 501(c)(3) nonprofit, tax-exempt organization.

Credit Cards: MC, V

Meals: Dairy-free vegetarian meals are included with residential programs.

Services: Chiropractic, pastoral counseling, naturopathy, colonic irrigation, facial and skincare, health lectures, group discussion, and classes in music, dance, art, meditation/relaxation, reflexology, iridology, yoga, massage, universal concepts, food combining, preparing raw meals, menu planning, and juicing, to name a few

Recreational Activities: Swimming, table tennis, tennis, basketball, hiking, and dancing

Facilities: A 900-acre wooded estate, including a three-story lodge, a main activity building, a health clinic, a hot tub, a dining hall and kitchen, an organic green house, basketball and tennis courts, walking trails, Big Sugar Creek, and a lake

Disability Access: None

Special Notes: The Wholistic Life Center is a smoking and drug-free environment.

Nearby Attractions: Branson, Missouri, home of many well-known country music stars, is reached within two hours. Beaver and Table Rock lakes are nearby for swimming, boating, picnicking, fishing, and camping.

Nearest Airport: Northwest Arkansas Regional Airport, AR

Getting There: Car rental is available at airport. Spa provides airport transfer service for a suggested donation of $25 each way. Driving from the north, take Highway 71 to Route 90 East; at intersection of Route KK, turn left into spa entrance. (1.5 hours)

Feathered Pipe Ranch

Feathered Pipe Foundation
P.O. Box 1682
Helena, MT 59624
406/442-8196; fax 406/442-8110
Email: fpranch@initco.net
Website: www.featheredpipe.com/ranch.html

For 22 years, the Feathered Pipe Ranch, located in the heart of the Montana Rockies, has symbolized the spirit of the feathered pipe—that of connecting with the circle of life—through its workshops and programs. The goal behind the Feathered Pipe Foundation—the nonprofit educational umbrella under which the ranch operates—is to provide learning experiences that provide the knowledge and commitment necessary for healthy living.

Programs are offered not only at the Montana home base but throughout the world, including Mexico's Isla Mujeres, and a yoga tour of India's "Spice Coast." Programs such as "Yoga in Paradise" are held at the Nabalam Hotel on the Mexican Caribbean. The resort is cozy, surrounded by tropical gardens, pristine beaches, and an outdoor platform for yoga sessions.

Ranch Seminars are held at either the Blacktail Ranch in Wolf Creek, Montana, or at the main ranch, the Feathered Pipe Ranch in the Montana Rockies. During ranch seminars, a broad spectrum of natural health, spirituality, and lifestyle topics are covered, such as power yoga, holistic health, shamanism, drum building, and natural healing. Guests also have time to take in a sauna and massage or to hike through the miles of forested mountains, pristine lakes, and abundant plant and wildlife. A short hike to the "sacred rocks" above the 110-acre ranch affords panoramic views.

Travel seminars are intended to foster personal growth while enabling guests to study ancient traditions and experience the healing energies of a place. Past workshops have included the four-day Power of Healing: Science, Nature and Spirit intensive session with Dr. Andrew Weil and Dr. Christine Northrup. Participants learn about the costs and benefits of traditional and natural medicine, how to prevent disease and promote health, herbs everyone should know, how to create health during menopause, how thoughts and feelings influence health and disease, and more.

Accommodations: Dormitory-style rooms that hold up to four persons; camping in tepees, tents, or yurts; a few double rooms with private or semiprivate baths available at an additional $300 and $200, respectively, per person.

Rates: Vary according to program chosen ($995–$1,895 per week). The cost for each program includes all instruction, lodging, meals, and general use of the bathhouse and ranch facilities. Discounts are available for longer stays. Scholarships are available for those who need financial assistance.

Credit Cards: MC, V

Meal Plans: Three organic, vegetarian meals are provided each day, with the option of chicken or fish.

Services: Health, spirituality, and lifestyle programs; therapeutic bodywork; meditation

Recreational Activities: Swimming, volleyball, hiking

Facilities: A 110-acre ranch with a main lodge, meeting rooms, tepees, yurts, tents, laundry facilities, a hot tub, a sauna, hiking trails, and a swimming pond

Disability Access: Yes

Special Notes: Smoking is not allowed.

Nearby Attractions: Helena, Montana; Yellowstone National Park; Glacier National Park

Nearest Airport: Helena, MT

Getting There: A detailed information packet, including map, is sent out after registration. Reservations are recommended. Car rental is available at airport. Spa provides round-trip van transportation. Driving from Great Falls and all points along I-15 South, take Exit 193. At exit, turn right onto Cedar Street/Highway 12 West; continue along Cedar Street/Highway 12 to Colorado Gulch; entrance is 2409 Colorado Gulch. (1.5 hours)

Kerr House

17777 Beaver Street, P.O. Box 363
Grand Rapids, OH 43522
419/832-1733; fax 419/832-4303
Email: NonnaGram@aol.com
Website: www.hostetler.net/kerr.htm

Laurie Hostetler, director of The Kerr House, knows how to do things right. A stay at this Victorian mansion that serves as a holistic rejuvenation center begins with breakfast in bed. Programs are primarily targeted for women, but occasional one-week, three-day, and weekend programs for couples, coeds, and men only are offered throughout the year. Only eight guests take the program at any one time to allow for a staff-to-guest ratio of about three to one. All programs are meant to leave guests with a renewed sense of life and self.

After the luxury of being awakened to the sight and smell of a wicker tray filled with wholesome natural foods, guests attend an exercise class at 8 A.M. Exercises take place in the mansion's picturesque loft and are meant to do more than get a body in shape. Better described as mind-body exercises, guests learn relaxation techniques, body appreciation, breathing exercises, and intensive stretches. Afterward, it's an herbal tea break and then off for a morning treatment, which could mean anything from reflexology to an herbal body wrap. Lunch is at noon, followed by quiet time and the option of a counseling session on how to reduce stress. Outdoor activities are encouraged in the afternoon, and guests can choose to walk along the nearby towpath. A yoga class is offered in the late afternoon, with time afterward to relax and prepare for dinner, which is served by candlelight in the formal dining room at 7 P.M. A whirlpool and sauna might follow, and perhaps listening to the melodies of a harpist plucking strings, before lights out at 11 P.M.

Accommodations: A maximum of eight guests in Victorian-style rooms with high ceilings, lace curtains, and antique furniture

Rates: One week is $2,150 for a semiprivate room or $2,550 for a private room.

Credit Cards: AE, D, MC, V

Meal Plans: Three meals are offered per day and are made with natural ingredients and no additives, dyes, white flour, or processed sugar. Breakfast is served in bed, and candlelight dinners are prepared in the evenings.

Services: Foot reflexology, body wraps, mud baths, massages, facials, exercise classes. Fifteen treatments are given in the five-day program, seven treatments in the three-day program, and four treatments in the weekend program.

Recreational Activities: Hiking

Facilities: Guests are housed in a renovated Victorian home equipped with massage rooms, exercise room with whirlpool, sauna, Nordic track system, and a treadmill.

Disability Access: No access

Special Notes: The staff-to-guest ratio is 3 to 1. Programs are primarily for women, although coeducational, couples, and men-only specialized programs are available.

Nearby Attractions: Shopping in Grand Rapids, Ohio, and exercise paths along the Miami and Erie canals, canal boat ride, train tour, and Fort Meigs

Nearest Airport: Toledo, OH

Getting There: Airport transportation is available. Call spa for information. Car rental is available at airport. Driving from Toledo, take US-20 Alt. Turn right onto S. Berkey Southern Road; right onto River Road/US-24; left onto OH-578; right onto OH-65 and spa entrance. (35 minutes)

Black Hills Health and Education Center

P.O. Box 19
Hermosa, SD 57744
800/658-LIFE (658-5433) or 605/255-4101
fax 605/255-4687
Email: bhhec@aol.com
Website: www.bhhec.org

The Black Hills Center, which claims 450 acres of creeks, canyons, and farmland, is located in what is described as the Banana Belt because of its year-round temperate climate. The center draws guests from around the country for its residential wellness programs. The 13- and 20-day programs, which are designed to help the mind, body, and soul, are based on the belief that God has given everyone eight natural remedies: nutrition, exercise, water, sunshine, temperance, air, rest, and trust in divine power.

The center has been particularly successful in controlling heart disease, diabetes, arthritis, hypertension, strokes, depression, addictions, osteoporosis, and obesity. The medically supervised programs begin with a complete physical examination, blood tests, and counseling. Hydrotherapy treatments are included in the program fee, and guests have access to a Russian steam cabinet, whirlpool, and showers with alternating hot and cold sprays. Outings to a local supermarket and restaurant teach how to choose and order healthy foods.

The day starts at 6:15 A.M. with an inspirational thought, followed by a medical lecture at 6:30 A.M. By 7:15 A.M., guests are garbed in exercise gear for aerobics, and by 8:15 A.M., they sit down for breakfast. At 9:15 A.M., a physiology lecture begins, and resistance training is scheduled for 10 A.M. A cooking lab is scheduled for noon, and a stress class follows at 1:30 P.M. An early dinner is served at 2:15 P.M., and guests walk through the valley trails. Hydrotherapy or massage treatments are scheduled for 4 P.M., and at 7 P.M., guests gather to share the day's experiences and to watch a health-related video.

Accommodations: 12 single and double rooms with private bath in a two-story lodge with modern furnishings. Motor home camping facilities are available as well.

Rates: The 20-day program is $2,315–2,600, the 18-day program is $1,620–1,800, and a five-day tune-up is $500.

Credit Cards: D, MC, V

Meal Plans: Two buffet-style vegan meals are served per day, with an optional third.

Services: Massage, hydrotherapy, medical consultations, health lectures, hot and cold fomentations, exercise rehabilitation, group discussions, and excursions to a natural indoor pool fed by a hot mineral spring

Recreational Activities: Hiking, walking

Facilities: Guest rooms, a cooking lab, a lecture room, a cafeteria, exercise equipment, a Russian steam cabinet, a whirlpool, and hot and cold showers with six sprays

Disability Access: Yes, specially equipped rooms are designed for people with disabilities.

Special Notes: Two medical doctors and three registered nurses are on staff. Smoking is not allowed indoors.

Nearby Attractions: Mount Rushmore, Crazy Horse Memorial, Badlands National Park, Reptile Gardens, Evans Plunge hot springs, Wind Cave National Park,

Custer State Park, and many Old West towns, such as Deadwood, where Wild Bill Hickok was shot

Nearest Airport: Rapid City, SD

Getting There: Complimentary airport transportation is provided with advance reservations. Driving from Rapid City, take Highway 79 South to Hermosa. Exit onto Highway 40; left onto Battle Creek Road; continue 2 miles to spa entrance. (1.5 hours)

The Christine Center

W8303 Mann Road
Willard, WI 54493
715/267-7507; fax: 715/267-7512
Email: christinecenter@tds.net
Website: christinecenter.org

The pristine natural setting and rustic hermitages of this rural Wisconsin retreat recommends the Christine Center as a vacation where guests take home "more than just a suntan." This accolade by the host of "Good Morning America," was not surprising considering that for more than 20 years the center has welcomed visitors from around the country who come for a quiet place to gain insight and perspective in a rejuvenating, spiritually-based community. The center was founded in 1980 with the aid of the Wheaton Franciscans in the Spirit of St. Francis, under the direction of Sister Virginia Mary Barta. Intended as a place for solitude and meditation, 20 cabins were built—each in a carefully designated forest setting—of local natural materials. In 1990, the center became an independent not-for-profit corporation embracing Unitive Spirituality, which recognizes the diversity and commonality of all spiritual traditions.

Workshops, which are scheduled throughout the year, address various aspects of health and personal growth. For example, retreats include the Healing Science of Homeopathy, Feminism and the Path of Meditation, and Sacred Dance. Private retreats offered at the Christine Center provide the solitude necessary to pursue personal goals in an environment of contemplation and renewal. Guests have the option of seeking spiritual guidance or working part of the day in exchange for discounted lodging. The Rejuvenation Retreats can last from a few days to a few weeks. Staff members consult with guests to design a schedule of activities intended to nurture the mind, body, and soul. Options include bodywork, meditation instruction, spiritual guidance, nutritional counseling, breathwork, and more.

Accommodations: 15 cabins ranging in size from a small rustic hermitage with a woodstove to a large cabin with gas heat, a full bath, and a kitchenette. All cabins have electricity; several are multiple occupancy, accommodating as many as five people. Campsites are available with bathroom and shower facilities.

Rates: $30–90, including meals, children under 6, free, 6–12 $10/day to 18, $18/day

Credit Cards: None accepted

Meal Plans: Three nutritionally balanced meals are prepared each day, primarily with vegetarian and whole foods.

Services: Workshops and seminars, individual and couples counseling, therapeutic massage, breathwork, dietary counseling, reflexology and neck release, jin shin do, transpersonal counseling, Rah energy balancing, and enneagram work

Recreational Activities: Long and short nature walks, biking, cross-country skiing, nearby swimming, climbing, canoeing, hiking, golf, and showshoeing (bring own equipment)

Facilities: A conference room, a meditation building, a dining room, a chapel, a pond, a creek, a nature trail, and nearby sleds and snowmobiles

Disability Access: Yes

Special Notes: Smoking is not allowed. Some scholarships and work/study are available. Children are welcome.

Nearby Attractions: Cross-country skiing, kayaking, remote Wisconsin woodlands

Nearest Airport: Eau Claire, WI

Getting There: Car rental is available at airport. Driving from Eau Claire, take I-94 to County Road M (Thorp); exit onto County Road GG; right on County Road G; 3 miles from Willards, follow signs to spa. (.5 hour) Driving from Minneapolis, take I-94 East to Osseo exit and onto Highway 10* East; continue for 14.8 miles to County Road I; continue for 14.7 miles; left on County Road G; follow one mile to spa entrance. (2.5 hours) ***Note:** County Roads have identical letters along Highway 10. Don't be confused if "G" appears shortly after entering Highway 10.

Antelope Retreat and Education Center

P.O. Box 156
Savery, WY 82332-0156
888/268-2732 or 307/383-2625

The Antelope Retreat Center, situated on a former working ranch in the Savery Creek Valley offers spiritually based wilderness retreats and vision quests designed to balance the body and soul. All programs give guests the opportunity to understand the interconnectedness between their own lives and the natural world. Located at the edge of the Medicine Bow National Forest, on the Western slope of the Rocky Mountains the ranch gives access to a variety of terrain; from alpine to desert. The rolling sagebrush hills, lush river valleys and meadows at the ranch extends multiple opportunities for solitude and solace.

John Boyer, who grew up on the ranch and founded the retreat center in 1986, says his goal is to share his love of nature and the inner quiet that can be accessed by being in touch with the land. Several programs are available including: nature awareness, creativity in nature and the wilderness quest. The wilderness quest allows participants to have supported time alone in the desert, preceded and concluded with a purifying sweat lodge ceremony in the Native American tradition. Nature awareness programs allow guests to venture out with a guide on long walks either to the mountains to the east or the desert to the west. During the walks, guides explain the physical and spiritual landscape. Those who hang back at the ranch can participate in Earth-centered meditation, sweat lodge ceremonies, listening exercises, or bioenergetics. All guests learn ways to develop a lifestyle that can be sustained without further environmental damage to the Earth.

Programs are offered from May to September, while retreats and vacation weeks are offered year round. Winters at the center offer an even greater sense of isolation and privateness as all of the dirt roads beyond the ranch are snowed in. Miles of cross country skiing is available through the pristine wilderness.

Accommodations: A five-bedroom log ranch house, secluded yurts, a shepherder's wagon, a small log house, and numerous camping sites are available. Private and group rooms, shared bathrooms

Rates: Vary according to accommodations and program. The daily rate is $60–120 per person; weekly rate is $400–1,200. All rates include meals and lodging. Monthly rates are also available.

Credit Cards: None accepted

Meal Plans: All meals are included in lodging rates. Healthy home-cooked meals are prepared using fresh garden vegetables, homemade breads, jams, and desserts. Vegetarian meals are available, and special needs foods can be provided by arrangement.

Services: Lifestyle assessment, bioenergetics, life coaching, wilderness fasting, sweat lodge ceremony, creativity workshops, nature awareness training

Recreational Activities: Hiking, swimming, cross-country skiing, gardening, fly fishing

Facilities: A 500-acre ranch with a 1890s log ranch house, secluded yurts, a shepherder's wagon, and gardens

Disability Access: No

Special Notes: Smoking is not allowed indoors. As a nonprofit organization, all costs exceeding program and operating expenses are credited to guests as a tax-deductible contribution. Scholarships are available.

Nearby Attractions: Steamboat Springs, Colorado; Red Desert; Flaming Gorge National Recreation Area; Dinosaur National Monument; Snowy Range; Saratoga Hot Spring and Resort; Little Snake River Museum; hiking, camping and fishing

Nearest Airport: Hayden/Steamboat Springs, CO

Getting There: Airport transportation is available. Call spa for details and driving directions.

Pacific

Chopra Center for Well-Being

7630 Fay Avenue South
La Jolla, CA 92037
888/424-6772 or 858/551-7788; fax: 858/551-7811
Email: info@chopra.com
Website: www.chopra.com/ccwbwelcome.htm

It's hard not to have heard of Deepak Chopra. Being the only author ever to land simultaneously on the *New York Times* bestseller lists for fiction and nonfiction is just one of his numerous achievements. Chopra's message—that unconditional health is within everyone's reach—can be found in books, videos, lectures, and television appearances. Because of his enormous appeal, PBS uses his video lectures during its pledge week. Chopra has helped bring Ayurveda into the mainstream and, with the opening of the Chopra Center for Well-Being, is now offering its benefits to the public.

The center is divided into three main elements. The first is patient care, which extends to anyone with immediate health concerns or who wants to feel rejuvenated. The anti-aging program is also an element of patient care. The second element is the development of educational programs. One such course, The Magic of Healing, lasts eight weeks and includes classes on nutrition, body types, meditation, psychophysiological techniques, eliminative procedures, herbal remedies, and looking at the human being in the context of environment, body, mind, and spirit. The third element is research, which benefits patients through the comfort of knowing that the most current technology is used in all services offered.

At this time, only two extended-stay programs are offered: Perfect Health, which is offered in both three- and five-day programs, and Ayurvedic Purification, which lasts for five days. Perfect Health begins with an orientation and includes natural cooking and wellness classes, primordial sound meditation, Ayurvedic therapy, yoga and breathing techniques, gourmet vegetarian meals, discussions on Chopra's Seven Laws of Spiritual Success, and personal empowerment sessions. Ayurvedic Purification includes a home preparation program, a mind-body medical consultation, an educational session with a nurse, traditional panchakarma, Ayurvedic meals, extended meditation practices, and yoga and breathing techniques.

Accommodations: Overnight accommodations are not available, but a concierge service arranges any lodging needs. Some hotels are within walking distance of the center.

Rates: Multiday programs are $1,250–2,750.

Credit Cards: MC, V

Meal Plans: Three organic, vegetarian meals per day are included with the residential program.

Services: Panchakarma treatments, Ayurvedic therapies, massage, body scrubs, facials, primordial sound meditation, mind-body medicine consultations, and children's programs

Recreational Activities: Walking on the beaches in La Jolla

Facilities: A spacious modern health center with classrooms, treatment rooms, a sauna, a steam room, a restaurant, and a music/bookstore

Disability Access: Facilities are accessible for people with disabilities, but guests with disabilities must bring an attendant to help massage therapists assist them on and off the tables.

Special Notes: Smoking is not allowed. The staff includes three medical doctors.
Nearby Attractions: San Diego Zoo, Wild Animal Park, beaches, parks
Nearby Airport: San Diego, CA
Getting There: Car rental and taxi available from airport. Driving from San Diego, take I-5 North to Ardath Road/La Jolla exit; Ardath Road becomes Torrey Pines Road; continue until road ends Girard Street; right on Girard; first left on Kline; go 1 block to Fay Avenue and the spa's entrance. (45 minutes)

Esalen Institute

Highway 1
Big Sur, CA 93920-9616
831/667-3000 (reservations 831/667-3005);
fax: 831/667-2724
Email: info@esalen.org
Website: www.esalen.org

On a 27-acre stretch of land between the Pacific Ocean and the coastal ridge of the Santa Lucia Mountains lies the Esalen Institute. The word *Esalen* comes from the Native American tribe known as the Esalen, who once made these breathtaking seaside grounds and natural hot springs their home. Since its founding in 1962, the institute's programs have revolved around the exploration of unrealized human capacity. Over the years, the center has gained renown for its blend of Eastern and Western philosophies and its experimental workshops. Philosophers, psychologists, artists, and religious thinkers have all made the winding coastal drive to Esalen, and some are still in residence today.

With such diverse programs as "Maps of the Jungle: Negotiating the Primitive Dimensions of the Workplace," "The Home Within the Heart: Ojibwe Tribal Healings," and "Core Holoenergetics: The Art and Science of Conscious Healing," the question is: How does one experience Esalen? For those who can't decide on one of the hundred or so programs, the program "Experiencing Esalen" is a good choice. It offers an introduction to therapeutic bodywork and healing practices, such as Gestalt, massage, sensory awareness, and meditation. Visits generally range from a weekend to five- or seven-day workshops. Longer stays are available with the Ongoing Residence program, as a seminarian, or through the work-study program.

Accommodations: Housing is shared with two or three persons per room and, in some cases, bathrooms are shared. Couples are housed together. Bunkbed rooms are available on a limited basis; meeting rooms are sometimes used as shared sleeping-bag space and may be available for workshop participants with limited financial means.

Rates: Vary according to length of stay, lodging, and program. The seven-day rate per person with standard accommodations is $1,370; the five-day rate is $885; and the weekend rate is $485. Bunks and sleeping bag rates, as well as scholarship assistance, are also available.

Credit Cards: AE, MC, V

Meal Plans: Three meals per day are served buffet style and incorporate fresh organic vegetables. Vegetarian options are available.

Services: Personal growth and holistic health workshops, including shamanic healing, Gestalt therapy, craniosacral therapy, Rolfing, Feldenkrais, Heller, Esalen, and deep-tissue massage; hiking; daily movement classes, including yoga, dance, and chi gong; and a children's program

Recreational Activities: Concerts, hiking, nature walks, swimming, and work-study programs

Facilities: A 27-acre oceanside campus with meeting rooms, an educational resources information center, treatment rooms, rustic lodges, a heated outdoor pool, beautiful redwood hot tubs with natural mineral water perched on the cliff above the ocean, a bookstore, and hiking trails. A completely new and renovated bathhouse and somatics center opened at the site of the original hot springs, which were wiped out in the 1998 El Niño storms.

Disability Access: A recently purchased vehicle now provides a means of transportation to the baths for those with physical limitations.

Special Notes: Smoking is not allowed in any accommodations or meeting rooms. Bringing a flashlight is recommended. Residential and work-study programs are available.

Nearby Attractions: Ventana Wilderness, Tassajara Zen Monastery, Los Padres National Forest, Big Sur State Park, Hearst Castle in San Simeon

Nearest Airports: San Francisco, San Jose, and Monterey, CA

Getting There: Transportation is available from Monterey Airport only. Service is limited to Friday and Sunday; contact spa for details; $30 each way. Driving from San Francisco and all points north, take Highway 101 South to Coastal 156; exit at Highway 1 South to Big Sur; spa entrance on right. (3+ hours) Driving from Morro Bay and all points south, take Highway 101 to San Luis Obispo then Highway 1 North to Big Sur; spa entrance on left. (1.5+ hours)

The Expanding Light

14618 Tyler Foote Road
Nevada City, CA 95959
800/346-5350 or 530/478-7518; fax: 530/478-7519
Email: info@expandinglight.org
Website: www.expandinglight.org

For 30 years, The Expanding Light has been the retreat center of Ananda Village, an intentional spiritual community where 350 residents make the teachings of yoga the basis of their daily lives. Ananda was founded in 1968 by Swami Kriyananda (J. Donald Walters), a direct disciple of Paramhansa Yogananda, author of *Autobiography of a Yogi.* The retreat center utilizes the teachings of Yogananda to inspire participants to have a deep, personal experience of their own higher essence through yoga and meditation, and to carry that inspiration back into their daily lives.

The Expanding Light welcomes people of all backgrounds who are looking for peace of mind. Yoga and meditation are offered daily, and staff members are always available for individual support. The various programs offered apply to all aspects of life, from health to relationships and career to spiritual development. Examples of programs include Making Meditation a Life Skill, Healing Yourself and Others, Simplify Your Life, How to Know and Trust Your Inner Guidance, Easy Vegetarian Cooking, Spirtualize Your Marriage, and The Healing Path of Yoga. Guests are free to participate as much or as little as they like; nothing is mandatory.

Accommodations: Standard (shared bathroom) and deluxe (private bathroom) rooms are available. Campsites and tents are also available, with modern bathhouses; campsites are level and shared. RVs are welcome, but no RV hookups are available.

Rates: Progam rates vary; two-day programs from $102–248 per person include accommodations, meals, and programs.

Credit Cards: MC, V

Meal Plans: Three lacto-ovo vegetarian meals (with dairy-free options) are prepared each day by Ananda cooks. Breakfasts and dinners are light; the main meal is lunch. The food is appetizing, with fresh salads, breads, and warm dishes served buffet-style. Tea, fruit, and juices are always available.

Services: Meditation, yoga, healing, and self-discovery. Personal retreats are available anytime and can be designed to fit individual needs. The Center for Radiant Health, part of Ananda, offers treatment options such as massage, Ayurveda, energy therapy, polarity, reiki, herbology, and counseling.

Recreational Activites: Hiking and swimming

Facilities: A retreat center with a large room for yoga and meditation, a dining hall, a bookstore, guest rooms, cabins, tent sites, and the Center for Radiant Health. A complete medical clinic is located five minutes away.

Disability Access: Yes; wheelchair ramps and grip bars are available; however, outdoor transit is via gravel paths.

Special Notes: All staff at the Expanding Light are Ananda members. Work exchange and work-study programs are available. Seniors receive a 10 percent discount on most programs.

Nearby Attractions: Hiking, nature walks, and swimming in the nearby Yuba River; the Tahoe ski area; shopping in Nevada City.

Nearest Airport: Sacramento, CA

Getting There: Foothill's Flyer (800/464-0808) provides airport service; $135 each way. Driving from Sacramento, take I-80 East to Auburn and exit on Highway 49. Continue north 36 miles; right onto Tyler Foote Road; left at "Anada Village" sign; left again at intersection and spa entrance. (2.5 hours)

The Golden Door Fitness Resort

P.O. Box 463060
Escondido, CA 92046-3077
800/424-0777 or 760/744-5777; fax: 760/471-2393
Email: gdres@adnc.com
Website: www.goldendoor.com

The Golden Door lies just six miles north of Escondido, in Southern California. Only rows of tall, closely set evergreens obscure the resort from the road, and yet once you are inside, the resort seems ideally sequestered and remote. The resort's 377 acres of gardens, groves, orchards, and hiking trails are reserved exclusively for the 39 weekly guests. With a staff that outnumbers guests four to one, personal attention is customized to each individual.

Sunrise hiking and breakfast in bed start off a typical Golden Door morning. The daily exercise program includes movement of high intensity balanced by periods of renewal and relaxation. The ancient arts of yoga, meditation, and tai chi have always been an integral part of the weekly program, along with walking and hiking. The property offers private hillsides with different graduated walks for each day of the week.

Other activities to choose from include pool exercises or water volleyball, weight training class, tap or jazz dancing, golf, tennis, or a walk through the labyrinth—a stone mosaic pathway that is a metaphor for one's journey through life and that helps quiet the mind. A guide is available to explain the labyrinth and help guests journey on the path themselves. Three hours each day are reserved for spa treatments, such as massages, facials, manicures, pedicures, skin scrubs, and herbal wraps. Cooking and nutritional classes are also offered.

The Golden Door offers special summer weeks, in addition to their regular program, with classes such as Hiking for Health and Joy, Journey through the Labyrinth, Yoga Week, Feldenkrais for Flexibility, Dance Celebration, Creative Writing Week, and Wonderful Water Workouts. Please call the resort for this year's summer calendar.

Accommodations: 39 private suites

Rates: $5,375 per person per week all inclusive. Summer weeks and Thanksgiving are $4,875 per person; the four-day coeducational special is $3,125 per person; the New Year's 10-day special is $5,375 per person.

Credit Cards: V only

Meal Plans: Three healthy, low-fat meals plus snacks are provided daily. All cuisines rely on freshly picked vegetables and fruits from their organic garden.

Services: Facials, herbal wraps, massages, and other spa services are available. A full-service salon provides hair styling, manicures, pedicures, and so forth.

Recreational Activities: Wonderful hiking trails. Various classes are offered each week, including aerobics, step aerobics, weight room classes, water classes, walking clinics, nutrition talks, dance, tai chi, yoga, and more.

Facilities: Three guest lounges, a dining room, a kitchen, indoor/outdoor exercise studios, the Dragon Tree Gym with Cybex equipment, two swimming pools, two tennis courts, a classical labyrinth, a Beauty Court, a bath house, a steam room, a sauna, and a therapy pool

Disability Access: No access

Special Notes: Men's weeks are five times yearly during March, June, September, November, and December; coeducational weeks are four times yearly during March, June, September, and December; all other weeks are exclusively for women.

Nearby Attractions: San Diego Wild Animal Park and Reserve, nearby beaches, golf

Nearest Airport: San Diego, CA

Getting There: From San Diego, take Highway 163 to I-15, north to the Deer Springs Road exit. Turn left onto Deer Springs Road and continue exactly one mile. Entrance is slightly hidden; look for break in trees at the one-mile mark; entrance is a large wooden gate. (45 minutes)

Harbin Hot Springs

P.O. Box 782
Middletown, CA 95461
800/622-2477 or 707/987-2477; fax: 707/987-9561
Email: reception@harbin.org
Website: www.harbin.org

In the 1880s, a stagecoach brought people suffering from gout, dyspepsia, and rheumatism to the Harbin Hot Springs Health and Pleasure Resort for the cure of "taking the waters." Hundreds of years before them, indigenous people had named Harbin *eetawyomi* (the hot place). More than 36,000 gallons of mineral water flow up to the Earth's surface each day from seven natural springs on the 1,160 acres of Harbin property, situated in a secluded mountain valley in Northern California. Heated by volcanic action, two hot springs feed the hot and warm pool complex, while cold springs feed the remaining pools and the resort's "tap water" tanks.

For 25 years, the Heart Consciousness Church has owned and operated Harbin Hot Springs, and the resort's operations are handled by a community of residents. Preferring to present itself as a retreat rather than a resort because of its homey, laidback atmosphere and clothing-optional policy, Harbin now offers workshops, seasonal packages, community living, or the opportunity to simply bathe in the hot, warm, and cold pools. The School of Shiatsu and Massage, also located at Harbin, brings students from Europe, Japan, and throughout the United States to study bodywork either for professional requirements or to expand their personal growth. The school's director, Harold Dull, is responsible for inventing watsu (the in-water form of shiatsu), which has proven to have profound rehabilitative results in treating emotional trauma, sleep disorders, and cerebral palsy. For those interested in retreat packages, they are offered during weekdays throughout the winter months and include lodging, a daily massage, and breakfast.

Accommodations: Private rooms, each with a unique design and either private or European-style bathrooms, cabins, dormitories, and campsites

Rates: $75–185 double occupancy; $30–90 single occupancy. Camping is $165 per week, $115 for children younger than 18. Day-visit passes are $15–20, $10–15 for children younger than 18.

Credit Cards: MC, V

Meal Plans: Breakfast is provided with the off-season package. On-grounds cafés and restaurants serve fresh, organic food from the garden.

Services: Holistic health and personal growth workshops, rebirthing, rebalancing, hypnotherapy, chiropractic treatments, and various types of massage, including Esalen, deep tissue, reflexology, shiatsu, and watsu; yoga, meditation, dance, 12-step meetings, and full and new moon celebrations

Recreational Activities: Hiking, swimming

Facilities: A 1,160-acre foothill estate, including the School of Shiatsu and Massage, rustic cabins, conference facilities, a vegetarian kitchen, a restaurant, a poolside café, two warm pools, a hot pool, a cold plunge pool, a dry sauna, a swimming pool, a redwood sundeck, a garden, and forest trails

Disability Access: No access

Special Notes: Bring a towel, a flashlight, sandals, and footwear appropriate for rocky terrain. The pool area is clothing optional; the dressing facilities are coeducational. Open fires, candles, and camp stoves are forbidden; smoking is allowed only in a designated area next to the parking lot. Inquire about the pool maintenance schedule.

Nearby Attractions: Wine country, galleries, Clearlake recreational area

Nearest Airports: Sacramento, Oakland, and San Francisco, CA

Getting There: Spa does not provide airport service. Car rental is available at airport. Street address is 18424 Harbin Springs Road, in Middletown. Driving from Middletown at Highway 29, turn left at Highway 175; right on Barnes Street (3 blocks); left on Harbin Springs Road. The spa's gatehouse is 2 miles up Harbin Springs Road. (10 minutes) Driving from Sacramento, take I-5 to Williams. Follow Highway 20 to Highway 53; left at Highway 53; exit at Highway 29 South; continue into Middletown. (3 hours) Driving from Oakland and the East Bay, take I-80 East past Vallejo to Highway 37. Exit Highway 37 after 2 miles at Highway 29; right at Highway 29; continue through Calistoga and into Middletown. (2.5 hours) Driving from San Francisco, take Highway 101 North through Santa Rosa. Exit at River Road/Mark West/Calistoga; right on Mark West Road (which becomes Potter Creek Road); left on Petrified Forest Road and into Calistoga; left on Foothill Boulevard; right on Tubbs Lane; left on Highway 29 into Middletown. (2.5 hours)

Heartwood Institute

220 Harmony Lane
Garberville, CA 95542
877/936-9663 or 707/923-5000; fax: 707/923-5010
Email: hello@heartwoodinstitute.com
Website: www.heartwoodinstitute.com

On a 240-acre campus surrounded by rolling meadows and forests of Douglas fir, oak, madrone, manzanita, and California bay laurel—replete with red tail hawks, wild turkeys, owls, bobtail cats, and foxes—lies the educational community of Heartwood. It is devoted to serving as a catalyst for planetary healing by helping people achieve physical, psychological, and spiritual well-being. "We believe that every personal healing is a step toward the healing of all," reads the institute's course catalog.

Several times throughout the year, group wellness retreats are offered at this 20-year-old institute. Retreats can revolve around spirituality, such as the Zen and Pure Land Meditation Retreat, or around physical health, such as the Polarity Cleansing Diet, which is intended for people who are ready to break their dietary habits and commit to a healthier lifestyle. Personalized Wellness Retreats can be arranged at any time throughout the year with advance notice. Guests can create their own schedule of private sessions in a wide variety of body therapies, Asian healing arts, and hypnotherapies with Heartwood's professionally trained and experienced staff.

As a school, Heartwood is recognized by many professional alternative health organizations nationwide, including the American Massage Therapy Association and the American Oriental Bodywork Therapy Association. In addition to the retreats, the general public is invited to join Heartwood's one- to three-week intensive sessions designed for holistic health professionals to study bodywork and massage, Asian healing arts, hypnotherapy, and addiction counseling. Each quarter, Heartwood also offers an 11-week program known as Life Exploration. This 200-hour course is designed as an opportunity to take time away from one's work and lifestyle to reflect on life and acquire the skills necessary for healing, wholeness, and self-actualization. Life Exploration is intended for refreshing the mind, body, and spirit, not as career training.

Accommodations: Private and shared preferred rooms come with sheets, pillows, comforters, and bath towels. Standard dormitory-style shared rooms have a communal bath. Campsites are available.

Rates: A weekend retreat is $240; preferred rooms with all linens furnished are $80 single or $130 double. The camping retreat fee is $55 per day and includes meals.

Credit Cards: MC, V

Meal Plans: Three meals, mostly organic vegetarian, are included daily. Guests may use the snack kitchen.

Services: Classes and workshops on bodywork and massage, including deep-tissue massage, shiatsu, Swedish, and Esalen; breathwork and jin shin jyutsu; transformational therapy and hypnotherapy; nutritional counseling; and lectures

Recreational Activities: Hiking, swimming, dances

Facilities: A 240-acre hillside campus with a log community lodge, a spacious deck, a dining room with piano, an outdoor heated swimming pool, a hot tub, a wood-fired sauna, guest rooms, and decks

Disability Access: No access

Special Notes: Pets are not allowed. Guests are advised to bring a sleeping bag, bed linens, towels, toiletries, a flashlight, snack foods, a day pack, rain gear, and seasonal clothing.

Nearby Attractions: Sinkyone Wilderness State Preserve; Humboldt Redwoods; Victorian architecture; museums, restaurants, and galleries in Arcata and Eureka

Nearest Airport: Eureka/Arcata, CA

Getting There: Shuttle service is available from the Garberville Greyhound station and Eureka/Arcata Airport for an additional fee. Call Hartwood for details. Driving from Garberville at the intersection of Redway and Harris Alder Point Road, turn right on Harris Adler Point Road. Continue 8 miles; bear right at fork onto Bell Spring Road; continue 8 miles; left on Island Mountain Road; after 4 miles follow signs to spa entrance. (1 hour) Driving from Eureka and points north, take Highway 101 South to the first Garberville exit and follow the above directions to spa. (2 hours) Driving from Santa Rosa, San Francisco, and points south, take Highway 101 North to first Garberville exit. Continue through town; stay left onto Redway and cross the highway; right on Harris Adler Point Road and follow the Garberville directions to spa. (4 hours)

Indian Springs Resort and Spa

1712 Lincoln Avenue
Calistoga, CA 94515
707/942-4913; fax: 707/942-4919
Email: info@indianspringscalistoga.com
Website: www.indianspringscalistoga.com

Situated on three thermal geysers and 16 acres of ancient volcanic ash, the land at Indian Springs has a tradition of purification and healing. Since 1860 the spa has offered mud baths, mineral tubs, steam rooms, and mineral pools, all supplied with pure mineral water from the three geysers on the property. It is one of California's oldest continuously operating pool and spa facilities.

Guests at Indian Springs enjoy 100-percent pure volcanic ash mud baths. The ash, which was deposited millions of years ago on the property, has been hand-sifted and carefully mixed with naturally heated geyser water until it reaches the perfect consistency to maintain an even warmth and provide buoyancy for your body. Taking a mud bath soothes minor aches and pains, increases blood circulation, relaxes muscles, and exfoliates the skin, leaving it soft and cleansed. Gentle music is piped throughout the treatment rooms, and the mud is sterilized after each use. A mud bath is usually followed by a mineral water soak in a Victorian tub, a geyser water steam bath, and a blanket wrap in a private room, which allows you to cool down and rest. A trained staff member is present at all times to guide people through the treatment and offer guests refreshing citrus and cucumber water drinks to help replace fluids lost during heat treatments. A variety of massages, facials, body polishes, and manicures and pedicures is also available.

Indian Springs is located within a hour and a half of the San Francisco Bay Area in beautiful Napa Valley. A great way to take care of yourself or someone special is by combining a spa treatment with a relaxing swim in the mineral pool, wine tasting at a nearby vineyard, followed with lunch/dinner at one of Napa Valley's many fine restaurants.

Accommodations: Guests stay in whitewashed cottages and bungalows.
Rates: $175–500 per night, depending on the bungalow and season
Credit Cards: MC, V
Meal Plans: A variety of restaurants is available in Calistoga within walking distance of Indian Springs.
Services: Massages, facials, body polishes, pedicures, manicures, and mud baths
Recreational Activities: Swimming, walking, hiking, shuffleboard, croquet, tennis, and biking
Facilities: A restored 1913 bathhouse, treatment rooms, an Olympic-sized mineral pool, mineral baths, bungalows, a clay tennis court, bicycle surreys, rose gardens, and hammocks
Disability Access: Access is limited; please call in advance.
Special Notes: Each massage technician has an average of more than ten years experience. All spa guests receive complimentary use of the Olympic-size mineral pool, beverages, and clean terrycloth robes.
Nearby Attractions: Wine tasting, several gift shops, and Napa valley restaurants in the area
Nearest Airport: San Francisco, CA

Getting There: Airport pick-up is not available at airport. Car rental is available at airport. Driving from San Francisco and points south, take Highway 101 North and onto Highway 37 North then Highway 121 East. Exit at Highway 29 and continue into Calistoga; right on Lincoln Avenue; spa entrance is on the right. (1.5 hours)

The Kenwood Inn and Spa

10400 Sonoma Highway
Kenwood, CA 95452
800/3-KENWOOD (353-6966) or 707/833-1293;
fax: 707/833-1247
Website: www.kenwoodinn.com

Recently rated as one of the top 10 wine country inns in the world, the Kenwood Inn and Spa has the ambience of an Italian country villa with peaceful Old World charm. Twelve suites are housed in Mediterranean-style buildings, which—along with the main building and dining room—cluster around a courtyard garden that features fountains located among mature rose and herb bushes, as well as persimmon, fig, and olive trees. This central courtyard is also the site of several lounge chairs, a full-sized swimming pool, and a hot tub.

Guests definitely come to this small, intimate setting to relax. Spa treatments are the only scheduled activities available besides breakfast. The five full-service treatment rooms, which are bathed in candlelight, are used for a variety of services, including massage, skincare treatments, body wraps and scrubs, aromatherapy, and an indulgent two-hour East Indian Ayurvedic healing treatment. Another favorite treatment among couples is the Ti Amo Togetherness Massage—a 90-minute massage for you and your partner, given in your suite complete with candlelight and champagne.

This inn is especially private and peaceful because of the design of the guest rooms and the buildings that encircle the center gardens and pool. The original four-room main building, which is cloaked in ivy, is now joined by three smaller Italian-style buildings, each containing 2–4 suites. Each suite contains European antiques, lush fabric treatments, feather beds and down comforters, a private bath, and a fireplace. Upstairs suites feature a balcony, whereas downstairs suites offer a private terrace. Relaxing in the courtyard, guests can sit under the olive trees and imagine that they are nestled in an Italian villa.

Accommodations: Twelve suites surrounding the garden courtyard. Each suite contains European antiques, feather beds and down comforters, a private bath, and a working fireplace. Upstairs suites feature a balcony, whereas downstairs suites offer a private terrace.

Rates: $295–395 per night, depending on the suite, night of the week, and season. Rates include a full breakfast daily, and a complimentary bottle of wine is provided upon arrival.

Credit Cards: AE, MC, V

Meal Plans: A Mediterranean-inspired breakfast is served each morning and is included in the room rate. Complimentary wine, cheese, and fruit are provided each evening in the courtyard for guests. Nearby restaurants are located within 15 minutes for other meals.

Services: Massages, body wraps, salt scrubs, facials, an ancient Ayurvedic body purification ritual, and a warm-oil treatment

Recreational Activities: Bikes and horses can be rented to tour nearby state parks and wineries.

Facilities: Twelve suites surrounding a courtyard, a dining room, a lounge, a library, five treatment rooms, a pool, and a hot tub

Disability Access: One guest room has disability access.

Nearby Attractions: The Inn is near the Kunde Estate Winery, landmark vineyards, and Kenwood vineyards. The historic town of Sonoma is just 15 minutes away.

Special Notes: In keeping with the romantic country setting, bringing children to the inn is not recommended.

Nearest Airports: San Francisco and Oakland, CA

Getting There: Car rentals are available at airports. Driving from San Francisco, take Highway 101, across the Golden Gate bridge to Highway 37 East toward Sonoma. Continue on Highway 37 to Highway 121 Sonoma Turnoff; left at the stoplight; follow signs to Glen Ellen/Arnold Drive through Glen Ellen; when you reach the end of Arnold drive, turn left onto Highway 12; spa entrance is 3 miles on the left. (1.5 hours) Driving from Oakland and the East Bay, take I-580 West towards San Francisco/San Rafael; cross Richmond Bridge and merge onto Highway 101 North; follow directions from Highway 37 above. (1.5 hours)

The Lodge At Skylonda

16350 Skyline Blvd.
Woodside, CA 94062
800/851-2222 or 415/954-8565; fax: 415/954-8567
Email: reservations@skylondalodge.com
Website: www.skylondalodge.com

Situated 35 miles south of San Francisco in the part of the peninsula that is redwood forest, The Lodge at Skylonda is a quality 16-room log and stone spa retreat. Skylonda was created to provide guests with a respite from the complexities of daily living. For those who would like to simply rest, relax, and do little, Skylonda offers a peaceful, stress-free environment. For those who like to be active, a variety of scheduled activities is offered each day. A typical day includes hiking, circuit training, tai chi, aquatics, yoga, and meditation. Daily massage, saunas, steam room, hot tub, and soothing body treatments are also available.

Hiking is a large part of the Skylonda program as a method for reaching new physical and spiritual heights. Guests hike with experienced guides on different adventures each day. Selected from the many footpaths and logging trails of the coastal range, the hiking program covers beautiful scenery. Guests set their own pace as they traverse vast meadows, climb steep ravines, or stroll among the native redwoods, Douglas firs, oaks, and madrones. Stretching is scheduled before and after each hike, and sessions of yoga and circuit training are recommended to recharge your energy.

Healthy and tastefully prepared gourmet meals also nurture one's energy and spirit. Skylonda's executive chef invites guests into the kitchen twice weekly for a delicious demonstration and tasting of healthy gourmet fare from appetizers to desserts, with lots of cooking tips in between.

Accommodations: 16 comfortable guest rooms, which open up to a private deck or patio with furniture. All baths have oversized soaking tubs and showers.

Meal Plans: Healthy, gourmet cuisine for breakfast, lunch, and dinner prepared by the executive chef. Appetizers are served in the great room every evening. Private dining and picnic lunches are available upon request.

Rates: $305–375 per person (double occupancy); rates reduced by 20 percent during "Winter Solstice" from November 1 to December 22, and from January 3 to March 31.

Facilities: A great room with a fireplace, a deck, a lending library, on-premise marked hiking trails and picnic spots, a 30-foot indoor swimming pool, an outdoor hot tub and deck, a sauna and steam room, and an exercise room with Cybex strength-conditioning equipment

Disability Access: Access is limited; please call in advance.

Services: Various massage options such as shiatsu, reflexology, Thai massage, and Trager; various body treatments such as sea salt glow, deep forest exfoliation, and hot stone therapy; facials and skincare treatments; hiking, aquatics, yoga, meditation, tai chi, and circuit training; and cooking demonstrations with the chef

Recreational Activities: Hiking, swimming

Special Notes: Smoking is permitted outside only. Complimentary wine tastings are presented twice monthly by a local boutique of the Association of Wine Growers of Santa Cruz County.

Nearby Attractions: Visits to local boutique wineries of the Santa Cruz mountains, which are home to more than 40 small, family-owned wineries; Half Moon Bay on the coast of the Pacific Ocean

Nearest Airports: San Francisco and San Jose, CA

Getting There: Towncar Airport Shuttle Service, 800/851-2222, is available from San Francisco, $37.50 each way. Taxi service is also available, Yellow CAB 888/595-1222, approximately $100 each way. Driving from San Francisco and points north, take I-280 South to Bunker Hill Drive. Turn left at stop sign; continue on Highway 92 West 2.5 miles to Highway 35/Skyline Boulevard; spa is in Woodside, 10.5 miles down on right. (1+ hours) Driving from San Jose and points south, take I-280 North. Exit at Highway 84/Woodside Road towards Woodside; left at first stop sign, Highway 84/Woodside Road then bear right to highway; continue 3 miles; right at Highway 35/Skyline Boulevard; spa is 1.5 miles on left. (1+ hours)

Mount Madonna Center

445 Summit Road
Watsonville, CA 95076
408/847-0406; fax: 408/847-2683
Email: programs@mountmadonna.org
Website: www.mountmadonna.org

In the rolling meadows and redwood forests of Santa Cruz County lies the Mount Madonna Center, a residential community offering spiritual and health retreats. In 1978, the Hanuman Fellowship originally purchased 355 acres of land with an expansive view of the Monterey Bay to form what would become the Mount Madonna Center, a community of people united by the study and practice of yoga. The center was founded with the goal of providing a place where people can explore yoga and other pathways of personal growth.

Mount Madonna is a threefold facility, functioning as a conference and retreat center, a private school, and a community. The center holds about 85 activities a year, including workshops, seminars, intensive sessions, rentals by outside groups, retreats, and other educational gatherings. Programs are primarily spiritual; however, each year several workshops are offered that focus on health and healing, including Ayurveda, as well as programs in dance, the arts, and psychology.

Yoga is a strong undercurrent at Mount Madonna, and many staff members have studied and practiced for more than 25 years under the direction of Baba Hari Dass. Guests on personal retreat can receive yoga instruction as well as acupuncture, massage, and other related services. Personal retreats of any length can be scheduled year-round at Mount Madonna and are an ideal way for people to take advantage of the beautiful natural setting and community resources. The center is an ideal location for academic research, personal projects, or simply a quiet place to recuperate.

Accommodations: Up to 500 beds in various facilities, including a studio, community lodge, guest house, and conference center. Both private and shared bathrooms are available. Campsites, tents, and RV hookups are also available.

Rates: Vary according to lodging; $25–92 per night, per person

Credit cards: None accepted

Meal Plans: Two healthy vegetarian meals and one snack per day are served cafeteria style.

Services: Retreats focusing on yoga practice and theory; seasonal celebrations; traditional Vedic healing methods; and swedan treatments consisting of body oiling, an herbal steam bath, a barley four rubdown, and a hot shower

Recreational Activities: Swimming, hiking, tennis, volleyball

Facilities: 355 acres with a private school for grades K–12, a library, conference and seminar rooms, a book and gift store, an Ayurvedic herb store, a wellness center, a hot tub, basketball courts, tennis courts, volleyball courts, a full-size gym, a garden, a greenhouse, a lake, and hiking trails

Disability Access: Yes; the facilities are accessible for people with disabilities.

Special Notes: Smoking is allowed only in designated outdoor areas.

Nearby Attractions: Santa Cruz, Monterey, Pacific Coast Highway, Carel, festivals, redwoods

Nearest Airports: San Francisco and San Jose, CA

Getting There: Airport pick-up is available for extra charge. Driving from San Jose, San Francisco, and points north, take Highway 101 South and exit at Gilroy and Highway 152. Continue west on Highway 152 to Mount Madonna State Park; drive through park and continue as road changes to Summit Road; Summit Road goes directly to spa. (1.5+ hours)

Optimum Health Institute of San Diego

6970 Central Avenue
Lemon Grove, CA 91945
619/464-3346; fax: 619/589-4098
Email: optimum@optimumhealth.org
Website: www.optimumhealth.org

A diet of live raw foods, exercise, whirlpools, and the opportunity to receive colonics, massages, and chiropractic care is what one can expect at the Optimum Health Institute. In three-week sessions, guests are taught the institute's philosophy that "the human body is self-regenerating and self-cleansing, and if given the proper tools with which to work, it can maintain its natural state of health." The program is structured to address the mental, physical, and emotional aspects of each person, with the ultimate goal of having each guest learn about the body and mind and how the two work together.

In the first week, some of the activities are daily exercise and attending classes that teach how to eat properly, build self-esteem, mentally and emotionally detoxify, and relax to help control pain. Daily exercise continues in the second week, but guests also learn how to grow sprouts, plant wheat grass, garden organically, prepare healthy foods, and plan menus. Communication skills and at-home personal follow-up are also addressed. In the third week, guests put their newfound knowledge to work in hands-on food preparation classes and classes about the mind-body connection and diet maintenance.

Since its founding in 1976, more than 50,000 guests have benefited from the institute's program. Testimonials of lowered blood pressure and blood sugar levels returning to normal are just some of the many responses shared by former guests. Staff members are passionate, knowledgeable, and experienced in the holistic health field.

Accommodations: Standard single, standard double, preferred single, preferred double, preferred deluxe, townhouse

Rates: $450–850 a week, depending on the level of accommodations. Rates include room, meals, and classes. Colonics, massages, and chiropractic care are available at additional cost.

Credit Cards: D, MC, V

Meal Plans: Three vegan, raw vegetarian meals, including sprouts, greens, fruits, vegetables, fruit juices, enzyme-rich Rejuvelac, and wheat grass juice, are served every day.

Services: Nutritional classes, massages, chiropractic care, and colonic hydrotherapy

Recreational Activities: Walking and enjoying the gardens

Facilities: Beachfront facility with main building, a lounge, an exercise room, and townhouses, a greenhouse, a hot tub, a skincare center, a whirlpool, lawns, gardens, and beach access

Disability Access: Limited; please inquire when making reservations.

Special Notes: The institute has a free open house every Sunday at 4:30 P.M., with a live-foods meal at 6 P.M. A three-dollar donation is requested. Smoking, alcohol, incense, and heavy perfumes are not allowed at the institute.

Nearby Attractions: San Diego Zoo, San Diego Wild Animal Park, Balboa Park, downtown shopping

Nearest Airport: San Diego, CA

Getting There: Airport and Amtrak pick-up at reduced rates with Orange Cab 619/291-3341. Reduced rates only applicable with advance arrangements. Driving from all points along I-5, exit to Highway 94 east. Take Massachusetts Exit; left at traffic light; right on Central Avenue; spa entrance on right. (15 minutes+)

Vichy Springs Resort and Inn

2605 Vichy Springs Road
Ukiah, CA 95482-3507
707/462-9515; fax: 707/462-9516
Email: info@vichysprings.com
Website: www.vichysprings.com

An old photograph of the Vichy Springs Resort shows Mark Twain in a summer suit, necktie, and Panama hat "taking the waters." Twain dips the tip of his long cane into the mineral water that pours from the Mendocino foothills and stares intently at the mouth of a cave. It is obvious that both the resort and the waters have been around for a long time.

The "champagne baths," as they are known at Vichy Springs, were first used by indigenous peoples thousands of years ago and are still sought for their healing and restorative qualities. The mineral baths contain the only warm and naturally carbonated water in North America, and their composition is exactly like that of the famous Vichy Springs in France. No chemicals have been added to the water. The mineral water bottled directly from the springs has been served at the White House.

After the 700-acre resort opened in 1854, it began to gain renown among well-known writers, philosophers, and politicians. Robert Louis Stevenson, Jack London, and Ulysses S Grant made Vichy a regular retreat spot. The current proprietors of Vichy Springs traveled through 135 countries to gain an intimate knowledge of what visitors need and seek. They then sought out the most unique springs in the United States and developed this small and understated resort for the subtle rest and healing people need today.

There are no set programs at Vichy. The naturally occurring springs are therapeutic in themselves and provide relief from a variety of maladies, including arthritis, gout, rheumatism, poison oak, burns, and the general stresses of everyday life. Combined with massage therapy, facials, hiking, and swimming, the benefits of this relaxing and healthy getaway accumulate.

Accommodations: Rooms or cottages with queen and/or twin beds

Rates: $105 single room; $140–175 double room, $205 suite, and $235 double cottage. Massage/facial rates are $70 for 60 minutes and $95 for 90 minutes. Day use of the mineral baths, swimming pool, and property is $35 for a day pass, $22 for two hours or less.

Credit Cards: All major credit cards are accepted.

Meals: A full buffet-style breakfast, with vegetarian options, is included.

Services: Therapeutic and Swedish massage, hand and foot reflexology, herbal facials

Recreational Activities: Volleyball, basketball, hiking, horseshoes, and swimming

Facilities: A 700-acre ranch estate with 10 private mineral baths, a communal hot pool, an Olympic-sized outdoor pool, massage and treatment rooms, four cottages, one suite, five acres of landscaped gardens, swings, badminton, horseshoes, a live stream, a waterfall, rolling hills, and miles of hiking trails

Disability Access: Yes

Special Notes: Bathing suits are required in all facilities. Pets are not allowed.

Nearby Attractions: Mendocino coast; lakes and wineries of Sonoma, Lake, and Mendocino counties; redwood forests (Montgomery Woods has the tallest trees in the world); water sports; and fishing

Nearest Airports: San Francisco, Oakland, and Sacramento, CA

Getting There: Car rental is available at all airports. Driving from San Francisco and Oakland, take Highway 101 North to Ukiah, then east on Vichy Springs Road and follow the Historic Landmark signs. (2.5 hours) From Sacramento, take I-5 North, to Highway 20 West, and Highway 101 South to Ukiah; follow above directions. (2.5 hours)

We Care Holistic Health Center

18000 Long Canyon Road
Desert Hot Springs, CA 92241
800/888-2523 or 760/251-2261; fax 760/251-5399
Email: info@wecarespa.com
Website: www.wecarespa.com

We Care is a family-owned holistic health center dedicated to total well-being through natural health practices. Guests are rejuvenated and detoxified through the combined use of herbs, an all-natural liquid diet, colonics, and massage. This approach is built around the recovery of an impaired immune system, but guests don't have to have an illness caused by a weak immune system to benefit from We Care's program. Founders Susana and Susan Lombardi believe that people who feel sluggish, bloated, or listless or who are prone to gas, indigestion, and constipation are already feeling the effects of immune system damage. Consequently, through participating in the We Care program, guests not only restore healthy immune function but also experience redoubled energy and the need to sleep less.

The Lombardis emphasize improving the mind, body, and spirit through cleansing, relaxation, exercise, and nutritional education. Although guests are technically fasting, they are not on a starvation diet. A regular stay consists of a liquid diet, daily colonic hygiene treatments, reflexology, and the use of products that act as solvents to remove toxins from the body. The cold-press raw fruit and vegetable juices, herb teas, and lemon water ensure that the body receives all the nutrition it needs and sometimes more than most people get from their normal diets. Guests also experience lymphatic massage, reflexology, herbal wraps, salt glows, yoga, mineral water baths, swimming, cooking demonstrations, and nutrition classes. Because it takes several days of cleansing before the body begins to release toxins, the program is one week long; daily and monthly rates, as well as a home cleansing program, are available.

Accommodations: Seven spacious private rooms with private bath, six small rooms with semiprivate bath

Rates: A three-day retreat is $360–815 depending on accommodations; an eight-day wellness package is $1,215–2,280. Discount rates are offered for double occupancy, We Care graduates, and travel agents.

Credit Cards: AE, MC, V

Meal Plans: We Care is a juice-fasting spa. Raw juices are offered hourly, as are herbal teas and detoxification drinks.

Services: Yoga classes, meditation, guided fasting, colonics, iridology, reflexology, massage treatments, salt glow rubs, herbal wraps, skin brushing, aromatherapy, energy clearing, nutrition and cooking classes, and more

Recreational Activities: Hiking, swimming, nearby golf

Facilities: A five-acre desert ranch with a sun deck, a kitchen, hot mineral pools, an outdoor swimming pool, a sauna, a mini-trampoline, a magnetic bed, a pyramid, a labyrinth, a medicine wheel, and desert hikes

Disability Access: No access

Special Notes: A satisfaction guarantee gives guests 24 hours to claim a refund, minus a daily rate charge. Smoking is not allowed.

Nearby Attractions: Joshua Tree National Monument; theater, concerts, and galleries of Palm Springs; botanical gardens; jeep tours; Palm Springs Aerial Tramway; golf courses and hikes

Nearest Airport: Palm Springs, CA

Getting There: VIP Taxi, 760/322-2264, provides airport service. Advance reservations are recommended. Car rental is available. Driving from Palm Springs Airport, exiting on Tahquitz Drive, turn right on Vista Chino; left on Palm Drive to Desert Hot Springs; right on Dillon; pass Mountain View (1 mile) and turn right on Long Canyon Road; spa entrance is at the end of Long Canyon Road. (.5 hour)

Wilbur Hot Springs

3375 Wilbur Springs Road
Wilbur Springs, CA 95987-9709
530/473-2306
Email: mail@wilburhotsprings.com
Website: www.wilburhotsprings.com

During the Victorian era, gold diggers, silver miners, stagecoach drivers, and weary travelers flooded the small town of Wilbur Springs, California, to sit in the natural hot mineral waters and rejuvenate themselves—and perhaps slug a shot of whiskey. Today, Wilbur Hot Springs, billed as a "sanctuary for the self," is a place where people who seek quiet can come to take the waters. The Colusi, Pomo, and Wintun tribes considered these panoramic ridge views and high meadows sacred healing grounds for centuries before Columbus found his way to America. Guests can experience the unmistakably therapeutic experience of a mineral soak amidst serene and remote countryside.

The retreat rests on a nature preserve in Northern California's Coastal Mountain Range. The hotel is solar powered and warmed by centrally located gas fireplaces. The lodge is a historic hotel, evidenced by the details of carved flowers in paneled wood within the guest rooms. The bathhouse, a quiet area at all times, is sheltered. Water is channeled into three long baths, with temperatures ranging from a mild 98 degrees Fahrenheit to a robust 112 degrees Fahrenheit. A large, cool-water mineral pool offers guests a break from the heat, and an outdoor hot mineral sitting pool is perfect for those who like to soak under the stars. A dry sauna is connected to the bathhouse by a sweeping wood deck. Licensed massage therapists are available with advance reservations.

Accommodations: 17 private guest rooms; one spacious suite with a private bath, kitchen, and three optional adjoining bedrooms; an 11-bed bunkroom; and campsites (available seasonally)

Rates: Vary according to lodging and time of visit. A single-occupancy room is $99 Sunday through Thursday, $147 Friday through Sunday and holidays. Rates include access to all facilities and unlimited use of the hot springs. A minimum stay of two nights is required for weekend bookings.

Credit Cards: MC, V

Meal Plans: Guests supply their own food and cook their meals in a commercially equipped kitchen. Dry spices, cookware, utensils, and dishes are provided.

Services: Esalen/Swedish and deep-tissue massage, hot- and cold-water mineral soaks

Recreational Activities: Hiking, mountain biking, stargazing

Facilities: A 240-acre private valley adjacent to a 15,000-acre nature preserve; a bathhouse; a cool-water mineral pool; an outdoor hot mineral sitting pool; a dry sauna; a redwood deck; a historic hotel; a kitchen; billiards; a music room with piano, guitars, and bamboo flutes; table tennis; two dining rooms; a library; and nature trails

Disability Access: Access is limited, please call in advance.

Special Notes: Wilbur Hot Springs is clothing optional behind the screened area. Guests supply their own towels, which are required, and all toiletries. Bunkroom guests must bring their own top bedding. Children younger than three years are not permitted in the baths.

Nearby Attractions: River rafting in the Cache Creek Canyon

Nearest Airports: San Francisco, Oakland, and Sacramento, CA

Getting There: Car rental is available at all airports. Driving from San Francisco, take Highway 280 to I-80 East towards Vallejo and Sacramento. Exit at Highway 16; left at intersection with Highway 20; right onto Bear Valley Road; left onto the Wilbur Silver Bridge; spa entrance is 1 mile ahead. (2.5 hours)

Anuhea Bed-and-Breakfast Health Retreat

3164 Mapu Place
Kihei, Maui, HI 96753
800/206-4441 or 808/874-1490; fax 808/874-8587
Email: anuhea@maui.net
Website: www.anuheamaui.com

Dr. Russell and Cherie Kolbo have blended their vision and talents to create Anuhea, a unique health and healing center located in a private home nestled on the hillside of Haleakala above Kihei/Wailea on the island of Maui.

A large hot tub is situated in the garden area for water therapy and/or relaxation. Other peaceful areas allow space to rest, read, or just be in tune with yourself and nature.

Dr. Russell Kolbo has been a practicing naturopathic physician and chiropractor for 28 years and specializes in allergies, metabolic imbalances, candida, parasites, and detoxification programs. Cherie Kolbo is a certified colonic hydrotherapist and instructor. She incorporates color, sound, and flower essence therapy in her healing sessions. Cherie and Russell have taught classes on tissue cleansing and proper food combining. Together, the talents of this team offer guests of Anuhea a comprehensive life-enhancing program. Services and programs are customized to meet your specific needs. They include personal health coaching, cleansing programs, colon hydrotherapy, and transformational bodywork and massage.

Accommodations: Five appointed rooms. Three rooms have private bathrooms (two have large soaking bathtubs) and two garden rooms share a bathroom and shower. All rooms can be arranged into king or twin beds and are equipped with refrigerators, TVs, and ceiling fans and air-conditioning.

Rates: Bed-and-breakfast rates are $75–120 per night. Personal program rates range from $145–185 per day (three meals included). Personal consultations, body work, and colonics are available for an extra charge. Group rates are also available.

Credit Cards: MC, V

Meal Plans: A healthy, gourmet breakfast comes with a night's stay. Meal plans for personalized programs are included in the program rate. Bottled water is provided in rooms as well as other areas of the house. Breakfasts are served on the lanai overlooking the gardens, with a partial view of the ocean.

Services: Cleansing and detoxification programs, personal health coaching, massage and therapeutic bodywork, consultations, and colon hydrotherapy

Recreational Activities: Anuhea is near major hotels, golf courses, restaurants, shops, and the beaches on Maui. The staff can arrange guided tours, hiking, whale watching (in season), sunset cruises, kayak adventures, and snorkeling.

Facilities: A private home, B&B-style retreat surrounded by tropical gardens. Five private rooms for guests, a large living room, hammocks, a large lanai, a colon hydrotherapy room, and a massage room. Other amenities include a washer and dryer, a guest phone, a fax machine, email, parking, a physical workout area, and beach equipment.

Disability Access: No access

Special Notes: Wedding services can be conducted on the premises.

Nearby Attractions: Wailea/Mekena/Kihei beaches, Haleakala crater, world-class hotels and restaurants, shops and galleries, Spa Grande at the Grand Wailea Hotel, and golf courses

Nearest Airport: Maui, HI

Getting There: Car rental is available at airport. Driving from airport, take Highway 350 for 6.5 miles and turn left on Highway 31. Continue on Highway 31 to Wailea; left at Mapu Place and spa entrance. (.5 hour)

Dragonfly Ranch

P.O. Box 675
Honaunau-Kona, HI 96726
800/487-2159 or 808/328-9570; fax: 808/328-2159
Email: dfly@dragonflyranch.com
Website: www.dragonflyranch.com

The Dragonfly Ranch is a bed-and-breakfast located two miles north of Honaunau Bay, site of a *heiau* (historic temple). The area is also an ancient "place of sanctuary" blessed with *mana* (spiritual power). It's hard to tell whether this spiritual power or the lush garden atmosphere makes Dragonfly the unique and restorative retreat that it is.

This unique "Swiss Family Robinson"-style getaway caters to tourists looking for authenticity and an adventure in living "inside the outdoors." Although two rooms are available in the main house, there is also a plush outdoor bed for guests on the lanai and several indoor/outdoor suites with a rustic Hawaiian-style feeling. For example, the Honeymoon Suite features a king-size bed with a mirrored canopy in a junglelike setting with ocean views. The bed and kitchen are screened in under a pavilion roof, with an adjoining indoor redwood living room. Tropical vegetation surrounds an old-fashioned outdoor bathtub and shower, and a private redwood deck overlooks rock walls, gardens, and meadows.

The Dragonfly staff are friendly and invite guests to join their *ohana* (family) in sharing fresh, organic meals together, picking papayas and veggies from the garden, planting seeds, pulling weeds, and connecting with Mother Earth. Owner Barbara "Kenonilani" Moore has spent 25 years creating this "expansion mansion" full of character. She and her staff of health care practitioners periodically offer and host workshops that can include numerous vibrational healing modalities such as music, flower essences, yoga, LomiLomi massage, and a colorful labyrinth walk inside the rainbowed illuminarim. In five pristine bays nearby, you can enjoy snorkeling, scuba diving, sailing, kayaking, whale watching, and visits from wild, friendly dolphins. Romantic sunsets inspire enchanting, magical evenings.

Accommodations: Two main rooms and three suites, the Writer's Studio, the LomiLomi Suite, and the Honeymoon Suite

Rates: Rooms range from $85–200 per night, including breakfast.

Credit Cards: MC, V

Meal Plans: Continental breakfast is included with the room rate.

Services: Massage, aromatherapy, colored light therapy, and lectures by local healers and teachers

Recreational Activities: Scuba diving, snorkeling, sailing, kayaking, dolphin swims

Facilities: A ranch with a tropical garden, illuminarian with labyrinth, a main house, and three studios

Disability Access: No access

Special Notes: Weddings or renewal vows can be accommodated.

Nearby Attractions: Pu'uhonuaa O Honaunau National Park—Ancient "Place of Refuge," kayaking, world-class diving and snorkeling on the Kona coast, dolphin swims

Nearest Airport: Hilo, HI

Getting There: Spa can provide airport transportation with advance notice. Driving from Hilo, take Highway 11 to Route 160; right on Route 160; spa is 1.5 miles on right. (40 minutes)

Grand Wailea Resort Hotel and Spa

3850 Wailea Alanui Drive
Maui, HI 96753
800/888-6100 or 808/875-1234, ext. 4949;
fax 808/874-2424
Email: info@grandwailea.com
Website: www.grandwailea.com

Failing to mention the Grand Wailea when talking about healthy vacations in Hawaii is like failing to mention the Chrysler Building when talking about New York City's finest architecture. The Grand Wailea Resort's Spa Grande, covering 50,000 square feet, is Hawaii's most extensive health and fitness facility. Opulence is the key word here, with some suites going for as much as $10,000 per night, but this doesn't mean that health and well-being are overlooked.

All visits to the spa begin with the Terme Wailea Hydrotherapy Circuit, which consists of a brief shower, a soak in a Roman tub for relaxation, a cold plunge, a steam and sauna, and a sit under the cascading waterfall shower. A specialty bath of either Moor mud, seaweed, aromatherapy, tropical enzymes, or mineral salts follows, all of which have curative properties. Guests also have the option of taking a traditional Japanese-style bath.

Several packages are available, ranging from half- to full-day treatments. Each package includes a sampling of spa services, from a LomiLomi massage to a seaweed body mask. Natural Hawaiian plants, such as kelp, ginger, and papaya, are used in treatments and are selected for their particular healing properties. The spa also offers a collection of Ayurvedic revitalization therapies. The goal is to help guests achieve an inherent balance and improve overall wellness, in addition to the luxury pampering. The abhyanga, pizichili, and shirodhara treatments, once reserved for the kings and queens of India, are intended to energize and detoxify. Private consultations are available in stress management, nutrition, movement therapy, transformative energetics, and more.

Accommodations: Deluxe rooms in a nine-story tower with ocean views and private decks

Rates: Vary according to room, services, and season. The Terme Wailea Hydrotherapy Circuit is $50 for hotel guests, $75 for nonguests. Rooms are $390–10,000 per night.

Credit Cards: AE, D, MC, V

Meal Plans: Meals are not included in packages, but gourmet spa cuisine is available à la carte.

Services: Various types of massage, including LomiLomi, shiatsu, Swedish; aromatherapy; reflexology; hydrotherapy; herbal baths; Ayurvedic body treatments; body wraps and scrubs; facials; salon services; and private consultations on health, nutrition, and stress management

Recreational Activities: Catamaran cruises, snorkeling, windsurfing, scuba diving, golf, kids' programs

Facilities: A 40-acre luxury resort with a nine-story hotel, a 50,000-square-foot spa with Roman-style whirlpools, 42 treatment rooms, six restaurants, exercise equipment, a weight-training room, a racquetball court, 11 tennis courts, nine swimming pools, three golf courses, billiards, and gardens

Disability Access: Yes

Special Notes: The resort employs more than 1,000 total staff members, with spa staff of about 59 massage therapists, five Ayurvedic body-workers, 17 aestheticians, 19 Terme attendants, and 18 program specialists.

Nearby Attractions: Seven Sacred Pools, Haleakala National Park, horseback riding

Nearest Airport: Maui, HI

Getting There: Spa can assist with airport transportation with advance notice. Driving from airport, take Highway 380 to Highway 350. Continue on Highway 350; left onto Highway 31; Highway 31 ends at Wailea Ike Drive. Turn right onto Wailea Ike Drive; left onto Wailea Alanui Drive. Spa entrance on right. (.5 hour)

Hale Akua Shangri-La Bed and Breakfast Retreat Center

Star Route 1, Box 161
Haiku, Maui, HI 96708
888/368-5305 or 808/572-9300; fax 808/572-6666
Email: shangrila@maui.net
Website: www.haleakua.com

Sitting in the cliffside hot tub at the clothing-optional Hale Akua Shangri-La Retreat Center, guests can relax while gazing into the Haleakala crater. The health and yoga center is dedicated to the rejuvenation of body, mind, and spirit and is designed as a place to experience nature while receiving therapeutic bodywork, learning relaxation techniques, and consulting with local healers. Maui's waterfalls, bamboo forests, lava beds, and snorkeling bays are all within hiking distance, and seasoned guides accompany those who request them. The Shangri-La does not have a set program. This is a place to relax and create your own schedule, with a host of healing activities available, including the services of local healers on an individual basis at an additional charge.

The grounds sit on a cliff 300 feet above the ocean, providing spectacular views of Maui. Magnificent sunrises over the ocean cast red and gold light on Haleakala crater. This property consists of two secluded acres surrounded by tropical vegetation, coconut palms, and towering bamboo gently swaying in the wind. There are hammocks to nap in, cliffside ozonated hot tubs, an ozonated swimming pool, and opportunities to find out-of-the-way magical Maui sites.

Accommodations: Three buildings holding 12 rooms in all, most with ocean views and a bathroom or half bath. One suite has its own kitchen/dining area. Both main buildings have fully equipped kitchens.

Rates: The daily rate is $55-150, with a two-night minimum. Weekly rates are $330-900 per week, plus the Hawaii state visitor tax.

Credit Cards: AE, D, MC, V

Meal Plans: Continental breakfast is included with the room rate. Guests are on their own for lunch and dinner. Restaurants are located 20 minutes away, but kitchens are well set up for cooking lunch or dinner.

Services: Licensed massage therapy, hiking (with guides if requested), horseback riding, whale watching, and miscellaneous guest services, including an astrologer, an acupuncturist, a healer, and more. Yoga classes are held daily except Sunday and are free.

Recreational Activities: Swimming, whale watching, kayaking, biking, nature walks

Facilities: A two-acre cliffside retreat center with a spacious main house, a cabana building, a flower cottage for body treatments, hammocks, two hot tubs, an outdoor ozonated pool, tropical flower gardens, and natural pools and waterfalls

Disability Access: No access

Special Notes: The resort is clothing optional, except for in the yoga room and kitchen/dining areas.

Nearby Attractions: Baldwin Beach, Haleakala crater, Seven Sacred Pools, shopping and dining in Makawao and Paia, Hana, bamboo forest, beaches, waterfalls, lagoons

Nearest Airport: Maui, HI

Getting There: Spa can provide details on airport transportation. Car rental is available at airport. Driving from airport, take Highway 36 toward Hana. Exit to spa just past the junction of Highway 365. (40 minutes)

Hawaiian
Wellness Holiday

P.O. Box 279
Koloa, Kauai, HI 96756
808/332-9244; fax: 808/332-9374
Email: drdeal@askdrdeal.com
Website: www.askdrdeal.com/wellnessholiday

Dr. Grady Deal is a holistic, nutritional chiropractor who holds a doctorate in psychological counseling and a master's in sociology. He is also a licensed massage therapist, a lecturer, a gourmet cook, and author of *Dr. Deal's Delicious Detox Diet and Wellness Lifestyle*. His wife, Roberleigh Deal, is a licensed massage therapist and professional astrologer and numerologist who has delivered health lectures throughout the country. Both work together to form the Hawaiian Wellness Holiday, a health vacation program, and the Hawaiian Metaphysical Vacation, a personal transformation program. Guests can participate in either vacations or in both simultaneously. The groups are kept small to allow for personal attention. The vacations are a great idea for people who want to give themselves a leg up on their personal journey to health.

The vacations are available in durations from three days to four weeks. The Hawaiian Wellness Holiday includes an initial nutrition, weight-loss, and health consultation that results in recommendations for correcting nutritional deficiencies and excesses and methods to improve lifestyle habits and health problems. A diagnosis is made to determine which diet and lifestyle habits have poisoned the body. Healthy foods, cleansing herbs, self-administered colonics, fasting, raw juicing, and lots of water usually follow the diagnosis. Guests are also tested for several conditions, such as free-radical pathology, which may result in joint stiffness, chronic pain, and arthritis. Massage, reflexology, chiropractic adjustments, and hot packs are also a part of the therapeutic bodywork. Other healing activities include hikes to sacred sites and energy vortexes, yoga, aquacise, aura balancing by Roberleigh Deal, lessons in Hawaiian history, and health and personal transformation lectures.

Accommodations: Single and double rooms with private bath in a condominium on Poipu Beach
Rates: Vary according to room. Three days costs $955–1,120 for single occupancy, $1,455–1,665 for double occupancy. One- to four-week options are also available, with three- and four-week rates eligible for a 10 percent discount.
Credit Cards: MC, V
Meal Plans: Three meals are provided each day, with the options of vegetarian, macrobiotic, raw foods, juice fasting, Fit for Life, or Dr. Deal's Delicious Detox Diet. Fish and eggs are available.
Services: Massage, chiropractic, reflexology, exercise equipment, detoxification programs, colonics, nutritional counseling, lectures and slideshow on health-related subjects, and cooking classes
Recreational Activities: Golf, tennis, horseback riding, bicycling, hiking, water sports
Facilities: Guests have access to the health spa at the Hyatt Hotel, which has a steam room, a sauna, a hot tub, exercise equipment, an outdoor pool, and beach access.
Disability Access: Yes

Special Notes: Smoking is not allowed in program areas.

Nearby Attractions: Waimea canyon, Kokee State Park, botanical garden, fern grotto, golf courses, helicopter tours, day cruises

Nearest Airport: Kauai, HI

Getting There: Complimentary airport service is available. Driving from airport, take Poipu Road to Poipu Beach. (15 minutes)

Kalani Oceanside Resort-Retreat

RR 2, Box 4500
Pahoa, Hawai'i, HI 96778
800/800-6886 or 808/965-7828; fax 808/965-0527
Email: kalani@kalani.com
Website: www.kalani.com

Located on 113 acres of rural and sunny southeastern Hawaii, this resort offers a variety of vacations, workshops, and retreats and is the only coastal lodging facility within Hawaii's largest conservation area. Orchid farms and botanical gardens border Kalani, and the sea cliffs in the surrounding coastal area allow close-up views of sea turtles, dolphins, and migrating whales. The resort, whose name translates as "harmony of heaven and earth," has been offering unique and comfortable getaways since 1975. Kalani is also a member of the Hawaii Ecotourism Association and seeks to protect the natural environment through cultural education and responsible travel. Their not-for-profit status means that Kalani not only provides visitors with rich, healing experiences but also helps support the well-being of local communities.

Guests come to Kalani either for any one of the myriad scheduled activities or simply to settle into a cottage and take advantage of its many services and facilities. For those traveling to Kalani for an unscheduled event, options include various types of bodywork, watsu (floating water shiatsu), tai chi, yoga, lei making, a natural steam bath, dolphin swims, and treks to rare thermal springs and spectacular waterfalls. Scheduled programs vary from year to year. Some samples of last year's offerings included a watsu training session, the Kalani Spa Wellness Week, and several weeklong yoga retreats. A residency program is also available for artists and volunteers.

Accommodations: There are 3 large lodges, 8 cottage units, and a 3 acre camping area with hot showers and restroom facilities. Each lodge features 8 comfortable rooms with private or shared baths.

Rates: Vary according to program and usually include room and board. Overnight rates range from $60–294 per night, double occupancy. Campsites are $30 per night.

Credit Cards: AE, D, DC, MC, V

Meal Plans: Three meals are served daily. Meals are $27 per day and can be purchased individually. Produce comes from the Kalani Honua organic garden, orchard, and local farms. The lodge has kitchen facilities available for use by guests.

Services: Various types of massage, including LomiLomi and watsu; counseling on nutrition, diet, and weight loss; health workshops; daily yoga; weekly mythology; and free hula lessons

Recreational Activities: Tennis, horseback riding, hiking, volleyball, golf

Facilities: A 113-acre oceanside estate with an outdoor pool, tennis courts, whirlpools, a sauna, conference spaces, an orchard, and proximity to thermal spring and natural steam baths

Disability Access: Yes

Special Notes: Smoking is allowed in designated areas only.

Nearby Attractions: Volcanoes National Park, King Kamehameha historic site, Mauna Kea observatory telescope, Hawaii Tropical Botanical Garden, MacKenzie State Park, thermal spring parks, Lava Tree Park

Nearest Airport: Hilo, Big Island of Hawai'i

Getting There: Airport transportation is provided by Kalani Oceanside shuttle, $30 per person, $50 minimum; or taxi service, $70 per 1-4 persons. Reservations recommended through spa. Driving from Hilo, take Highway 11 to 130; by-pass Pahoa; at Kalapana take Highway 137, 5 miles to sign and entrance. (45 minutes)

JW Marriott Ihilani Resort and Spa at Ko Olina

92-1001 Olani Street
Kapolei, Oahu, HI 96707
800/626-4446 or 808/679-0079; fax: 808/679-0080
Website: www.marriott.com

This AAA Five-Diamond resort fronts four lagoons on Oahu's sunny western shore. Spanning 640 acres, the resort features elegant rooms, secluded beaches, tennis courts, and a variety of restaurants. It is also the home of the JW Marriott Ihilani Spa, which was voted one of the "Top Spas in the World" by readers of *Condé Nast Traveler* and *Travel & Leisure* magazines. In addition, the resort's 18-hole championship Ko Olina Golf Club has been heralded as one of "America's Top 75 Resort Courses" by *Golf Digest* magazine.

The JW Marriott Ihilani Spa is the only full-service resort spa on Oahu, offering services and treatments that are uniquely part of the Hawaiian tradition and lifestyle, using products harvested from the *honua* (earth) and the *mosan* (ocean) on the islands. A unique treat offered at the spa is thalassotherapy—an underwater massage from 180 pulsating jet streams utilizing warm seawater. In addition, Ihilani Spa offers other hydrotherapies, such as grand jets, Vichy and Swiss showers, and Roman pools.

Traditional massage therapies, such as Swedish and deep-tissue massage, are also available, as well as Hawaiian LomiLomi—a technique passed down by Hawaiian *kupuna* (elders) using kneading strokes and body manipulations. Pampering body treatments, such as island floral herbal wrap, green tea detoxifying wrap, or Hawaiian sea salt glow, rejuvenate guests.

In addition to Ihilani's pampering treatments, customized individual and group fitness, stress reduction, and nutritional programs are also available to suit guests' needs. Guests can use the outdoor lap and water exercise pool and comprehensive fitness center outfitted with strength and cardiovascular equipment. Treatments in acupuncture, tai chi classes, and "kekiono"—a three-hour service using neuroemotional techniques to address wellness of the body, mind, and spirit—are also offered.

Accommodations: A five-star hotel with 387 guest rooms and luxury suites, one beachfront suite, 10 Ihilani suites, 20 Naupaka junior suites, and six Deluxe Spa rooms. Rooms offer views of the ocean, lagoon, mountains, or golf course.

Rates: Various packages are available. The Aloha package is $363–429 per night (single or double occupancy), with a two-night minimum, and includes a $60 dining credit per day, use of the spa fitness lanai, and unlimited aerobics classes. A Taste of Ihilani is $498–565 per night (single or double occupancy), with a two-night minimum, and includes a choice of one activity per day, per person. The Hawaiian Harmony option is $497–564 per night (double occupancy), with a three-night minimum, and includes the choice of three 50-minute spa services per person, unlimited classes, and use of the spa.

Meal Plans: Four restaurants are available. Cuisine choices include Mediterranean dishes, fresh fish, authentic cuisine from regional Japan, and casual dining at the golf club.

Services: Massage and spa treatments, salon services, fitness classes, hula lessons

Recreational Activities: Golf, tennis, swimming, snorkeling, diving, fishing, sailing, horseback riding

Facilities: A full-service destination spa with an outdoor lap pool, a steam room, a sauna, relaxation lounges, Swiss and Vichy showers, grand jets, Roman pools, a fitness center, six championship tennis courts, a golf club with an 18-hole golf course, four restaurants, a hotel with nine meeting rooms, and a 5,530-square-foot ballroom

Disability Access: Yes; full access is available.

Special Notes: The Keiki Beachcomber Club at the hotel has been built exclusively for children ages 4–12 and offers programs such as kite-flying, tide pool exploration, snorkeling, golf, tennis, swimming, outdoor games, art projects, video games, and computer learning.

Nearby Attractions: Pearl Harbor, Waikiki, Neighbor Island excursions, downtown Honolulu

Nearest Airport: Honolulu, HI

Getting There: Call spa for details on airport transportaion and driving directions. Car rental is available at Honolulu airport. (.5 hour)

Breitenbush Hot Springs and Retreat

P.O. Box 578
Detroit, OR 97342
503/854-3314; fax: 503/854-3819
Email: office@breitenbush.com
Website: www.breitenbush.com

This Oregon Cascades retreat is as famous for its location as it is for its atmosphere. Guests can soak in a natural hot mineral spring lined with large, smooth stones overlooking a valley with a glacial river cutting through it and the forested mountain slopes. Or they can float in one of the four Medicine Wheel tubs in the "sacred circle" and receive a watsu treatment under a sky full of brilliant stars. This is Breitenbush Hot Springs and wildlife sanctuary, set in one of the last temperate rainforests in the world.

A 70-year-old lodge is the center of activity on this 86-acre holistic health retreat, providing space for guests to read one of the many library books on an oversized couch in the study or to feast on a fresh vegetarian lunch in the dining room. Shared community spaces include the Sanctuary, or sacred temple, where daily well-being programs such as meditation and yoga are held. The Forest Shelter is commonly used for workshops and yoga, and floor-to-ceiling glass provides an incredible view of the forest. The Vista Healing Arts Center is where guests come for a variety of therapeutic bodywork and energy healing treatments, such as LomiLomi, craniosacral therapy, somatoemotional release, or reiki.

People come to Breitenbush for one- and two-hour workshops, for unscheduled Personal Visits, or for one of the many weekend workshops held throughout the year. The annual Women's Renewal Weekend, limited to 20 women, is intended to relax and renew guests with healing arts and laughter. Women learn techniques to promote relaxation, stress reduction, and spiritual awareness, such as partner massage, group discussion, polarity energy balancing, conscious eating, and expressive movement. Because the center is situated just below the Pacific Crest Trail, backpackers have been known to drop down for a hot mineral bath and a soothing massage.

Accommodations: Cabins with heat and electricity are available for 2–4 people; 20 tents with mattresses and campsites are also available.

Rates: $55–90 per night for adults. Children's rates range from no fee to $30.

Credit Cards: MC, V

Meal Plans: Three organic vegetarian meals are served each day.

Services: Meditation, relaxation techniques, dance, yoga, music therapy, recovery programs, healing rituals, herb walks, drum circles, journaling

Recreational Activities: Hiking, cross-country skiing

Facilities: Natural hot springs, a steam and sauna, a sweat lodge, a community temple, a healing arts center, a greenhouse, an organic garden, a kitchen, and a dining villa

Disability Access: Access is limited; please call in advance.

Special Notes: Bring warm bedding, towels, a pillow, a flashlight, a swimsuit, rain gear and boots, a plastic water bottle, slip-on shoes and a robe, caffeinated beverages if desired, and snacks sealed in critter-proof containers. Smoking is allowed only in designated areas.

Nearby Attractions: Mount Jefferson Wilderness, Gorge Trail, Lake Detroit recreation area, Pacific Crest Trail, cross-country skiing

Nearest Airport: Portland, OR

Getting There: Car rental is available at airport. Driving from the airport, take I-5 to Salem, Exit 253; head east toward Detroit on Highway 22; left on Highway 46; at Detroit, 10 miles, just past Cleator Bend Campground, turn right; over the next few miles the road will split three times, stay left at every fork to spa's entrance. (2 hours)

Annapurna Inn and Retreat Center

538 Adams Street
Port Townsend, WA 98368
800/868-ANNA (868-2662) or 360/385-2909
Email: annapurna@Olympus.net
Website: annapurnaretreat.com

The Sanskrit name *Annapurna* refers to the goddess of fertility and nutritional healing. What better way to describe this warm and relaxed retreat in one of the Northwest's most picturesque harbor towns? An organic garden filled with plums, echinacea, yarrow, strawberries, and more surrounds the inn, while a cottage in back houses a luxurious tiled steam bath and wood sauna. A sign at the front door tells guests which of the six rooms—each named for their individual character—will be theirs.

After checking in, guests are invited to take a steam bath and sauna. Eucalyptus oil in the bath clears congestion while the steam relaxes, physically preparing guests for the three-day retreat. In the morning, guests find breakfast plates filled, literally, with the fruit of owner Robin Sharan's labor. Along with live organic gourmet cuisine comes reflexology, therapeutic massage, nature walks, educational videos, and yoga classes. Combine this with in-room whirlpool baths, and you get a small piece of heaven. Other healing modalities available include detoxification/gall bladder cleansing, wheat grass therapy, hands-on healing techniques by a Master Intuitive Healer, and various bodywork sessions.

The Annapurna Inn provides an example of sustainable living that is in tune with the earth and uses only inert or environmentally friendly cleaning products, full-spectrum lighting, filtered shower heads, and live organic gourmet cuisine with filtered water for all food and beverages. Accommodations at the inn are available on an overnight basis in addition to the retreat package. It is best to leave Seattle with a few hours of sunlight left for the two-hour trip in order to witness the drama of the Olympic Peninsula's mountainous ridge and to see the densely forested pine groves and pastoral meadows along the way.

Accommodations: Six rooms, three with private baths and three with semiprivate baths

Rates: $108–128 (private bath); $80–95 (semiprivate bath). All rates include spa facilities and breakfast. Three-day retreat, $252–552, includes one-hour reflexology, two yoga classes, 90-minute massage, two nights' stay, and two breakfasts.

Credit Cards: MC, V

Meals: Daily organic vegan breakfast. Other meals—vegan and live-food style—are served on request ($15–30 per meal).

Services: Reflexology, therapeutic massage, craniosacral therapy, yoga classes, and seminars on nutrition and reflexology

Facilities: Conferencing for groups up to 18, sauna and steam bath; garden

Disability Access: Full access is available.

Special Notes: Smoking is not allowed.

Nearby Attractions: Hiking through scenic Northwest terrain, kayaking in Puget Sound, whale watching

Nearest Airport: Seattle

Getting There: Airport transportation is provided by Pennco Transport, 360/583-3736. Driving from Seattle, take the Seattle Bainbridge Ferry to Bainbridge Island. Once on the island, follow signs to Hood Canal Bridge; cross bridge and continue straight; right to Port Townsend and onto Water Street into the old part of town; left on Monroe, 2 blocks up; left on Clay, 2 blocks up; spa entrance is at the corner of Clay and Adams on left. (2 hours)

Harmony Hill Retreat Center

7362 East SR 106
Union, WA 98592-9781
360/898-2363; fax: 360/898-2364
Email: hh@hctc.com
Website: www.harmonyhill.org

The Harmony Hill Retreat Center is located on scenic Hood Canal in Western Washington. Situated on 12 acres, the retreat site offers magnificent views of the Olympic Mountains, lush gardens, beach access, scenic walking paths, and comfortable facilities. Guests are always welcome to walk the three permanent labyrinths, two outdoor and one indoor. Harmony Hill's mission is to inspire and facilitate physical, emotional, and spiritual health in people seeking well-being. They offer three-day Labyrinth Retreats, three-day Renewal Retreats for Health Care Professionals, and five-day Transformative Retreats for those Living with Cancer and their Caregivers, as well as provide private group and individual retreat facilities. The program is designed to support both those dealing with cancer and their companions, in finding emotional, spiritual and physical healing.

The Harmony Hill Cancer Retreat serves as a supportive adjunct to medical treatment. This retreat includes a daily support group led by professional co-leaders, during which participants have an opportunity to explore the issues, questions, concerns, and feelings raised by the experience of cancer. The daily schedule also includes gentle movement, such as yoga or qi gong, deep relaxation, guided imagery, self-exploration with art and sandtray, and evening programs on complementary care. Participants are deeply nurtured by an experienced and caring staff, provided with delicious healthy food, offered an optional massage, and buoyed by the shared support of others dealing with cancer.

Accommodations: Up to 10 may be accommodated in the main house; a cottage sleeps up to six. Single and double occupancy rooms are available. A 30-foot diameter yurt serves 35 day guests.

Rates: Vary for different programs. Harmony Hill relies on donations for about half of its revenue. Financial contributions beyond the cost of actual programs and services are eligible for a tax deduction.

Credit Cards: MC, V

Meal Plans: Three home-cooked vegetarian meals, plus snacks and beverages, are offered each day. Meals are often prepared with produce fresh from the organic gardens.

Services: Massage, yoga, qi gong

Recreational Activities: Hiking

Facilities: The main house (historic lodge), a cottage, a library, three gardens, a greenhouse, a 30-foot-diameter yurt, three labyrinths, and walking trails

Disability Access: The main house is wheelchair accessible.

Special Notes: Smoking is not allowed in any of the buildings. Harmony Hill, a non-profit Wellness Center, depends upon both individual donations and community grants to reach out to those deeply affected by cancer. Contributions and volunteer work is welcomed.

Nearby Attractions: Olympic Mountains and Wilderness, Olympic National Forest, Victoria's Restaurant

Neareast Airports: Bremerton and Seattle, WA

Getting There: Car rental is available at airports. Driving from Seattle and all points along I-5, drive toward Tacoma. Exit at SR toward Bremerton; follow SR 16 past Port Orchard exits; continue until your see "Bremerton National Airport" signs; right on SR16 toward Twanch State Park; continue approximately 13 miles; spa entrance is 5 miles past Twanch State Park. (2 hours)

Southwest

Canyon Ranch Health Resort

8600 East Rockcliff Road
Tucson, AZ 85750
800/742-9000 or 520/749-9000; fax 520/749-7753
Website: www.canyonranch.com

Cacti, mesquite, acacia, and palo verde trees make up the desert landscape surrounding the 70 acres of Canyon Ranch. Built around a spacious hacienda in the foothills of the Santa Catalina Mountains, this renowned health spa was voted the world's best by readers of *Condeé Nast Traveler* magazine. The staff, which outnumbers guests three to one, consists of physicians, psychologists, registered dietitians, exercise physiologists, and certified health educators and bodyworkers.

Since its founding in 1979, Canyon Ranch has developed many lifestyle programs emphasizing the relationship between body, mind, and spirit. The one-week Life Enhancement Program, offered year-round, is designed to address health objectives. Elements of the package include nutrition and diet management consultations, behavioral health classes, exercise physiology consultations, and movement therapy. Canyon Ranch also occasionally offers weeklong programs that address specific health issues, such as arthritis, heart disease, asthma, and women's health.

Guests select their own schedule of activities from the wide array of options, including tai chi, yoga, chi kung, meditation and breathing, tennis, basketball, mountain biking, golf, horseback riding, spa treatments, and seven gyms containing ultramodern fitness equipment. Prospective visitors are asked to sign up for activities in advance after making reservations. Evening talks are given by noted psychologists, authors, naturalists, and other specialists.

Accommodations: 180 casitas and suites. Modern Southwestern furnishings and desert colors decorate all rooms. The Life Enhancement Center has special quarters for 25 people. All rooms are air-conditioned.

Rates: Vary according to room, season, and package. Seven-night packages begin at $3,640 per person during the high season for a double-occupancy room, meals, and use of the spa, resort facilities, and some services.

Credit Cards: AE, D, MC, V

Meal Plans: Three healthy gourmet meals plus snacks are served daily. A vegetarian option is available.

Services: More than 40 fitness classes are offered each day, as well as movement therapy, exercise physiology, medical and behavioral health services, consultation on nutrition and diet, holistic health and body composition, biofeedback, 15 types of massage, herbal and aromatherapy wraps, hydromassage, salon services, private sports lessons, and handwriting and tarot card reading.

Recreational Activities: Hiking, swimming, mountain biking, horseback riding, basketball, golf, and tennis

Facilities: A 70-acre desert retreat with adobe-style cottages, a demonstration kitchen, a creative arts center, a health and healing center, and a 62,000-square-foot spa complex, including a lounge, seven gymnasiums, aerobic and strength training rooms, squash and racquetball courts, eight tennis courts, a basketball court, four pools, a yoga/meditation dome, sauna, steam, and inhalation rooms, whirlpools, private sunbathing areas, walking trails, cactus gardens, streams, pools, and fountains. A golf package is available at the Raven, which is an 18-hole golf course located five minutes away.

Disability Access: Yes; all facilities provide access for people with disabilities.

Special Notes: The minimum allowed age of guests is 14. Alcoholic beverages are not permitted in public areas; smoking is not allowed indoors or in public areas. Approximately 800 total staff members are all licensed and certified. The staff-to-guest ratio is 3 to 1.

Nearby Attractions: Santa Catalina Mountains; Arizona-Sonora Desert Museum; Biosphere 2; Nogales, Mexico; jeep rides; Sabino Canyon; Mount Lemmon

Nearest Airport: Tuscon, AZ

Getting There: Spa provides complimentary airport service with 48-hour advance notice. Driving from Tuscon airport, exit to Valencia Road. Turn right on Valencia and continue to Kolb Road; left on Kolb and continue into Tanque Verde; right on Sabino Canyon Road; left at Sabino; go 3 miles to Snyder Road; right on Snyder and continue to Rockcliff and follow signs to spa entrance. (.5 hour). Driving from Phoenix, and all western points; take I-10 East to Tucson. Exit at Ina Road East; continue along Ina Road as it becomes Skyline Drive then Sunrise Drive; right on Sabino Canyon Road; left on Snyder Road; right on Rockcliff and follow signs to spa entrance. (2 hours)

Centre for Well-Being at the Phoenician

6000 East Camelback Road
Scottsdale, AZ 85251
800/888-8234 or 480/423-2405; fax: 480/947-4311
Website: www.thephoenician.com

Make no mistake, this Mobil Five-Star resort is a luxury destination. Yet *Town and Country*—just one of many magazines to comment on the Centre for Well-Being at the Phoenician—called it "one of the most healing and nurturing spots on the planet." How does a member of the prestigious Starwood Luxury Collection manage to offer healing modalities? This facility accomplishes its goals through detoxification and Ayurvedic rituals, through the use of herbs and mud long prized by Native Americans in the Southwest for their therapeutic properties, through classes in herbology and nutrition, and through a lifestyle consultation that focuses on mind-body connections. Specialized one-, four-, and eight-day programs focus on the principles of well-being and creating balance in everyday life.

The center is located on 250 acres of pools, fountains, and lawn and a two-acre cactus garden containing 350 varieties of cactus and succulents. Although this world-class resort would never describe itself as a healing center alone, many profoundly therapeutic treatments are available on the spa menu, for example, neuromuscular therapy, lymphatic massage, and the centuries-old practices of jin shin jyutsu, reflexology, and shiatsu. Neuromuscular therapy is recommended for those who have chronic pain, headaches, or injuries such as whiplash and tennis elbow; lymphatic massage helps remove toxins and activates the body's natural immune system. Jin shin jyutsu, reflexology, and shiatsu all reportedly reduce fatigue, release muscular aches, and restore well-being.

Accommodations: 581 guest rooms, 62 suites, four presidential suites, and seven villas. Rooms include Berber carpeting and authentic McGuire furniture with Philippine leather strapping. Every piece of art and décor is hand-selected.

Rates: Vary according to lodging, program, and season. A standard single guest room is $195 in summer, $435 in fall, and $525 in winter.

Credit Cards: AE, D, MC, V

Meal Plans: The "Choices" cuisine breakfast is included in some programs.

Services: Massage and body therapies from various traditions, health consultations, neuromuscular therapy, craniosacral therapy, jin shin jyutsu, reflexology, reiki, body wraps, body scrubs, facials, tai chi, salon services, personal training, astrology, tarot card readings, meditation

Recreational Activities: Hiking and biking

Facilities: A 250-acre resort with museum-quality fine art and antiques, a business center, a ballroom, a multimedia theater, three boardrooms, 23 breakout rooms, nine dining facilities, a fitness room, a Swiss shower, whirlpools, a sauna, a steam room, 24 treatment rooms, a meditation atrium, a golf course, a croquet lawn, an oversize chess board, a basketball half-court, lawn bowling, billiards, nine swimming pools, a tennis garden, a water slide, a necklace lake, lagoons, waterfalls, and a cactus garden

Disability Access: Yes; wheelchair accessible

Special Notes: Nonsmoking rooms are available upon request.

Nearby Attractions: Camelback Mountain, Desert Botanical Garden, Phoenix Zoo, Frank Lloyd Wright's Taliesin West, Heard Museum, Phoenix Art Museum, Sedona arts and spiritual community

Nearest Airport: Phoenix, AZ

Getting There: Airport service is available through the spa's Guest Services department, ext. 3666; $25 each way. Driving from the airport and downtown Phoenix area, take 44th Street north to Camelback Road. Right on Camelback Road (East); left onto Phoencian Boulevard and spa entrance. (20 minutes)

The Merritt Center

Merritt Lodge of Payson
P.O. Box 2087
Payson, AZ 85547-2087
800/414-9880 or 520/474-4268; fax: 520/474-8588
Email: betty@merritt-az-retreat.org
Website: www.merritt-az-retreat.org

With her radiant smile and long silver braid running down her back, Betty Merritt looks like everyone's dream grandmother. Merritt is a bodywork therapist and self-renewal consultant who founded the Merritt Center and Lodge with her husband, Al, 10 years ago to provide a secluded, natural setting for people to find rejuvenation and self-empowerment. The center, located 90 miles north of Phoenix within the Tonto National Forest, hosts year-round classes, workshops, and experiential programs for groups and individuals seeking personal growth. The programs also provide free time for lolling in a hammock under the shade of black walnut trees, taking a guided hike through ponderosa pines, or relaxing in a whirlpool under the stars.

The Heart Renewal Program is one of the dozen programs focused on wellness and is beneficial for people who want to evaluate their lifestyles and learn methods and strategies for improving health. Because it encourages changing long-lived and sometimes detrimental habits, the program asks guests to bring a spouse or close friend to support the process. Program facilitators include a board-certified cardiologist, a registered dietitian, a nurse, and Betty Merritt.

Over the course of a weekend, guests learn how the heart and related systems work together, as well as lifesaving tips on how to handle an emergency situation. Other topics include how to cope with stress, the benefit of alternative therapies in healing, how exercise can strengthen the heart, how emotions and beliefs affect health, and how to create a support system of family and friends. Guests also take home a plan to help them continue implementing positive lifestyle changes. The program is designed to complement an existing health routine and is not meant to be a substitute for medical treatment.

The center's other programs offering a holistic approach to living include Women's Journey, Relationship Enrichment for Couples, Empowerment Coaching, Creating your Purpose, Take Charge of your Life, Spiritual Fasting, and Wisdom Questioning.

Accommodations: Lodge with 12 rooms containing twin or king-size beds
Rates: Lodging and meals, single occupancy, $75 per day; double occupancy, $115 per day
Credit Cards: MC, V
Meal Plans: Three buffet-style meals are provided each day. Special diets are accommodated with advance notice.
Services: Personal growth seminars and workshops, Swedish massage, Kiatsu emotional release work, healing touch therapy, tai chi, meditation, drumming, Native American healing ceremonies, and hatha yoga
Recreational Activities: Walking and hiking
Facilities: A large multipurpose meeting room and living room with fireplaces, a library, a veranda, a dining room, a sleeping porch, an outdoor hot tub on the deck,

hammocks, a meditation garden, a sweat lodge, and an exercise room. Walking trails are located nearby.

Disability Access: Access is limited; please call.

Special Notes: Merritt recommends bringing all-terrain shoes, a swimsuit, seasonal layers of clothing, books, tapes, and a cassette player.

Nearby Attractions: Tonto National Forest, Mogollon Rim, Grand Canyon, Sedona Red Rocks

Nearest Airport: Phoenix, AZ

Getting There: Car rental and taxis, to Payson, are available at airport. Driving from Phoenix airport, take Highway 202 to Country Club/Highway 87 turn north (left). Stay on Highway 87 for about 65 miles into Payson. (1 hour). Driving from Payson and points South, along Highway 87, right onto Highway 260; after 3 miles, turn left onto Valley Road; left on Haught Road; spa is third property on the left. (.5 hour)

Miraval, Life in Balance Resort and Spa

5000 East Via Estancia Miraval
Catalina, AZ 85737
800/825-4000 (reservations 800/232-3969) or
520/825-4000; fax: 520/825-5163
Email: miravalaz@aol.com
Website: www.miravalresort.com

Set amid the Santa Catalina Mountains, just 30 miles north of Tucson, lies Miraval, a spa and holistic lifestyle resort. Although traditional and luxurious spa treatments are available, Miraval promotes a philosophy of well-being through harmony among the body, mind, and spirit.

Personal guides assist guests in choosing a program combining stress management, self-discovery, and luxury resort recreational activities that complement one another and promote balanced well-being. Packages include lodging, meals, airport transfer, one personal service or fitness consultation per night, all resort programs and activities, and 24-hour room service. More than 120 activities are offered, ranging from aerobic exercise to Zen meditation. A common theme running throughout virtually all of the curricula is the philosophy of "mindfulness," which can simply be described as paying attention to the moment. An introductory class is offered to lay the foundation for this awareness-promoting principle.

A day at Miraval can begin with a morning meditation timed to greet the rising sun. A buffet breakfast of fresh fruit, juices, cereal, and yogurt might precede a class in Desert Mandala, in which guests learn traditional and contemporary techniques of sand painting. Music and storytelling accompany the process to relay an understanding of how nature reflects the many facets of human experience. A hot-stone massage might follow, using smooth, warm basalt stones. After lunch there is time for chi nei tsang, the Asian abdominal massage. For the ambitious, zero balancing and acupuncture can be squeezed in before dinner. Guests might choose to end the day with a marine hydrotherapy bath and body wrap.

At Miraval, every service and amenity—from early morning hiking in the Santa Catalina Mountains, to hot stone massages, to a quiet breakfast on your private patio—is designed to heighten the senses and to make you more aware of living in the moment.

Accommodations: Single and double occupancy in luxury, casita-style rooms and suites with Southwestern décor. Some suites have whirlpools and fireplaces.

Rates: $300–1,050 per person, per night

Credit Cards: AE, D, DC, MC, V

Meal Plans: Three gourmet spa meals are included each day, including complimentary in-room snacks and beverages. A variety of dietary needs and tastes are accommodated.

Services: Massage, hydrotherapy, body wraps, scalp treatments, facials, manicures, pedicures, and more than 120 activities, including tai chi, yoga, sand painting, and meditation

Recreational Activities: Mountain biking, horseback riding, aerobics, and cooking classes. Golf is just 10–15 minutes away at either Mountain View Golf Club at Saddlebrook or The Golf Club at Vistoso.

Facilities: The 135-acre desert resort offers 106 casita-style suites and rooms, three swimming pools including a tri-level pool with cascading waterfalls, horseback-riding stables, a full-service restaurant, a fully equipped fitness center, two tennis courts, a volleyball court, a croquet lawn, hiking trails, biking paths, and a fully staffed Personal Services Center.

Disability Access: Six rooms are especially designed to accommodate people with disabilities.

Special Notes: The minimum allowed age of spa guests is 17. Tipping is not permitted. Pets are not allowed.

Nearby Attractions: Biosphere 2, Sonoran Desert Museum, Tombstone, Sabino Canyon, Mission San Xavier del Bac

Nearest Airport: Tucson, AZ

Getting There: Spa provides complimentary airport transportation with advance reservations. Driving from Tucson, take I-10 North to Tangerine Road; East on Oracle Road; East on Golder Ranch Road; North on Lago del Oro Parkway; spa entrance is on right. (.5 hour)

The Spa At Camelback Inn, Marriott

5402 East Lincoln Drive
Scottsdale, AZ 85253
800/922-2635 or 408/948-1700; fax: 480/951-8469
Website: www.camelbackinn.com

The Spa at Camelback Inn is set in the foothills of Mummy Mountain and offers spectacular views of Mummy and Camelback Mountains, for which the inn is named. Surrounded by 125 acres of the lush Sonoran desert, the spa provides a soothing Southwest desert landscape. It is not only a bonus for the guests of the hotel but also a healing destination in itself.

The 27,000-square-foot European Health Spa offers the following comprehensive services: 10 types of skincare treatments, such as a rejuvenating Spiralina facial, herbal enzyme deep-cleansing treatment, and a fresh cell anti-aging facial; 10 types of body care treatments, such as a desert honey wrap, aloe vera rehydrating body treatment, and a full body mud mask; eight types of massage therapies, such as maternity massage, shiatsu, and hot stone massage; a full-service salon offering hair, nail, and makeup services; a fitness center with daily exercise classes, such as tai chi, yoga, step, and meditation; and a heated outdoor lap pool, saunas, steam rooms, hot whirlpools, and cold plunges.

The spa's wellness and fitness center offers a comprehensive analysis of your fitness and well-being with a Personalized Aerobic Lifestyle System, designed by Dr. Kenneth H. Cooper, founder of the Institute for Aerobic Research and Cooper Clinic of Dallas, Texas. Also available is the Physicalmind Method Training Session, based on the Pilates method, during which a trained instructor teaches you to regulate and control breathing, correct postural alignment, and strengthen back and abdominal muscles.

Guests at the Camelback Inn stay in 453 Pueblo-style casitas nested between the two landmark mountains. Spa packages include Spa Renewal Week, the Spa Getaway package, the Spa Revitalizer, the Sonoran Retreat, and the Relaxation package. In addition to the spa, the resort has 36 holes of golf, seven restaurants and lounges, three pools, and six tennis courts.

Accommodations: 453 casitas, 27 suites
Rates: Vary with packages; Relaxation package starts from $419 per night (single or double occupancy); Spa Getaway package is $479 per night (single occupancy) or $559 per night (double occupancy); Spa Renewal Week for six nights and seven days is $3,220 per stay (single occupancy) or $4,480 per stay (double occupancy). More package options are offered.
Credit Cards: All major credit cards are accepted.
Meal Plans: Spa packages include some meals. Otherwise, the hotel has seven restaurants on the premises.
Services: Massage, skincare treatments, body care treatments, full-service salon, fitness and wellness evaluation, body composition analysis, yoga, tai chi, and step aerobics
Recreational Activities: Tennis, golf, basketball half-court, shuffleboard, swimming, walks, hiking nearby
Facilities: A 27,000-square-foot European Health Spa, state-of-the-art fitness and exer-

cise facilities, six tennis courts, an 18-hole golf course, three swimming pools, and a children's playground

Disability Access: Yes

Special Notes: Free parking is available for hotel guests; seasonal children's programs and childcare referrals are offered.

Nearby Attractions: Shopping in Old Town Scottsdale, horseback riding, Jeep tours, hot air ballooning, Heard museum, Scottsdale Center for the Arts, hiking

Nearest Airport: Phoenix, AZ

Getting There: Airport service is provided by Transtyle Taxi, 800/410-5479, $25 each way. Located 10 miles northeast of Phoenix Sky Harbor Airport in Paradise Valley. Driving from Phoenix airport, take Highway 153 North; highway becomes N. 44th Street; left on Tatum Boulevard; right on Lincoln Drive; spa entrance on left. (.5 hour)

Tree of Life Rejuvenation Center

P.O. Box 1080
Patagonia, AZ 85624
520/394-2520; fax: 520/394-2099
Email: healing@treeoflife.nu
Website: www.treeoflife.nu

The Tree of Life Rejuvenation Center is an innovative rejuvenation, spiritual, and educational eco-retreat center whose staff is committed to the integration of all healing life forces for complete body, mind, spirit, and planetary renewal. The metaphor of the "Tree of Life" is one of working with all the forces in our lives, such as air, earth, sun, water, love, wisdom, joy, peace, right livelihood, and the Divine Presence. Gabrial Counsens, MD, founder and director of the center, has practiced holistic medicine and psychiatry for 30 years. He is the author of several books, including *Spiritual Nutrition and the Rainbow Diet, Sevenfold Peace, Conscious Eating,* and *Depression-Free for Life.* His disciplines of study and practice include nutrition, naturopathy, homeopathy, acupuncture, Ayurveda, and individual, couples, and family therapy.

The Tree of Life occupies 166 acres on a beautiful mesa in the Patagonia mountains, 60 miles south of Tucson, Arizona. The center's innovative chefs use the bountiful effective microorganisms (EM)–based organic gardens to prepare live-food, kosher, gourmet, vegetarian cuisine. The setting supports inner discovery as one partakes of the Menu of Awakened Living: live-food preparation classes, an organic gardening appreciation experience, yoga, meditation, breathing exercises, hiking, sunset meditations, a new moon sweat lodge, chanting and celebrations, or just taking time to be. Guests may also choose to incorporate juice fasting, panchakarma Ayurvedic treatments, and various techniques of bodywork into their "Tree of Life Experience." Several self-healing courses and retreats are offered that empower participants with the tools and awareness to take responsibility for their healing and conscious living.

Accommodations: Simple, regionally inspired, environmentally friendly, private rooms with shared bath are offered in the casita guest house.

Rates: $139 per day includes lodging, cuisine, and daily programs. Special rates are offered.

Credit Cards: AE, M, V

Meal Plans: Three vegetarian, live-food meals, which are designed to optimize rejuvenation, are offered each day.

Services: Individualized, holistic health consultations, fasting, yoga, panchakarma, massage, detoxification programs, nutritional counseling, zero-point process psychospiritual counseling, meditation instruction, live-food preparation instruction, and organic gardening appreciation classes

Recreational Activities: Hiking and gardening

Facilities: A simple, scenic high desert center with a holistic health clinic, a live-food café, a meditation temple, a yoga facility, rejuvenation treatment facilities, hot tubs, a sweat lodge, outdoor meditation and ceremonial areas.

Disability Access: Access is limited; please call in advance.

Special Notes: Smoking is not allowed.

Nearby Attractions: Saguaro National Park, Tombstone, Colossal Cave, and a Nature Conservancy Preserve that is world famous for birding

Nearest Airport: Tucson, AZ

Getting There: Airport service is available through Larry's Airline Taxi, 520/977-7999. Driving from Tucson, take I-10 East to Highway 83 South, to town of Sonoita; right on Highway 82, to Patagonia; left on 3rd Avenue; left on McKeown which becomes Harshaw Road; spa is on right. (1 hour)

Ann Wigmore Foundation

P.O. Box 399
San Fidel, NM 87049
505/552-0595; fax: 505/552-0596
Email: livingfoods@wigmore.org
Website: www.wigmore.org

Dr. Ann Wigmore was the founding mother of the Living Foods Lifestyle. After 35 years of research, Wigmore drew a correlation between disease and the toxicity and nutritional deficiencies resulting from cooked and processed foods, drugs, and a negative mental attitude. Her theories proved successful, as evidenced by testimonials from people suffering from various chronic and degenerative diseases, such as arthritis, hypoglycemia, chronic fatigue, and cancerous tumors.

The lifestyle consists of a live-food organic diet that includes the famous Energy Soup, made with sprouts, buckwheat greens, apples, avocado, and more. Wheat grass is an essential element of the living-foods program, which is believed to have profound detoxifying effects. The diet also excludes all breads, meats, dairy products, and cooked or processed foods. The diet does include dehydrated crackers and cookies, which provide texture in the diet, along with the salads.

In addition to the diet, students go through an internal cleansing process while taking classes in growing greens and wheat grass, composting and soil management, indoor gardening, sprouting, food combining, self-improvement, positive thinking, breathing, stress reduction, colon care and enemas, detoxification, foot massage, and more. The environment is supportive and family-like, with all staff members having gone through the program themselves. The standard program is 11 days, commencing every other Monday and culminating with a "chanpagne" feast for graduation. The center is adjacent to two indigenous tribes, where guests often visit Sky City on the weekends, while on a watermelon fast.

Dr. Wigmore was director of the Ann Wigmore Foundation in Boston for more than 30 years. In 1994, she died from smoke inhalation when the foundation caught fire. At that time, the Boston school closed, and the property was sold to acquire the new site in New Mexico. The Ann Wigmore Foundation has been in operation at San Fidel since May 1999.

Accommodations: 15 rooms, single and double, with private and shared baths in a simple two-story dormitory-style building
Rates: The two-week program is $800–1,500.
Credit Cards: MC, V
Meal Plans: Three live, organic, vegan meals are included per day.
Services: Living-foods program, colonics, yoga, self-sufficiency skills, relaxation, and transformational and cultural activities
Recreational Activities: Hiking
Facilities: A two-story lodge with classrooms, a kitchen, a dining room and community space, a hot tub, a sauna, an outdoor organic garden, and an indoor greenhouse
Disability Access: Access is limited; please call in advance.
Special Notes: Smoking and alcohol are not allowed.
Nearby Attractions: Sky City; University of New Mexico's observation towers; dining, galleries, museums, and shopping in Santa Fe

Nearest Airport: Albuquerque, NM

Getting There: Spa will provide airport transportation with advance notice and additional fee. Driving from Albuquerque, take I-40 West to Exit 100; left toward San Fidel; follow road to Route 66/Highway 124; continue through stop sign and follow 2.5 miles (San Jose loop); follow signs to entrance. (1 hour)

Ayurvedic Institute

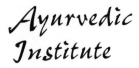

P.O. Box 23445, 11311 Menaul Blvd. NE
Albuquerque, NM 87112-1445
505/291-9698; fax 505/294-7572
Email: info@ayurveda.com
Website: www.ayurveda.com

The snow-covered Sandia Mountains rise to the east of the Ayurvedic Institute. Founded in 1984 as an educational nonprofit corporation, the institute has expanded each year, adding new courses, treatments, and facilities. A two-year course in Ayurveda is offered, as is a rejuvenating panchakarma cleansing program at the institute's healing center. Dr. Vasant Lad, an Ayurvedic physician, teaches many courses at the institute, and panchakarma clients are welcome to attend his evening health lectures while they participate in the program.

The healing center at the institute offers five-day panchakarma programs, which are designed to bring the body, mind, and spirit back into balance. The program begins with an orientation, consultation, and pulse diagnosis with Dr. Lad or his assistant, after which an individualized series of treatments is recommended, as is a special diet, herbal teas, yoga, and health classes. Panchakarma therapies include an oil massage performed by two therapists in synchrony, herbal steam baths, herbal skincare, and a treatment that involves pouring warm oil onto the forehead. Oils and specific services are chosen according to the individual's unique constitution. Although extremely relaxing, the treatments act as vehicles to more or less force toxins to travel out of the tissues and into the gastrointestinal tract, where they can be eliminated. Guests also meet with department staff throughout the week to discuss the Ayurvedic diet and lifestyle and monitor progress. Because of the program's immense popularity, scheduling for panchakarma is normally made 1–3 months in advance, although a waiting list is available for cancellations.

Accommodations: A nearby house accommodates 3–4 panchakarma clients. Because the house is booked well in advance, a list of motels and bed-and-breakfasts is available. Some bed-and-breakfasts will arrange to drive you back and forth to the institute for an additional fee.

Rates: Daily panchakarma services, without lodging, are $240 per day, $1,200 per week. Lodging rates vary; inquire for details.

Credit Cards: MC, V

Meal Plans: All meals are included with panchakarma treatment; diet is designed to support the prescribed regimen of therapy.

Services: Orientation, consultation, and pulse diagnosis with an Ayurvedic specialist; herbal steam treatments; herbal skin treatments; Ayurvedic treatments, such as abhyanga, netra basti, shirodhara, and nasya; color therapy; marma point therapy; therapeutic and Ayurvedic massage; private yoga lessons; and evening health lectures

Facilities: The institute consists of a large single structure divided into classrooms, offices, a store, a health center, a meditation room, and a panchakarma department; hiking trails are also available.

Disability Access: Yes

Special Notes: Smoking is not allowed.

Nearby Attractions: Restaurants and sightseeing in Albuquerque, Santa Fe, and Taos; downhill skiing; hiking; boating

Nearest Airport: Albuquerque, NM

Getting There: Airport transportation is available through Airport Express, ticket counter is located on the lower level of the airport across from the Southwest baggage claim carousel; $15 each way. Taxi service, $25, and car rental is also available at airport. Driving from the airport, take Sunport Loop SE out of the airport, slight right onto Sunport Boulevard SE; stay straight onto Girard Boulevard SE; right on Gibson Boulevard SE; left on San Mateo Boulevard SE; right on Mehaul Boulevard NE, continue to entrance. (25 minutes)

Riverdancer Inn

16445 Scenic Highway 4
Jemez Springs, NM 87025
800/809-3262 or 505/829-3262
E-mail: reservations@riverdancer.com
Website: www.riverdancer.com

The Riverdancer Inn is a small adobe-style inn located on five acres at the base of the Virgin Mesa, which rises 2,000 feet to the ancient pueblo sites at the top. A natural landscape, wildflowers, and a stream meander from the front of the property to the Jemez River behind the Riverdancer. From the inn property you hear the rustle of dancing leaves, birds singing, and the gentle splashing of water over rocks and boulders in the river.

The atmosphere at Riverdancer is casual, friendly, and energetic; clothing is loose, layered, and comfortable. One can visit Riverdancer as a bed-and-breakfast or create a personal healing retreat with the guidance of owner Lindsay Locke and her staff. As a therapist and healer, Lindsay helps you design your creative retreat offering art therapy, meditative nature walks, rituals, yoga, and tai chi, along with massage, a variety of energy techniques, and seaweed wraps. Breakfast and dinner are included for personal retreat packages. Customized programs are also available for those who want to detoxify with juices and herbs. In keeping with the interrelatedness of body-mind-spirit, Riverdancer offers expressive means to clarify goals or to clear negative and/or limiting patterns; participate in guided visualization or meditations; connect with spirituality in nature; reconnect with your creativity; and rejuvenate your body with therapeutic treatments, movement, and vegetarian whole foods.

Accommodations: Six guest rooms, all of which open onto a garden courtyard with a flowing fountain, birds, fruit trees, and seasonal flowers. Each room is comfortably furnished and has its own private bathroom with amenites such as hair dryer and toiletries, TV, telephone, air-conditioning, and ceiling fan. The floors are radiantly heated in the winter. The Zia suite (sleeps four) with a hot tub in the private bath is also available.

Rates: Rooms start at $109 per night. The basic retreat package (includes queen or twin room accommodations, two meals per day, a one-hour massage/energy treatment, and a one-hour personal creative session) is $275–296.97 (single) and $455–488.61 (double). Rates are lower during the off-season from November 1 through March 15.

Credit Cards: D, MC, V

Meal Plans: Vegetarian whole foods are served. Breakfast is offered daily, and dinner is included for retreat packages. Restaurants are nearby for other meals.

Services: Massage, reiki, craniosacral work, and seaweed wraps

Recreational Activities: Trout fishing, hiking, skiing

Facilities: A great room with a kiva fireplace, six guest rooms surrounding a courtyard, a Zia suite, and a restored barn/art studio

Disability Access: Yes

Special Notes: No smoking or pets are allowed on the property.

Nearby Attractions: Riverdancer is near the quaint, centuries-old village of Jemez Springs, situated in a quiet valley that was created by ancient volcanoes and carved by the elements. The area's hot mineral waters are located one mile away at the Bodhi Mandala Zen Center, with four serene pools, and at the 130-year-old Jemez Springs Bath House, offering private tubs.

Nearest Airport: Albuquerque, NM

Getting There: Call spa for details on airport transportation. Driving from Albuquerque, take I-25 North to Highway 44 at Bernalillo (Exit 242); keep left at exit ramp split; left onto Highway 44; right at Highway 4; continue along Jemez River and into Jemez Springs village; spa entrance is 1 mile south of village. (1.5 hours)

Ten Thousand Waves

P.O. Box 10200, 3451 Hyde Park Road
Santa Fe, NM 87504
505/982-9304; fax: 505/989-5077
Email: info@tenthousandwaves.com
Website: www.tenthousandwaves.com

For centuries the Japanese have known about the health benefits of "taking the waters," and at Ten Thousand Waves in Santa Fe, this ancient tradition of healing and relaxation takes place against a backdrop of New Mexico's serene and beautiful Sangre de Cristo Mountains. Voted as one of the 10 Best Spas in the United States in a *Travel & Leisure* magazine readers' poll, this Japanese health spa features mainly relaxation and enjoyment. The hot tubs at Ten Thousand Waves are kept sparkling clean by the state-of-the-art purification system utilizing ultraviolet light, hydrogen peroxide, ozone, and copper/silver ions. The water is clear enough to read the face of a quarter on the bottom of the tub. Chlorine is not used in any tub or cold plunge.

Therapeutic massage is also provided, offering relief from physical pain, stress reduction, and deep relaxation. As for healing modalities, Ten Thousand Waves also offers watsu, the in-water form of massage. The treatment involves cradling, pulling, and stretching and applying pressure to "energy centers," described in the Taoist creation myth. Watsu has proved to be a valuable treatment in aquatic rehabilitation, especially for cerebral palsy and sleep disorders and for people recovering from stroke, injury, or emotional disabilities.

Spa treatments are also available. The 5,000-year-old Ayurvedic tradition is drawn on with the East Indian cleansing treatment. First, hot oil scented with sandalwood, orange, and lavender is massaged into the skin. Then, calamus root powder is massaged in as a stimulant, mild exfoliant, and rejuvenator. Afterward, guests are wrapped in hot linens soaked in herbs, allowing the calamus and essential oils to penetrate the skin and pull the toxins out.

Accommodations: Eight lodging suites, each housing 1–5 people. All rooms include a phone, mini-refrigerator, coffeemaker supplied with gourmet coffee and tea, real wood-burning fireplaces, and access to laundry facilities.

Rates: Vary according to services. Lodging is $155–205 per night.

Credit Cards: D, MC, V

Meal Plans: No meals are provided, although a healthful snack bar is available on the premises. Santa Fe has a variety of excellent restaurants to choose from nearby.

Services: Private and communal hot tubs, massage, watsu, facials, herbal wrap, salt-glow scrub, East Indian cleansing, and Japanese Hot Stone Massage

Recreational Activities: Hiking, skiing

Facilities: A seven-acre spa with Japanese- and Southwest-style treatment rooms and a lodge; outdoor hot tubs spaced all over the mountain, including Japanese-style wood tubs

Disability Access: Yes. Several of the massage rooms, tubs and houses are equipped to accommodate individuals with disabilities. Please mention any special needs when making your reservations.

Special Notes: Ten Thousand Waves is the closest luxury accommodations to the Santa Fe ski area. Discounts are available for New Mexico residents.

Nearby Attractions: Bandelier National Monument; Abiquiu; Taos; Santa Fe museums, galleries, restaurants, and other attractions

Nearest Airport: Santa Fe and Albuquerque, NM

Getting There: Taxi service and car rental is available at airports. Driving from Santa Fe airport, take I-25 North to Exit 282 and onto South St. Francis Drive. Turn right onto Paseo de Peralta; left on Washington Avenue; right on Artist Road (becomes Hyde Park Road); spa entrance 3 miles on left. (.5 hour) Driving from Albuquerque, take I-25 North to Old Pecos Trail exit, follow Old Pecos Trail to third light stay right; road becomes Old Santa Fe Trail; right onto Paseo de Peralta, follow above directions to spa. (2 hours)

Vista Clara Ranch Resort and Spa

HC 75, Box 111
Galisteo, NM 87540
505/466-4772; fax: 505/466-1942
Email: vclara@newmexico.com
Website: www.vistaclara.com

Vista Clara Ranch is named appropriately. The ranch affords 80-mile views across the Dali-esque New Mexico landscape. The site of the ranch itself is considered sacred by the Tewa Indians. Closed as the ultra-chic spa that drew an elite celebrity clientele in 1990, the ranch reopened in 1993 as a fully self-sustained nonprofit wellness center and spa. All profits benefit the Juvenile Diabetes Foundation. Expansion plans include programs in nutritional education, an organic greenhouse, an observatory for guests to learn about astronomy, a multitude of conservation equipment, and more.

The ranch aims to nurture the growth of wellness in mind, body, and spirit. Designed primarily for baby-boomers, programs focus on maintaining good health and anti-aging therapies. The diverse spa menu reflects the belief that each guest needs to learn about and experiment with health treatments to discover what works best for him or her in achieving optimal wellness. This approach includes all facets of living, including a nutritious diet, proper exercise, body therapies, spiritual discovery, and the development of the mind. Through these facets, it is hoped that guests gain an understanding of how mind, body, and spirit are connected in a holistic sense and how personal wellness is connected with the wellness of the Earth. Native American spiritual ceremonies are recent additions to the programs, including a traditional sweat. Native American facilitators conduct the ceremonies, following traditions handed down over many generations.

The eight-day package includes accommodations; three gourmet spa meals plus two snacks per day; six massage therapies; three body therapies; two beauty treatments; fitness classes and nature hikes; use of all facilities, including steam, sauna, and Swiss shower; astrological chart and reading; and round-trip transportation from Santa Fe.

Accommodations: View rooms with balconies, hardwood floors, two double beds, and a full bath; lower-level with king and double rooms with hardwood floors, a full bath, and a private garden

Rates: The four-day package is $700–950; the eight-day package is $1,750–2,300.

Credit Cards: MC, V

Meal Plans: All meals are included with the package. The on-premise restaurant serves Southwestern cuisine.

Services: Therapeutic bodywork, shiatsu and Swedish massage, salt scrubs and herbal wraps, craniosacral therapy, personal trainers, Native American ceremonies, astrology, salon services, yoga, tai chi, and activity and fitness classes

Recreational Activities: Horseback riding, nature and petroglyph hikes

Facilities: 80 acres with a pueblo-style adobe main lodge, dining rooms, an ozonated pool, a glass-enclosed outdoor hot tub, a fully equipped gym, a kiva room, a sweat lodge, an orchard, a pond, and an organic vegetable and herb garden

Disability Access: Yes

Special Notes: Smoking is allowed only in designated outdoor areas.

Nearby Attractions: Santa Fe shopping, dining, and museums; downhill skiing; historic Indian ruins; petroglyphs

Nearest Airport: Santa Fe, NM

Getting There: Complimentary airport service is provided. Car rental and taxi service is also available at airport. Driving from Santa Fe, take I-25 North to El Dorado Exit/U.S. 285. Continue on U.S. 285 South; right on Highway 41 for 4 miles to spa entrance on left. (25 minutes) Driving from Albuquerque, take I-25 North and exit at I-40 East. Continue on I-40 for 35 miles and exit at Highway 41 North; continue for 30 miles and through the town of Galisteo; spa entrance is one mile out of Galisteo on right. (1 hour)

Alamo Plaza Spa at the Menger Hotel

204 Alamo Plaza
San Antonio, TX 78205
210/223-5772; fax: 210/228-0022
Email: alamospa@swbell.net
Website: www.alamoplazaspa.com

One cannot visit the Alamo Plaza Spa without experiencing a classical kur treatment—a program encompassing relaxing spa treatments and a series of rejuvenating all-natural body therapies. Kneipp herbal baths and wraps, an essential element of the kur treatment, were developed by Bavarian priest Father Sebastian Kneipp more than a century ago. Kneipp combined his knowledge of herbs and water therapy to develop the practice of warm bathing and wraps with aromatic natural herbs. Kneipp believed that the effects of a detrimental lifestyle could be reversed through a combination of healthy eating, exercise, sunlight, and adequate rest.

Dr. Jonathan Paul de Vierville, director of the Alamo Plaza Spa, studied and trained at the Kneipp School in Bad Worishofen as well as in Karlsbad (The King of Spas), Czech Republic, and consequently adapted popular European traditions for this hotel amenity and day spa. De Vierville, author of *American Healing Waters,* believes that spas should serve the whole person. "Traditional and classic spa treatments in places like Bath, Karlsbad, Baden-Baden, and Vichy are profoundly relaxing while regenerating and enriching one's physical, mental, emotional, spiritual and social energies," he says. "I see the programs at Alamo Plaza Spa as a significant resource for anyone desiring time and space for rest, relaxation, renewal, restoration, and total regeneration."

The San Antonio Kur Spa Program is the ideal way to experience de Vierville's spa philosophy. It combines spa services with healthful treatments and cultural activities. Guests also have access to a heated outdoor pool, a tropical shaded patio, a solarium, a heated whirlpool, and exercise and fitness rooms. The full day and evening can include a visit to San Antonio's historical sites, art museums, cultural activities, and seasonal festivals.

Accommodations: Standard and deluxe rooms with twin or king-size beds in the 320-room Menger Hotel, including the historic 19th-century wing

Rates: Vary according to program. Call spa for rates.

Credit Cards: AE, D, MC, V

Meals: Breakfast and lunch are included in the spa program. Meals are a combination of vegetables, fresh fruit, and high-protein and whole-grain foods.

Services: Massage, kur spa program using Kneipp herbal essences, body scrubs, herbal wraps with Egyptian linens, hand and foot reflexology treatments, facials, stress reduction treatments, movement therapy, lifestyle and nutritional counseling, mind-body programs, and dream and journal-writing workshops

Recreational Activities: Golf, self-guided walking and jogging

Facilities: A Finnish sauna, a steam room, an aquifer-filled swimming pool, a heated whirlpool, a tropical palm-shaded patio and solarium, an exercise and fitness room, a ballroom and conference facilities, and gardens

Disability Access: Yes; spa and hotel facilities are accessible.

Special Notes: Smoking is not allowed in the spa.

Nearby Attractions: San Antonio's Riverwalk, Institute of Texan Cultures, HemisFair Water Park, Tower of the Americas, Alamodome, Mexican Cultural Institute, Guadalupe Cultural Arts Center, river barge cruises,performing arts centers, museums, and galleries

Nearest Airport: San Antonio, TX

Getting There: Airport Service provided by SA Trans, 210/181-9900, $8 each way. Taxi service and car rental is available at airport. Driving from San Antonio airport, take I-37 South. Exit at Houston Street; right on Houston Street; left on Bonham; spa is located on the grounds of The Menger Hotel. (20 minutes)

Cooper Wellness Program

Cooper Aerobics Center
12230 Preston Road
Dallas, TX 75230
800/444-5192 or 972/386-4777; fax: 972/386-0039
Website: www.cooperaerobics.com

Dr. Kenneth Cooper, whose 18 books have sold more than 30 million copies in 41 languages, is founder and director of the Cooper Aerobics Center. A 63-room Colonial-style hotel houses guests at this 30-acre health retreat in Dallas, Texas. Programs are tailored to the unique needs and goals of each guest. The Cooper Wellness Program was developed for anyone committed to rejuvenation, fitness, and good health. The program specializes in stress management, nutrition, preventive medicine, and overall well-being. Each day, guests learn strategies intended to guide them toward lasting good health, based on Dr. Cooper's philosophy that: "It is easier to maintain good health through proper exercise, diet, and emotional balance than it is to regain it once it is lost." Options include the four-day Wellness Retreat or 1–2 weeks of the Wellness Program.

The weeklong program starts with a physical fitness assessment or a comprehensive preventive medicine physical, followed by a workshop. Workshop topics vary daily and range from successful lifestyle changes to maximizing natural immunity. Two personal fitness training sessions are included in the program, as are presentations by Dr. Cooper or Dr. Tedd Mitchell, the center's medical director. Also included are three nutritious gourmet meals, plus snacks and dining opportunities at nearby heart-healthy restaurants. Guests attend lectures in goal setting and motivation, take cooking classes, learn relaxation techniques, and receive a wellness workbook and a Cooper T-shirt. Special one-day-only programs are offered with short courses on specific health behaviors that provide an encapsulated version of the longer wellness weeks.

Accommodations: Standard single and double rooms with king-size beds in a full-service guest lodge; one- and two-bedroom suites have private baths and king-size beds.

Rates: Vary according to room and program. The four-day program is $2,095; the two-week program is $3,595. Lodging is not included in the package price. Rooms range from $110–260.

Credit Cards: AE, D, MC, V

Meal Plans: Three calorie-controlled gourmet meals, plus snacks, are served per day.

Services: Wellness workshops and health lectures on subjects such as health, wellness, and total well-being; relaxation and stress-management techniques; massage; motivation and goal setting; healthy dining and cooking classes; nutrition assessment; comprehensive medical examinations; hearing and vision tests; strength training; swimming and water exercise; yoga, tai chi, and boxing

Facilities: Fitness center with weight-training equipment, a sauna, a steam room, two heated outdoor pools, a whirlpool, lap pools, four lighted tennis courts, a racquetball court, padded indoor and outdoor jogging tracks, walking trails, and a duck pond

Disability Access: Yes; ramps and elevators provide access to all areas.

Special Notes: One- to two-day special corporate retreats are available. Smoking is not allowed indoors.

Nearby Attractions: White Rock Lake, Dallas Museum of Art, Fort Worth Science Center, Dallas Arboretum and Botanical Garden

Nearest Airport: Dallas/Fort Worth, TX

Getting There: Taxi service and car rental is available at airport. Driving from airport, take the North exit to Highway 635 East towards Dallas; exit on Preston Road; spa entrance is 1 mile on left. (.5 hour)

Lake Austin Spa Resort

1705 South Quinlan Park Road
Austin, TX 78732
800/847-5637 or 512/372-7300; fax: 512/266-1572
Email: info@lakeaustin.com
Website: www.lakeaustin.com

About 20 miles from Austin lies the Lake Austin Spa Resort; however, this resort would be more aptly named the Colorado River Spa Resort because this body of water collects in the gentle bends of Texas hill country to form a popular site for water-skiing, sculling, and canoeing. It is no coincidence that the spa offers the Healing Waters body treatments, which are open to both in-residence spa guests and day visitors. The treatments are intended to reduce stress, increase inner strength, and revitalize the mind, body, and spirit. All treatments are based on ancient healing techniques, such as Ayurveda and thalassotherapy.

Packages at the spa resort are also designed to rejuvenate the whole person and include lodging, meals, and snacks; unlimited fitness and discovery programs; spa treatments; and personal consultations and/or training sessions. Guests have the option to do as much or as little as they like, such as climbing aboard a 15-person Northern Explorer canoe to glide over the waters of Lake Austin, which turn a stunning green and gold in the afternoon.

In addition to the spa's regular programming, the Gathering of Wise Women program is offered in the fall. The program pools the resources of a panel of experts to examine women's health issues. Surgeons, dermatologists, oncologists, nurses, psychologists, dietitians, and noted speakers gather for four weeks in October to share knowledge and explore new ground. The spa has compiled a collection of its best recipes into the cookbook *Lean Star Cuisine,* which is available at the spa. Seasonal cookbooks are also available during summer cooking schools.

Accommodations: 40 rooms facing the lake in connecting cottages with comfortable furnishings, down comforters, and private baths. Some include private gardens with hot tub. The Lady Bird Suite reflects hill country luxury with a living room, a fireplace, a sitting area, and a hot tub that seats six.

Rates: Nightly room rates start at $440. Group rates and mother/daughter packages are available. A $500 nonrefundable prepayment is required at the time of booking and is applied toward the remainder of your stay. A minimum stay may apply for peak periods.

Credit Cards: AE, D, DC, MC, V

Meal Plans: Three low-fat gourmet spa meals are served each day.

Services: Personal growth and stress-reduction programs, holistic health workshops, nutritional counseling, massage, hydrotherapy, aromatherapy, reflexology, body polishes and wraps, tai chi, cooking classes, toning and stretching

Recreational Activities: Hiking, tennis, gardening, water biking, canoeing, lake cruises, nature walks, kayaking, sculling

Facilities: Indoor and outdoor pools, lakeside exercise equipment, fitness center, an activity center, tennis courts, a sauna, a steam room, hydrobikes, small boats, walking trails, organic gardens, a garden library, and a lakeside living room

Disability Access: Full access is available.

Special Notes: Smoking is allowed only in outdoor, nonpublic areas. The minimum allowed age of spa guests is 14.

Nearby Attractions: Steiner Cattle Ranch, Lady Bird Johnson Wildflower Research Center, winery tours

Nearest Airport: Austin, TX

Getting There: Taxi service and car rental is available at airport. Driving from Austin, take I-71 West to Highway 360 North to Highway 2222 West; exit onto Highway 620 South and turn onto Quilan Park Road; spa entrance is at end of road on left. (1 hour)

Optimum Health Institute of Austin

265 Cedar Lane
Cedar Creek, TX 78612
800/993-4325 or 512/303-4817; fax 512/303-1230
Email: austin@optimumhealth.org
Website: www.optimumhealth.org

Like it's California counterpart, the Optimum Health Institute of Austin offers a diet of live raw foods, exercise, whirlpools, and the opportunity to receive colonics, massage, and chiropractic. The institute, which officially opened in March 1996, is a mission of the Free Sacred Trinity Church and educates guests about the institute's philosophy that "the human body is self-regenerating and self-cleansing and, if given the proper tools with which to work, it can maintain its natural state of health."

The three-week program is structured to address the mental, physical, and emotional aspects of each person, with the ultimate goal of having each guest learn about the body and mind and how the two work together. In the first week, some of the activities are daily exercise and attending classes that teach proper food combinations, how to build self-esteem, how to mentally and emotionally detoxify, and relaxation techniques to help control pain. Daily exercise continues in the second week, but guests now learn how to grow sprouts, plant wheat grass, garden organically, prepare healthy foods, and plan menus. Communication skills and at-home personal follow-up are also addressed. In the third week, guests put their newfound knowledge to work with hands-on food preparation classes. Guests also take classes about the mind-body connection and diet maintenance.

Since its founding in 1976, more than 50,000 visitors have benefited from the institute's program. Testimonials of lowered blood pressure and blood sugar levels returning to normal are just some of the many results former guests have shared. Staff members are passionate, knowledgeable, and experienced in the holistic health field.

Accommodations: Single and double rooms with private baths in a new 20,000-square-foot, two-story, Southwestern-style lodge built around a grand atrium

Rates: $550–750 per week

Credit Cards: MC, V (but the salon does not take credit cards)

Meal Plans: Three raw vegan meals (sprouts, greens, fruits, vegetables, fruit juices, enzyme-rich Rejuvelac, wheat grass juice) are served daily.

Services: Colonic hydrotherapy, massage, chiropractic, detoxification, nutritional/cooking classes

Facilities: 14 wooded acres, with a main lodge containing a community living room, an outdoor pool, a hot tub, an exercise room, a salon, and walking trails through cedar and oak trees

Recreational Activities: Walking and enjoying the gardens

Disability Access: Yes

Special Notes: Buildings were designed and are maintained as environmentally clean as possible. Smoking is not allowed.

Nearby Attractions: L. B. Johnson Library, golf, shopping in downtown Austin, three 18-hole golf courses, Lady Bird Johnson Wildflower Research Center, winery tours

Nearest Airport: Austin, TX

Getting There: Airport transportation is provided through Star Shuttle, 512/303-5505 and Austin Cab, 512/736-7748 or 775-7705. Driving from Austin, take Highway 71 East toward Bastrop (15 miles); pass Fina Gas station on right and turn right onto access road (Frontage Road); continue 1 mile; right at Still Forrest Road and continue to spa entrance at the end of the road. (20 minutes)

The Last Resort Retreat Center

P.O. Box 707
Cedar City, UT 84721
435/682-2289

The Last Resort is, well, at the end of the road. A road winds 30 miles up a mountain from Cedar City to the home of Abhilasha and Pujari, dubbed The Last Resort. The retreat center is the culmination of Abhilasha and Pujari's efforts to create a place where people can come to heal, to reflect on different aspects of their lives, and to revitalize themselves. In an intimate log home, guests participate in daily yoga and meditation, group and individual discussion, guided hikes, and relaxation. Abhilasha, a nutrition teacher and gourmet cook, studied with the renowned health and nutrition expert Dr. Bernard Jensen. Pujari, also a student of Dr. Jensen's, is a rebirther, counselor, therapist, and meditation teacher. He has conducted therapy groups in India and throughout the United States since 1974.

Five different types of workshops and retreats are scheduled throughout the year: the Vipassana Meditation Retreat, the Yoga Retreat, the yearly Spring Cleaning Retreat, a relationship workshop, and a natural foods cooking workshop, which is designed to help guests develop good eating habits and eliminate cravings, while learning to prepare natural, whole foods. Participants learn how to create tasty, well-balanced meals using a variety of whole grains, fresh vegetables, beans, and other natural ingredients. Classes lasting 2.5 hours are held twice a day and cover topics like nutritious food combining, how to cook with tofu and tempeh, and how to cook a healthy meal in less time with proper planning. A morning meditation and yoga class is also part of the daily regimen. The Spring Cleaning Retreat is held in June and includes 3–4 days of juice fasting, colonics, light yoga, and silent meditation every morning and evening. One morning is spent trekking down to the Pah Tempe Hot Springs for a luxurious mineral water soak. Guests also watch videos by well-known experts on health and nutrition.

Accommodations: Up to 10 in a log home with private and dormitory-style rooms

Rates: Vary according to program. The Vipassana Meditation Retreat is $450 for five days, $700 for 10 days, and $1,700 for 30 days; the Yoga Retreat is $750 for seven days.

Credit Cards: None accepted

Meal Plans: Two balanced vegetarian meals, plus snacks, are offered each day.

Services: Vipassana meditation, yoga, natural foods cooking classes, relationship workshops, and nutrition and health education

Recreational Activities: Hiking

Facilities: A large log home on a ridge overlooking Sunset Cliff, a dry sauna, a hot tub, mineral baths, and hiking trails

Disability Access: Yes

Special Notes: Smoking is not allowed. Pujari offers phone counseling, with appointment times scheduled between retreats.

Nearby Attractions: Pah Tempe Hot Springs; central to the major national parks of Utah, such as Bryce Canyon, Cedar Breaks, Dixie, and Zion

Nearest Airports: Cedar City and Salt Lake City, UT

Getting There: Taxi service and car rental is available at both airports. Call spa for additional information on airport transportation into Duck Creek Village and spa. Driving from Salt Lake City, take I-15 South to Cedar City. In Cedar City, take Highway 14 for 30 miles into Duck Creek Village and follow signs for spa. (40 minutes)

Red Mountain Resort and Spa

1275 E. Red Mountain Circle
Ivins, UT 84738
800/407-3002 or 435/673-4905; fax: 435/673-1363
Website: www.redmountainspa.com

For more than two decades, the Red Mountain Resort and Spa has nestled at the foot of the red sandstone towers near the entrance to Snow Canyon State Park (named for its early settlers, not for the "white stuff"). The facility sits at the mouth of Snow Canyon's red sandstone cliffs, beneath the towering peaks of 10,000-foot Pine Valley Mountain.

This premier resort, known as an adventure spa, features an array of health and fitness programs from adventure hikes to aerobics, biking, personal training, meditation, and massage. The focus is on education in proper nutrition and exercise as the path to stress reduction, weight loss, and complete lifestyle improvement. Guests participate in classes on cooking, grocery shopping, mind-body awareness, time and stress management, and disease prevention. Outdoor fitness excursions, healthy supportive meals, informative presentations, and a full complement of spa services provide a comprehensive, rewarding experience in body and mind.

Programs begin with individualized health and fitness evaluations. Based on the results of this assessment, guests are placed in groups that participate in activities that are geared aerobically to their needs. This evaluation also identifies fitness areas that need improvement. A wide variety of exercise options, promoting weight loss, cardiovascular health, and total body fitness, have been prepared for guests. Options include walking tours, scenic and challenging hikes for all fitness levels, biking tours/mountain biking, fitness and weight training, spinning, swimming, yoga, tai chi, tennis, water aerobics, land aerobics, football, and resistance training. Total health is promoted by educating guests about healthy diet choices that complement active lifestyles.

Accommodations: Luxury hotel-style accommodations include double or quad rooms or single, double, and trio casitas

Rates: A four-day stay ranges from $685–1,360 per person, depending on accommodations; a seven-day stay is $995–1,995; a 10-day stay is $1,420–2,850; and a 14-day stay is $1,860–3750.

Credit Cards: AE, D, MC, V

Meal Plans: Three balanced, nutritious meals are served daily and include buffet-style breakfast and lunch and seated dinner. A variety of lifestyles—vegetarian and otherwise—are accommodated.

Services: 30 fitness classes, spinning, tai chi, yoga, aerobics, spa services, beauty salon, weight training, cooking classes

Recreational Activities: Hiking, mountain biking

Facilities: An outdoor and indoor swimming pool, a hot tub, a cardiovascular center, a learning center, a retail sports shop, and a conference center for group activities

Disability Access: Yes; full access is available.

Special Notes: A 21-day weight loss program is available. A full-service medical facility is located 20 minutes from the resort for those with medical requirements.

Nearby Attractions: Snow Canyon State Park, Zion National Park, Bryce Canyon

National Park, North Rim Grand Canyon National Park, Capital Reef National Monument, Valley State Park, Lake Mead, Dixie National Forest, historic St. George, and Southern Utah

Nearest Airport: St. George, UT

Getting There: Airport transportation to St. George and Las Vegas is provided by St. George Shuttle, 800/933-8320 and Autobus, 800/500-9785. Car rental is available at Las Vegas airport. (2.5 hours) Driving from Las Vegas, take I-15 North to St. George, Exit 6 onto Bluff Street; left on Bluff Street; left at Snow Canyon Parkway, entrance is 3.5 miles. (2.5 hours) **Note:** Driving from Salt Lake City not recommended due to extensive road construction (5 hours)

International

Ayurvedic Spa

Babaji's Kriya Yoga Ashram
196 Mountain Road C.P. 90
Eastman, Quebec, Canada J0E 1P0
450/297-0258; fax 450/297-3957
Email: Babaji@generation.net
Website: www.babaji.ca

The five-year-old Ayurvedic Spa, also known as Babaji's Kriya Yoga Ashram, offers holistic health programs through the ancient Indian practice of Ayurveda. In Canada's secluded northeastern countryside, the ashram is located on top of a mountain, with panoramic views of nearby mountains and pristine forest land. Guests of the 40-acre Ayurvedic Spa have access to a private lake and panoramic mountaintop views. The spa's founder, Gaetane Annai Govindan, is a therapist whose background includes training in polarity, therapeutic touch, energetic osteopathy, Chinese auriculotherapy, and focusing. After a near-death experience during a relatively minor surgical operation in 1983, Govindan was diagnosed with cancer. These dramatic experiences inspired her to pursue tantrism, metaphysics, and Taoist yoga, a method of journeying within the body. Through these efforts, Govindan's cancer was cured, and she later studied at the Aluva Ayurvedic Hospital in Kerela, India.

An underlying emphasis is placed on rejuvenating the body, mind, and spirit, healing chronic illnesses, and reinforcing the immune system. The unique constitution of each guest is considered, and a well-rounded method of addressing the physical, emotional, mental, and spiritual is applied. Programs last from 1–7 days and include traditional detoxification methods and instruction in diet, exercise, breathing, and meditation. Based on a personalized approach, the initial evaluation includes an examination of the pulse, eyes, and tongue. Depending on an individual's needs, detoxification, herbal oil massage, sauna, therapeutic whirlpool bathing, herbal supplements, and diet recommendations are prescribed. In addition to traditional Ayurveda, Govindan offers some of the healing modalities that underlie her professional background, such as energetic osteopathy and Chinese auriculotherapy.

Accommodations: Up to 35 guests can be accommodated in 11 rooms with private and shared bathrooms.
Rates: $300 per day, including lodging, meals, and treatments
Credit Cards: V only
Meal Plans: All meals consist of a diet designed to support the therapeutic regimen.
Services: Initial evaluation of pulse, eyes, and tongue; detoxification treatments; Ayurvedic oil massage; herbal steam baths; polarity therapy; energetic osteopathy; hands-on harmonization and Chinese auriculotherapy; herbal supplements; yoga classes and training
Recreational Activities: Forest walks and hikes, swimming, and kayaking
Facilities: 40 acres with a private lake, a two-story lodge, a treatment center, a whirlpool, and a sauna
Disability Access: Yes
Special Notes: Smoking is not allowed indoors.
Nearby Attractions: Mount Orford; Lake Memphramagog; dining, theater, and nightlife in Montreal

Nearest Airport: Montreal, Quebec

Getting There: Spa provides airport transportation with advance notice. Call for reservations and cost. Car rental is available at airport. Driving from Montreal airport, take Route 20 East toward downtown Montreal. Cross Champlain Bridge and go onto Route 10; take Exit 100 and continue two miles to spa. (1.25 hours)

Centre de Santé d'Eastman

895 Chemin des Diligences
Eastman, Quebec, Canada J0E 1P0
800/665-5272 or 450/297-3009; fax: 450/297-3370
Email: courrier@spa-eastman.com
Website: www.centredesante.com

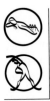

Since 1977, Centre de Santé d'Eastman has offered award-winning anti-stress vacations. The center is located about one hour southeast of Montreal in the rolling countryside of the Eastern Townships. The bucolic estate provides guests with a stunning view of Mount Orford, and only 10 of its 315 acres are used for lodging and facilities. No more than 35 guests at a time stay at this former Quebécois farm in seven buildings spread out a couple of hundred feet apart. Despite its location in the heart of French-speaking Canada, all staff members speak English. Horseback riding is offered year-round, as well as 15 kilometers of hiking trails. Indoor and outdoor pools are located on site, and guests can plunge into the swimming hole in summer. Many optional activities are available, including Hammam (steam bath), health walks, and personal training sessions. Although a terrycloth robe and comfortable rooms with private bath are an option, guests wanting complete seclusion can opt for a stay in l'Ermitage, a room with only running water, a woodstove, and an oil lamp.

Spa treatments are broken into categories, such as the Bodily Approach sessions, which include Feldenkrais, reflexology, and polarity therapy. Take Stock and Stock Up workshops are held every morning, and topics range from applied kinesiology to an introduction to focusing, self-healing techniques, and self-awareness through writing. The seven-night Health Relaxation Stay includes lodging, three gourmet vegetarian meals per day, a body peel with marine sediments, a full body wrap with essential oils, a full body wrap with algae, lymphatic draining, two hydromassage baths with algae or essential oils, two massages, a hydrotherapy massage, two oxygen and steam baths with essential oils, a facial, a pressotherapy session, two Take Stock and Stock Up sessions, three Bodily Approach sessions, three anti-stress walks, daily fitness walks, and six evening activities, such as sleigh rides, healthy diet secrets, or tai chi.

Accommodations: Standard single and double rooms in the main house and small hamlets. Some rooms have fireplaces and sitting rooms.

Rates: Vary according to room and package. À la carte treatments range between $18–70. Health getaways range between $650–1,28, including lodging (double occupancy), meals, and services.

Credit Cards: AE, MC, V

Meal Plans: All meals are included with residential programs and consist of three nutritionally balanced gourmet meals per day.

Services: Massage therapy, hydrotherapy, aromatherapy, reflexology, reiki, lymphatic manual drainage, algotherapy, fangotherapy, body exfoliation and wraps, pressotherapy, colonics, anticellulite treatments, salon services, fitness training, health consultations, and psychological counseling

Recreational Activities: Guided and solo nature walks, cross-country and downhill skiing, horseback riding, swimming, golf

Facilities: A 315-acre estate with 45 private rooms and 30 independent enclosures for spa treatments, a vibromassage table, two oxygen baths, a Hammam bath, indoor and outdoor pools, and two gazebos for outdoor massages

Disability Access: Yes; full access is available.

Special Notes: Smoking is allowed only outside.

Nearby Attractions: Mount Orford; Lake Memphramagog; Theatre de la Marjolaine; theater, shopping, dining, and nightlife in Quebec City

Nearest Airport: Montreal, Quebec

Getting There: Spa provides airport transportation with advance notice. Call for reservations and cost. Driving from Montreal Airport, take Route 20 East toward downtown Montreal. Cross Champlain Bridge and go on to Route 10; take Exit 100 and follow signs to spa. (1 hour)

The Hills Health Ranch

P.O. Box 26, 108 Mile Ranch
British Columbia, Canada, V0K 2Z0
250/791-5225; fax: 250/791-6384
Email: thehills@bcinternet.net
Website: www.spabc.com

The Hills Health Ranch combines a down-to-earth rustic ambience with luxury spa services and wellness programs. In the heart of the Canadian wilderness, this health and fitness resort provides true country charm. An authentic Indian tepee is the gathering site for sing-along parties, and guests can learn new steps at Texas line-dancing parties. Swiss-style chalets look out over 20,000 acres of heavily forested hills, mountain lakes, and meadowlands with grazing horses and cattle. Guests who venture out on horseback with their guides ride past eight different lakes on the Horseback Holiday. An elevation of 3,400 feet and a dry climate are especially beneficial for people with respiratory disorders.

More than 20 homeopathic and aesthetic treatments, indoor and outdoor fitness programming, daily wellness workshops, and low-fat gourmet spa cuisine are offered. Programs range from weekend spa spoilers to 11-day retreats that adhere to an extensive daily agenda. For people who are committed to serious weight or lifestyle changes, 30-day intensive programs are available. Programs address a wide range of lifestyle issues, such as wellness kick-start, smoking cessation, stress reduction, successful aging, and injury rehabilitation. Programs include lodging, low-fat meals, daily hiking and skiing in season, personal training sessions, medical consultations, a complete fitness test and lifestyle assessment, daily wellness workshops, and daily indoor and outdoor fitness activities. Optional treatments include massage, clay packs, and reflexology.

Accommodations: 26 deluxe rooms and 19 individual Swiss-style chalets

Rates: Space must be confirmed by a deposit of $100 or 25 percent of the program fee at least two weeks in advance. Cancellations must be received in writing 30 days in advance for a full refund.

Credit Cards: AE, MC, V

Meal Plans: Three low-fat, calorie-controlled gourmet spa meals are provided daily.

Services: Massage, full-body mud packs, herbal wraps, aromatherapy, hydrotherapy, scalp treatments, salt scrubs, reflexology, facials, manicures, pedicures, aerobics, yoga, daily guided walks and hikes, and wellness workshops

Recreational Activities: Horseback riding, hiking, mountain biking, canoeing, swimming, lake fishing, ice-skating, skiing, snowboarding, tubing, sleigh rides, dog sledding, Texas line dancing, hayrides, and campfires

Facilities: Indoor pool, hot tubs, saunas, aerobic studio, 16 spa treatment rooms, two dining rooms, a lounge, three meeting rooms, five lakes, a downhill and cross-country snowpark, and a ski shop

Recreational Activities: Downhill and cross-country skiing, daily guided hikes

Disability Access: Yes; full access is available.

Special Notes: Smoking is not allowed in the spa or dining room. Guests should bring warm clothes and all-terrain shoes.

Nearby Attractions: Barker Village, Helmicken Falls, Gibraltar Gold Mine

Nearest Airport: Williams Lake, BC

Getting There: Spa provides airport services, $60 each way, reservations required. (.5 hour)

Hollyhock

P.O. Box 127
Mansons Landing, Cortes Island
British Columbia, Canada V0P 1K0
800/933-6339 or 250/935-6576; fax: 250/935-6424
Email: hollyhock@oberon.ark.com
Website: www.hollyhock.bc.ca

A fire circle, a coastal wilderness, sandy beach, and days left open and unplanned—just like camp except more refined. This holistic learning center on tiny Cortes Island, just 90 miles north of Vancouver, British Columbia, draws internationally acclaimed authors, healers, and artists as guest speakers for its 70 or so workshops each year. Open evenings allow guests who have come for a little quiet and a soak in the hot tub a chance to meet other guests and learn new skills. Hollyhock allows plenty of time for quiet introspection, although evidence of the communal atmosphere shows in the invitation to guests to bring musical instruments and art materials.

Visitors come to Hollyhock for everything from meditating to gathering plants in the surrounding woods for a workshop on herbal medicine. A wide range of five-day workshops provide the opportunity for guests to test the waters of an arts-and-culture, wellness, wisdom practices, leadership, or business workshop. Programs begin with guests gathering at the two-story cedar lodge on the opening evening for an informal welcome. The next day starts with an optional 7 A.M. yoga class followed by meditation, and at 10 A.M. workshop sessions get underway. After lunch, sessions resume around 3 P.M., and a presentation by a workshop leader or Cortes Island instructor begins at 8 P.M. Before catching the ferry or seaplane home, guests can take a bird walk with an experienced naturalist or hop in the 12-passenger *Harlequin* for a group row over to a nearby inlet.

Accommodations: Lodging for up to 80 in private single rooms with private baths on the beach; private single rooms with shared bath on the beach or forest, or in orchard cabins; double-occupancy cabins; or shared rooms for 3–6 with choice of ocean or forest views (men and women are assigned to separate rooms). Tent space is available; the campground has a bathhouse. Guests must bring their own tents and bedding.

Rates: Vary according to lodging, program, and season. Meals and accommodation packages range from US$47–142 per person per day. Five-day program tuition ranges from US$280–530.

Credit Cards: MC, V

Meal Plans: Three gourmet vegetarian meals per day are served buffet style. Seafood is served twice a week; evening barbecues are held once a week.

Services: Arts and culture, wisdom practices, wellness, leadership, and business workshops and seminars, massage and bodywork, aromatherapy, natural skin care, yoga, meditation

Recreational Activities: Wilderness tours, walking, hiking, kayaking, sailing

Facilities: Outdoor hot tubs overlooking the ocean, an orchard with a sanctuary, sailboats, and trails

Disability Access: Wheelchair access is limited.

Special Notes: Smoking is not allowed indoors. Guests must bring flashlights and warm casual clothing. A beach towel, rain gear, and all-terrain shoes are recommended. In addition to retreats, elderhostel and work-study programs are available.

Nearby Attractions: Easter Bluff; shopping, restaurants, and museums of Victoria; petroglyphs; waterfalls; lakes; old-growth forests

Nearest Airport: Vancouver, B.C.

Getting There: There are several ways to reach Cortes Island, depending on your budget and desired travel time. Option one: taking a seaplane from Vancouver, North West Seaplanes, 800/690-0086 and Kenmore Air, 800/543-9595, is the quickest and most expensive choice. (1 hour) Option two: fly to Campbell River then water taxi to island. (2 hours) Option three: drive to Campbell River then take a couple ferries to island. This is the longest but least expensive route . (6 hours) Spa can provide additional directions and details.

Macrobiotics Canada Health and Healing Center

Rural Route 3
Almonte, Ontario, Canada K0A 1A0
613/256-2665; fax: 613/256-4985
Email: None, to encourage the lost art of personal contact
Website: macrobioticscanada.ca

For those who may be wondering exactly what macrobiotics is, Wayne Diotte, founder of Macrobiotics Canada Health and Healing Centers, has this reply: "It is a way of approaching life. Simply translated from the Greek, *macrobiotics* means 'great life.' Understanding and balancing the energy of our daily food relationships, environment, and activities is an enjoyable and rewarding focus of macrobiotics." Diotte's philosophy is to offer a larger view—a way of perceiving, pursuing, creating, and experiencing the best possible life full of energy, good humor, and adventure. "The spirit and essence of macrobiotic philosophy," adds Diotte, "is to use unifying principles to harmonize and unify the body, mind, and spirit in order to create health, freedom, and peace—first within our own being, then within our family, our society, and finally within our world community."

Over a day, a week, or longer, individually designed residential programs are offered at the center to facilitate natural healing and awaken participants to the richness of life. Programs can contain any combination of educational consultations, macrobiotic shiatsu, cooking classes, breathwork, issue-focused counseling, ginger compresses, do-ins, yoga, meditation, and pampering facials. Many physical health benefits are derived from the program. For example, in macrobiotic shiatsu, meridians are massaged by thumb, hand, elbow, or foot pressure, with the resulting benefit of regulating and balancing the capacity of the organ systems. Ginger compresses—which consist of a topical application of fresh, hot ginger water—dispel cold, stimulate circulation, and assist in the breakdown of fat deposits. Do-In is a self-massage technique that reportedly increases circulation and digestion and strengthens muscles, organs, and nerves. Breathwork involves one-on-one sessions that teach breathing techniques, aiding in the release of accumulated toxins within the tissues.

Evenings include group discussions, campfires, recreational activities, and entertainment provided by the more musical and theatrical guests. A picnic on the banks of a river is scheduled at least once during the conference, and a farewell brunch winds up the week's activities.

Accommodations: Up to 40 guests in either shared rooms at a nearby conference center or an on-site three-bedroom cottage or a five-bedroom house. A limited number of campsites are also available.

Rates: $95–395 per person, per day, according to services.

Credit Cards: MC, V

Meal Plans: Three macrobiotic meals are included with the residential program.

Services: Health and dietary consultations, shiatsu, compresses, breathwork, palm healing, facials, yoga, meditation, counseling, cooking classes

Recreational Activities: Hiking, boating, swimming, canoeing, skiing

Facilities: A five-acre rural village with three hand-built wood-frame buildings, treatment and seminar rooms, four kitchens, organic gardens, walking trails, and a river

Disability Access: Yes

Special Notes: Clients from around the world are accommodated after the program through telephone follow-up. Collaboration with medical professionals, chiropractors, naturopaths, and various healers can be arranged on clients' behalf.

Nearby Attractions: Clear lakes and rivers, skiing, recreation areas; downtown Ottawa's world-class museums and galleries, festivals; skiing and golfing

Nearest Airport: Ottawa, Ontario

Getting There: Complimentary airport service is available with advance reservations. Driving from points along Highway 401 and Ottawa, take Highway 417 West. North of the town of Almonte, left on March Road; right onto Martain Street; left on Blakney Road; spa is third building on right. (.5+ hours)

Mountain Trek Fitness Retreat and Health Spa

P.O. Box 1352
Ainsworth Hot Springs
British Columbia, Canada V0G 1A0
800/661-5161 (reservations) or 250-229-5636
fax: 250/229-5246
Email: inquiry@hiking.com
Website: www.hiking.com

Fresh mountain air, incredible hiking, vegetarian cuisine, and the spa's wonderful massage treatments make Mountain Trek Fitness Retreat a rejuvenating vacation spot. This exclusive mountain lodge offers a spacious, comfortable, 16-bedroom lodge on the shores of Kootenay Lake, overlooking the Pucell Mountains. Whether you're there for rest and relaxation, getting in shape by hiking along mountain trails, or to jumpstart a healthy eating regimen, you'll find support at this unique fitness and health spa.

Since 1990, Mountain Trek has been offering guests all kinds of programs geared toward holistic rejuvenation. The retreat's guiding philosophy, according to owner Wendy Pope, is to offer a "vacation for the body and mind." Mountain Trek coordinates programs that focus on the essentials of a healthy lifestyle: fresh air, cardiovascular exercise, flexibility and strength workouts, healthy energized food, relaxation, and rest. Previous programs offered include Nateshvar's Yoga Tree Retreat, Spa Cuisine Cooking Course, Weight Loss Spa Retreat, Fit 'n' Fast Two-Week Program, Natural Health Vacations, Snowshoe 'n' Spa Vacation, and Tesh Trek Challenge Boot Camp week for those who want to challenge their heart, soul, and body with intensive yoga, hiking, and biking, followed with a massage. Gentle hiking/walking programs are also available.

Seasonal activities at Mountain Trek include snowshoeing and cross-country skiing in the winter and an assortment of year-round hiking that is suited to every ability level. A daily yoga class is part of the routine, as is eating healthy vegetarian cuisine, daily massages, and access to Ainsworth Hot Springs, a five-minute walk from the lodge.

Accommodations: 12 private rooms with private bath in a rustic, comfortable cedar lodge with fireplace lounge

Rates: Vary by program. A standard hiking week is approximately US$2,000.

Credit Cards: MC, V

Meal Plans: Gourmet cuisine with healthy, low-fat dishes, chicken and fish options, vegetarian dishes, or vegan selections.

Services: Swedish massage treatments, aromatherapy, reflexology, and "Nature's Path," which is a consultation with a licensed Naturalpathic Physician.

Activities: Backcountry hiking, walking, mountain biking, lake kayaking, exploring caves, snowshoeing, and a variety of outdoor sports

Facilities: 34 acres of forested property; the main cedar lounge with 16 bedrooms, fireplace lounge, and dining room with lake view; outdoor hot tub; sauna; gym; yoga studio; and weight room

Disability Access: No access

Special Notes: Mountain Treks' website, provides practical, basic information about hiking in general, as well as information about the spa.

Nearby Attractions: A five-minute walk from Ainsworth Hot Springs; the historic town of Nelson, located one hour away, has cute shops.

Nearest Airport: Castlegar, B.C.; Spokane, WA

Getting There: Spa provides transportation from both airports—Castlegar (1.5 hours), Spokane (4 hours). Call for reservations and cost. Car rental is available at airports. Spa will provide driving directions.

Salt Spring Centre

355 Blackburn Road
Salt Spring Island
British Columbia, Canada, V8K 2B8
250/537-2326; fax: 250/537-2311
Email: ssc@saltspring.com
Website: www.saltspringcentre.com

Since 1981, the Salt Spring Centre has provided rest and rejuvenation weekends for women, yoga retreats, Ayurvedic health treatments, and daily yoga, as well as renting its facilities out to various organizations for seminars and retreats. This nonprofit yoga center was inspired by Baba Hari Dass, a monk and teacher who has not spoken since 1952 and communicates by means of a small chalkboard. Following his example of self-less service, the center's aim is to provide a nurturing environment for the pursuit of the creative and healing arts—all within a context of spiritual growth. The Dharma Sara Satsang Society, a group that practices the principles of ashtanga yoga, manages and maintains the center.

The center is located in the middle of the largest of the Canadian Gulf Islands, Salt Spring Island, British Columbia. On 69 acres of organic garden, orchard, and woodlands, guests have a view of the mountains and wild meadows. A fully restored heritage farmhouse accommodates 21 guests, and the health facility overlooking the garden can house four more. Camping is available during the summer months. A wood-fired sauna and therapeutic body treatments, including Ayurvedic Swedan—a rejuvenating balsam steam and bodywork session—reflexology, and facials using ingredients made from the organic garden, add to the appeal of the Salt Spring Centre.

Ongoing yoga classes are offered, as are retreats focusing on health, Ayurveda, yoga, and relaxation. Women's weekends, which include Ayurvedic Swedan or massage, reflexology, two yoga classes, a wood-fired sauna, facials, delicious vegetarian meals, and an inspiring evening program with topics such as Healing Herbs for Women, Ayurvedic Self-Massage, and Aromatherapy for Women, are scheduled throughout the year.

Accommodations: The fully restored three-story heritage farmhouse sleeps up to 21 people. The Garden House is a new health facility that sleeps four. A yurt or small cabin can sleep five. Campsites with washroom and shower facilities are available during summer.

Rates: Vary according to the program. The Women's Weekend is $360 Canadian, which includes shared accommodation, meals, three health treatments, yoga classes, sauna, and evening program. Private rooms are available at an additional cost.

Credit Cards: Not accepted

Meal Plans: For most programs and retreats, three organic vegetarian meals per day are served buffet style. Vegan options are available.

Services: A variety of health treatments, yoga posture classes, meditation and Pranayama classes, and Satsang

Recreational Activities: Nature trails, also close to swimming lakes and a golf course

Facilities: 69 acres with a 1,500-square-foot main seminar room and a smaller meeting room, organic gardens, a dining room, a health facility, and forest trails

Disability Access: No access

Special Notes: The national bestseller *Salt Spring Island Cooking: Vegetarian Recipes from the Salt Spring Centre* is available by mail order. Smoking, alcohol, meat, and eggs are not permitted on the property.

Nearby Attractions: Artist's market in town, two golf courses, fishing and swimming lakes, shopping, dining, hiking, biking, kayaking, and more

Nearest Airport: Vancouver or Victoria, B.C.

Getting There: Transportation is available from Salt Spring Island Ferry building. Call spa for details and reservations. Ferries operate between Vancouver's Tsawwassen terminal and Long Harbour on Salt Spring Island. (1.5–3 hours) BC Ferries, 888/BCFerry, operates from Vancouver Island to Salt Spring's Fulford Harbour. (35 minutes) Ferry reservations recommended. Driving from either ferry landings, continue along Fulford Ganges Road; at Blackburn Road, turn left from the direction of Fulford Harbor and turn right from Long Harbour; follow Blackburn Road to spa entrance. (10 minutes)

Self-Realization Meditation Healing Centre

736 Creekside Crescent
RR1 - S4 - C5
Gibsons Landing
British Columbia, Canada V0N 1V0
phone/fax: 604/886-0898

Self-Realization Meditation Healing Centres can be found all over the world. Mata Yogananda and Peter Sevonanda founded the original center in Somerset, England, more than 30 years ago with the goal of helping everyone overcome illness and stress in a supportive and loving environment. The centers were established to teach meditation as a means of tapping into the universal consciousness and consequently empowering individuals to create a life of health and happiness.

The Centre at Gibsons Landing is located on the beautiful Sunshine Coast near Vancouver, close to the sea, and with easy access to mountain walking. Workshops, courses, and several types of retreats are offered at the center and are particularly beneficial for people experiencing life changes, burnout, and chronic physical illness. Natural spiritual healing and progressive counseling are used to bring the whole person into a state of balance, which results in a progressive improvement of the individual's ailment. Relaxation, healing, meditation, personal development, and silent retreats are among program choices.

All healing retreats are individually designed to meet the unique needs of each guest. Mornings usually start with meditation at 7 A.M. and a whole-foods vegetarian breakfast at 9 A.M. Healing treatments, personal counseling, or yoga begins at 10 A.M., followed by free time, which is considered essential for absorbing the healing treatments. Guests can walk along one of the many ocean and forest trails, read in a sitting room with a woodstove, or listen to music quietly. A light lunch is served at 1 P.M., and afterward guests learn relaxation techniques or participate in hatha yoga. Late afternoon is open for more free time, which could mean exploring the library or meditation room or relaxing in the garden overlooking the ocean. Guests gather for dinner at 6 P.M., and evening activities include yoga and meditation.

Accommodations: Warm, comfortable single and double rooms

Rates: Prices vary. A typical healing or counseling session is $40; full room and board can be $62.50 per night.

Credit Cards: None accepted

Meal Plans: Home-cooked whole and vegetarian foods. All diets can be accommodated.

Services: Natural spiritual healing, counseling, hatha yoga, meditation, stress management, workshops, courses, healing and spiritual retreats

Recreational Activities: Walking, hiking

Facilities: Library; meditation room; yoga room; guest sitting room with a woodstove; organic garden; and sundeck

Disability Access: No access

Special Notes: The center cannot care for patients requiring medical and nursing assistance. Silent retreats are scheduled throughout the year, including Christmas and Easter.

Nearby Attractions: Ocean beaches, forest trails, Gulf Islands, mountains, small fishing, and village of Gibsons Landing

Nearest Airport: Vancouver, BC

Getting There: Spa provides transportation from the Langdale Ferry Landing on the Sunshine Coast. BC Ferries, 888/BCFerry, operates between Langdale and Horseshoe Bay on Mainland Vancouver (40 minutes). Ferry reservations recommended. Driving from Langdale ferry landing, take Highway 101 into Gibsons Landing. (15 minutes)

Serenity by the Sea

225 Serenity Lane, RR2
Galiano Island 42-14
British Columbia, Canada V0N 1P0
800/944-2655; fax: 250/539-2655
Email: serenity@gulfislands.com
Website: www.serenitybythesea.com

Serenity by the Sea is more an effect than a name for this year-round haven perched on Galiano Island, located midway between Vancouver and Victoria in the Canadian Gulf Islands. In the surrounding woodlands and on remote beaches, guests can spot otters, mink, seals, and eagles. The goal of owners Shera Street and her partner, Amrit Chidakash, is to provide a casual and holistic approach in an intimate setting so guests can quickly feel "at home" and safe. Street and Chidakash, both artists and healers, facilitate most workshops. Both have experience in reiki, yoga, meditation, life transitions counseling, journal writing, Gestalt therapy, and mask making. Although primarily a retreat specializing in core relaxation, emotional balancing, and creative self-discovery, individual programs are tailored to balance the mind, body, and spirit. Reiki, breathing awareness for stress management, daily yoga, and meditation are also offered.

A unique style of massage is available that focuses on the body, breath, and energy. Known as core relaxation, the technique was developed by Chidakash on the basis of his belief that stress and trauma result in contraction throughout the body. By creating space in the joints, where contraction tends to focus as "stiffness," the body can shed stress and begin the healing process. The massage focuses on using subtle stretches and pulsing rhythms to open joints and release energy blockages. The result is an expansive feeling of energy flowing throughout the whole body.

In addition to personal healing retreats, several weekend programs are offered throughout the summer at Serenity that aim mainly to foster creative self-discovery. At all times of the year, custom creative programs can be tailored for people to enjoy during their stay. Health, however, is often a fundamental aspect of the programs, as in the workshop "For the Love of Touch," which explores the idea that touch and healing are as natural as breath. "We want to provide a space where contracted bodies, pressured emotions, and withdrawn spirits will expand naturally and heal themselves," says Chidakash. If space is what he wants to provide, he has certainly managed it with a cliffside hot tub; airy, light-filled rooms with ocean and garden views; and access to tremendous natural Northwest beauty through kayaking, sailing, and hiking.

Accommodations: Two large rooms and one self-contained chalet
Credit Cards: MC, V
Meal Plans: Vegetarian breakfast is provided for guests, except those staying in the self-contained chalet.
Services: Bodywork, reiki, toning bowls, yoga, meditation, creative therapies
Recreational Activities: Walking; kayaking; fishing
Facilities: A multilevel home situated within feet of the ocean, cascading spiral steps down to the ocean, a tub on a cliffside terrace overlooking the ocean, art work, and hammocks
Disability Access: No access

Special Notes: Smoking is allowed only in designated areas.

Nearby Attractions: Forest, creek, waterfall, shopping, dining, theater in Victoria and Vancouver, rainforests

Nearest Airports: Vancouver and Victoria, BC; Seattle, WA

Getting There: Car rental is available at airports. Taxi service available at Galiano Island ferry landing. BC Ferries, 888/BCFerry, operates between Galiano Island and Vancouver's Tsawwassen terminal (50 minutes); Vancouver Island's Swartz Bay (50 minutes); and from Anacortes or Port Angeles through Vancouver. Seattle is a 2.5 hour drive from Vancouver. Driving from Galiano Island ferry landing, take Galiano Drive 1.5 miles (3 kilometers); right on Porlier Pass Drive; at "The Pottery," left onto Ganner Drive; bear left to end of Ganner and spa entrance. (15 minutes)

Sivananda Ashram Yoga Camp

673 8th Avenue
Val Morin, Quebec
Canada JOT 2R0
819/322-3226; fax: 819/322-5876
Email: HQ@sivananda.org
website: www.sivananda.org

The Sivananda Ashram yoga camp is a place to relax, exercise, learn and meditate. The programs of the ashram are based on Swami Vishu-Devanandas's five points for a holistic evolution of body, mind, and soul, which include proper exercise, proper breathing, proper relaxation, proper diet, and positive thinking and meditation.

The yoga camp was founded in 1962 and is one of five ashrams founded by Swami Vishnu-Devananda to carry on the teachings of his master, Swami Sivananda of Rishikesh. The center offers year-round programs, providing guests with the opportunity to participate fully in the ashram routine, experiencing both its joys and its challenges. The daily program is based on classical yogic teachings passed down through the ages from guru to disciple.

The ashram offers a year-round schedule of morning and evening meditation, plus two yoga and pranayama classes daily. During special times throughout the year, such as Christmas, Thanksgiving, and Easter, the Yoga Retreat offers specialized programs on themes of peace, heath, parapsychology and spiritual practices. Special guests are invited to enhance the retreat with lectures, workshops, and classes. (Call for program descriptions.) Families with children are welcome at the Yoga Camp with parental supervision.

Accommodations: There are two buildings with guest rooms: a new ecologically built straw bale lodge with comfortable shared rooms each with a private bathroom, and an older building with smaller rooms and separate bathrooms. Several rustic cabins are also available, and camping is welcome for those who bring their own tents.

Rates: US$45 per person, per night or US$285 per person, per week for a shared room; US$30 per person, per night or US$170 per person, per week for tent space.

Credit Cards: AE, V

Meal Plans: The Yogic vegetarian diet consists of pure, simple, natural foods with the least negative impact on the environment and the least pain to other beings. Some of the vegetables and herbs are grown in the Ashram gardens, whereas other produce is obtained locally in season. Meals are lactovegetarian but do not use garlic, onions, vinegar, or eggs. Drinking water comes from an 80-foot-deep artesian well. Herb teas are always available.

Services: Yoga, meditation classes

Recreational Activities: Swimming, hiking, snow-shoeing, or cross-country skiing. Local activities include canoeing, cycling, and lake swimming in summer and fall and downhill skiing and skating in winter.

Facilities: 250 forested acres of Canada's Laurentian Mountains. Abundant wildlife, tended gardens, secluded shrines, an ecologically built straw bale lodge, a temple, a swimming pool, and a sauna

Disability Access: Yes; full access is available.

Nearby Attractions: Ski resorts and parks

Special Notes: To maintain the purity and spiritual purpose of the ashram, guests and residents are asked to follow the schedule of events in the daily program.

Nearby Airport: Montreal, Quebec

Getting There: Call spa for details and cost of transportation from Montreal airports to Val Morin. Driving from Montreal, take the Laurentian Autoroute (Highway 15 North); leave highway at Exit 76; follow signs to entrance. (1 hour)

Spa Concept Bromont

90 rue Stanstead
Bromont, Quebec
Canada J2L 1K6
800/567-SPAS (567-7727) or 450/534-2717
fax: 450/534-0599
Email: info@spaconcept.ca
Website: www.spaconcept.qc.ca

Spa Concept Bromont is a health center located in the Chateau Bromont, just one hour from Montreal in the heart of Canada's Eastern Townships. Invigorating mountain air and halcyon countryside await guests at this center geared toward relaxation, beauty, and remineralization.

In addition to health profiles, casual kinesiology and colonics, guests are offered a variety of massage therapies—Swedish, shiatsu, polarity, jin shin do, lymphatic drainage, reflexology, Californian, and orthotherapy. Waterfall massages and massages designed especially for pregnant women and children are also offered.

Another important aspect of their services are beauty treatments. Specialized aestheticians provide customers with calming and soothing experiences: a 90-minute facial with mini foot massage (back or breast treatments also available); body peeling with dead sea salt; body wrap with seaweed, mud, or clay; manicure, pedicure, makeup, and waxing. The newest addition is the Rejuvenating Scalp Treatment, which provides a deep moisturization of the scalp and cellular revitalization. It includes a complete examination, exfoliation, and massage and scalp cleansing adapted to the customer's hair/scalp type.

A range of treatments complement the relaxing care at no extra charge—thermomassage baths, Japanese mattress reenergizing session, pressotherapy, Vibrosaun bed, vibromassage chair, and paraffin treatment for hands and feet. All packages include a Finnish sauna with showers and an herbal tea pause in the solarium. Combining these treatments, the spa offers a wide range of packages from half-day to five-day stays. Guests can also customize their stays with à la carte treatments. The facility also offers indoor and outdoor swimming pools, hot tubs, a racquetball court, volleyball, and an exercise room.

Accommodations: 152 single and double standard rooms with queen-size beds, and six executive rooms. The option of smoking or nonsmoking rooms is available.

Rates: Packages range from Canadian $209–1,369 per person, double occupancy

Credit Cards: AE, MC, V

Meal Plans: Three nonvegetarian meals are provided per day: a nutritionally balanced breakfast is served buffet style, lunch is healthy spa cuisine, and a low-calorie dinner is served at the table.

Services: Lifestyle evaluations, energy testing, various types of massage, aromatherapy, reflexology, polarity therapy, lymphatic drainage, colonics, algotherapy, balneotherapy, herbal wrap, body peel, facials, aquacise

Recreational Activities: Volleyball, mountain biking, nearby downhill and cross-country skiing, horseback riding, hiking

Facilities: A lodge with an atrium, a swimming pool, indoor and outdoor hot tubs, men's and women's saunas, squash and racquetball courts, a pool table, shuffleboard, and horseshoes

Disability Access: Yes

Special Notes: A wide range of packages are available: half day, 1 day, 2 day, 3 day, 4 day, and 5 days. Some insurance receipts are accepted for massage services.

Nearby Attractions: A complete aquatics park with slides, hiking and mountain-biking trails, horseback riding, several golf courses, and downhill and cross-country skiing

Nearest Airport: Monteral, Quebec

Getting There: Car rental and taxi service is available at airport. Driving from Montreal, take Highway 20 East. Exit at Lazerendry Verdun, cross Champlain Bridge; and enter Highway 10; take Exit 78; spa four miles ahead. (1 hour)

Omega Institute for Holistic Studies Maho Bay

Maho Bay Resort (Omega in the Caribbean)
150 Lake Drive
Rhinebeck, NY 12572
800/944-1001 or 845/266-4444; fax: 845/266-3769
Email: registration@eomega.org
Website: www.eomega.org

The Omega Institute, based in New York, offers its winter programs at the Maho Bay Resort on the Island of St. John in the U.S. Virgin Islands. While still participating in one of Omega's myriad personal growth and holistic health seminars, guest can lie on a massage table set up on crystal-white sands and listen to the gentle lapping of the Caribbean's aquamarine waves as they receive a deep-tissue massage. The Maho Bay Resort is located within the boundaries of the Virgin Islands National Park.

The island of St. John is one of the most serene islands in the Virgin Islands. Two-thirds of the island is protected as part of the U.S. National Park System. Finding a secluded spot on the pristine beaches will not be difficult. Maho Bay Resort is perfectly situated at the seaside. Mahogany and bay trees surround the tropical tent village, and guests are free to snorkel through coral reefs or hike to the ruins of 18th-century sugar mills.

Caribbean programs, considered an Omega learning vacation, have been offered for 23 years. Escaping the mainland's often cold and dreary winter days, is an ideal revitalizing opportunity for the body and mind. Beginning the first week of January, the eight-day, seven-night programs continue for four weeks. About seven different programs, from yoga to writing, take place each week. You can focus on one program or sample them all. Fees include tuition, meals, and accommodations. Other programs include stress reduction, shamanism, meditation, Afro-Cuban dance, and bodywork.

As at the upstate New York campus, a typical day starts with optional meditation, tai chi, yoga, dawn program movement. These early morning sessions are held by the warm Caribbean and blends in with the sounds of an awakening island. After breakfast in an open-air pavilion, workshops begin. The day usually ends at 5 P.M. then dinner is served an hour later. Omega's natural foods chefs also migrate to the Caribbean to prepare daily buffets of vegetables and tropical fruits.

Accommodations: Single and double canvas cottages with comfortable furnishings

Rates: The average weeklong course is $1,100, which includes lodging and food. A $100 weekly discount is offered to guests who wish to stay longer.

Meal Plans: Three vegetarian meals are prepared daily using natural foods and fresh tropical fruit. Fish and dairy are optional. Meals are served community style, overlooking the sea.

Services: Workshops on personal growth and spiritual development, including yoga, meditation, art, writing, dance, and stress reduction

Recreational Activities: Snorkeling, swimming, hiking

Facilities: Canvas cottages, a network of boardwalks connecting the resort to beaches, miles of marked hiking trails

Disability Access: No access

Special Notes: Guests are asked to bring a flashlight, all-terrain shoes, and bug spray. Smoking is not allowed indoors.

Nearby Attractions: Virgin Islands National Park, Annaberg Plantation, Bordeaux Mountain rainforest, catamaran trips, dining and nightlife on St. Thomas, coral reefs of Trunk Bay

Nearest Airport: St. Thomas, U.S. Virgin Islands

Getting There: Call spa for details on airport transportation. Fly to St. Thomas and take the ferry to St. John.

Hostería Las Quintas Resort Spa

Blvd. Diaz Ordaz 9, Cantarranas
c.p. 62440, Cuernavaca
Morelos, Mexico
877/QUINTAS (784-6827); fax: 888/772-7639
Email: lasquintas@hlasquintas.com
Website: www.hlasquintas.com

The Hostería Las Quintas Resort Spa is located in the colonial city of Cuernavaca. Eighty terrace rooms are nestled throughout the walled estate property, which includes 80,000 square feet of lush gardens, with a variety of exotic flowers and trees in harmony with the resort's classic Colonial architecture. Elegant, yet casual facilities offer enjoyment and spa rejuvenation.

A typical stay begins with a medical and fitness evaluation to create an individual program based on your specific needs. A fitness consultant then provides you with an exercise routine in the modern gym or an aquatic workout in one of the two heated pools surrounded by tropical gardens. Once you finish your exercise routine, you begin your treatments, perhaps starting with a steam bath or sauna, followed by a high-pressure cold shower. Then you are given an exfoliating body scrub with natural products such as oatmeal, apricot, honey, and salt. If you feel stressed and need a detoxification treatment, you may try the fangotherapy wrap, which is a full-body mud mask using mud from the Dead Sea, or an algae seaweed wrap, which remineralizes your body. If you simply need relaxation and pampering, you may want a Swedish massage with aromatherapy to help you relax and destress, or a shiatsu massage. After finishing your body treatment, you are taken to the facial treatment area, where one of the licensed cosmetologists evaluates your skin and suggests a treatment according to your needs, such as hydrating, anti-age, acne, nutrition, or alpha-hydroxy acid peeling. Your day is complete with a visit to the full-service hair and nail salon.

Eco-tours are available departing from the hotel at 9 A.M. each morning and returning at approximately 2 P.M. in time for lunch and afternoon spa services. A different tour is offered each day of the week, including visits to the Pyramids of Tepoztlan; Las Estacas Natural River, where many movies such as *Tarzan* have been filmed; a city tour of Taxco, which has hundreds of silver shops; the archeological site of Xochicalco; and a city tour of Cuernavaca.

Accommodations: 80 individually decorated terrace rooms include ceiling fans, remote color television with U.S. cable service, a service bar, and a safety box. Some rooms have a hot tub, a sitting area, or a fireplace.

Rates: Two-night Stress Relief is $665 single, $559 double; four-night Supreme Pampering is $1,247 single, $1,035 double; four-night Eco-Fitness is $1,403 single, $1,191 double; seven-night Eco-Fitness is $2,269 single, $1,898 double; seven-night Healthy Lifestyle is $2,119 single, $1,748 double. Other packages are also available.

Credit Cards: AE, MC, V

Meal Plans: The hotel restaurant serves regional and international spa cuisine, including buffet brunches with Mexican trio music.

Services: Full spa services, including massage, facials, body scrubs and wraps, and a salon with a variety of hair and nail services; eco-tours; and daily classes, such as yoga, tai chi, aerobics, aquaerobics, latin dancercise, Spanish, arts and crafts, and meditation

Recreational Activities: Hiking, swimming

Facilities: Two heated swimming pools, an outdoor hot tub, a sauna, two boutiques, nine conference rooms, a full-service spa and salon, and a gym

Disability Access: No access

Special Notes: "Survival Spanish" classes are available for guests.

Nearest Airport: Mexico City, Mexico

Getting There: Contact spa for details on airport transportation. Spa is located in the colonial city of Cuernavaca, 53 miles from the Mexico City airport. (1 hour)

Hotel Qualton Club and Spa Vallarta

Km 2.5 Av. las Palmas, Fco Medina Ascencio
Puerto Vallarta, Jalisco, Mexico 48300
52/332-44-44; fax 52/332-44-447
Email: qualton@pvnet.com.mx
Website: www.qualton.com/mexico/vallarta/
index.htm

Located in a seaside complex of one of Mexico's most cultured cities, Hotel Qualton Club and Spa Vallarta provides an ideal mixture of relaxation and enjoyment. Once you check into the hotel, you become a member with full membership benefits, which include the daily schedule of free classes, such as yoga, step aerobics, water aerobics, a tennis clinic, and a full circuit of strength training equipment. Fitness evaluations and medical consultations by professional staff who test your aerobic capacity, strength, flexibility, and blood pressure are also available before you start an exercise regime.

The spa offers a variety of massages, facials, herbal wraps, and other salon treatments in packages or à la carte. Body treatments include exfoliation with salt and loofah, herbal mud treatment, marine algae body wrap, and stone therapy massage, to name a few. In addition, chiropractic sessions, acupuncture, and Bach flower remedies are also available by appointment. After a day of pampering, venture down Puerto Vallarta's cobblestone streets, with red tile roofs, and flowering bougainvilleas that cascade from balconies. In the center of town, facing the Bay of Banderas, stands the Church of The Lady of Guadalupe with its unique crown that is an important symbol of Puerto Vallarta. While enjoying the night life, it is common to hear the Mariachi playing in town.

This all-inclusive hotel is large, with 14 stories in the main building and two adjacent five-story buildings, but somehow the garden atmosphere creates a quiet, self-contained complex. Most of its 218 rooms have an ocean view with balcony or terrace with a king-size bed or two double beds. All meals, drinks, and nightly entertainment at the hotel come with the daily rate membership. Three on-premise restaurants serve international cuisine. A favorite experience for those who love the ocean is to dine at the beach restaurant.

Accommodations: 212 rooms and four suites; air conditioning, safe deposit box, direct dial telephone and satellite TV with remote control.

Rates: $75 daily per person for double occupancy, which includes three meals; $90 per person for single occupancy; $60 per person for triple occupancy.

Credit Cards: AE, D, MC, V

Meal Plans: Three meals are served daily either buffet or à la carte, plus afternoon snacks and beverages are provided.

Facilities: A gym with 24 weight stations, a swimming pool, a sauna, a hot tub, a steam bath, a spa, and tennis courts

Disability Access: Rooms with handicap access and non smoking are available.

Services: Massage and spa treatments, yoga, meditation, chiropractic sessions, acupuncture, Bach floral therapy, scuba lessons, step aerobics, water aerobics, and a tennis clinic

Recreation Activities: Tennis; golf; horseback riding; scuba diving; non-motorized watersports

Special Notes: Hotel guests receive complimentary spa admission; Puerto Vallarta enjoys a pleasant sunny climate all year round.

Nearby Attractions: Downtown discos, night clubs, shopping, restaurants, and the beach

Nearest Airport: Puerto Vallarta, Mexico

Getting There: Contact spa for details on airport transportation. Located in the hotel zone of Puerto Vallarta about 10 minutes from the airport and 10 minutes from downtown.

Maya Tulum Retreat and Resort

U.S. Contact:
P.O. Box 1496
Conyers, GA 30012
888/515-4580 or 770/483-0238; fax: 770/785-9260
Email: reservations@mayantulum.com
Website: www.mayantulum.com

Maya Tulum Retreat and Resort is located on the Caribbean seashore of Mexico's Yucatan Peninsula. Guests sleep in simple cabanas built in traditional Mayan style blended into tropical gardens with beautiful views of the sea and jungle. Set up with a round palapa yoga room which faces the ocean, this retreat center hosts several yoga teachers and other weeklong programs throughout the year such as Reike, Continuum Movement and Transformational therapy. There is a daily Yoga and meditation program open to all guests whether they are participating in a group program or not. Also offered at Maya Tulum are individual sessions in various types of bodywork, spa treatments and traditional Mayan healings.

The resort is located at the entrance of Sian Ka'an Biosphere Preserve (Mayan for "where the sky is born"), a protected area with miles of empty beaches, rainforest, mangroves, and vast lagoons. It is home to hundreds of species including birds, peccaries, tapirs, alligators, manatees, iguanas and sea turtles. At The resort itself there is a wonderful stretch of white sand beach. The combination of tropical jungle, the Caribbean seashore and Maya Tulums lovely thatch roof cabanas in this private setting make this retreat an ideal place for those who appreciate nature, healing and relaxation.

Accommodations: Guests stay in cabanas that are built in the traditional Maya style blended into tropical gardens. Each cabana has views of the sea and jungle. Three styles of cabanas are available: standard, deluxe, and super deluxe.

Rates: Standard $60–70; deluxe $70–85; and super deluxe $90–130, meals, yoga, and healing programs are not included.

Credit Cards: AE, MC, V

Meal Plans: Buffet-style meals. Three vegetarian meals a day with fresh fish, seafood, and lobster served à la carte.

Services: Treatments include reflexology, shiatsu, facials, body scrubs and wraps, and traditional Mayan healing.

Recreational Activities: Swimming, snorkeling, diving, turtle watching, and boat trips

Facilities: Two meditation/group meeting rooms for various size workshops, a restaurant, spa treatment rooms, sleeping cabanas, and a small boutique

Disability Access: No access

Special Notes: Caguama turtles nest on nearby beaches in May, June, and July. Please do not touch them or their eggs.

Nearby Attractions: Mayan archaeological sites; Pyramids of Coba

Nearest Airport: Cancun, Mexico

Getting There: Tulum is located 1.5–2 hours south of the airport. Airport transportation is available through the spa, $195 RT up to three passengers. (1.5-2 hours)

Punta Serena

Km. 20 Carretera Federal 200
Tenacatita, Jalisco, Mexico
C.P. 48989
800/551-2558 or 52/335-150-20; fax: 52/335-150-50
Email: info@puntaserena.com
Website: www.puntaserena.com

Perched high atop a mountain in Pacific Mexico overlooking Tenacatita Bay and the surrounding tropical jungle landscape, lies Punta Serena (serenity point), a refuge for relaxation and renewal. Punta Serena is an adults-only holistic retreat that provides a comfortable and nurturing environment for rest, introspection, and restored wholeness.

A stay at Punta Serena includes meals and snacks; use of the hot tubs, the swimming pool, the sauna, and the gym; spiritual awareness programs such as yoga, tai chi, chi kung, and chakra work; guided daily meditation sessions; health and natural healing classes; herbal remedies; the experience of a Temazeal native Mexican sweat lodge and purification ceremony; a river cruise through the surrounding jungle; and horseback riding along the beach. All this is offered by a team of dedicated holistic teachers and a professional staff of warm, caring people. Massage and bodywork are also available for additional fees.

Guests at Punta Serena stay in spacious bungalows nestled in the foothills of the Sierra Madre mountains. The sound of the surf breaking against the rocky shore and the songs of exotic birds can be heard throughout the retreat setting, which promotes rest, introspection, and restored wholeness. For those who want more lively entertainment, a variety of evening shows at a nearby resort are complimentary to all Punta Serena guests.

Accommodations: 21 smoke-free rooms, some of which are in spacious two- and three-bedroom villas with balconies and/or terraces

Rates: Vary with packages. The three-night Rejuvenation Program is $525 single, $435 double; the five-night Rejuvenation Program is $875 single, $725 double; the seven-night Rejuvenation Program is $1,225 single, $1,015 double. Rates are reduced in the off-season from April 23 through December 23.

Credit Cards: AE, DC, MC, V

Meal Plans: An open-air restaurant serves a healthful menu and vegetarian cuisine. A juice bar serves snacks, fruit juices, and drinks throughout the day.

Services: Massage, acupressure, reflexology, reiki, fitness programs, guided meditation, yoga, tai chi, chi kung, and chakra work

Recreational Activities: Horseback riding, tennis, swimming, hiking, and a jungle tour through the mangroves on a boat

Facilities: A swimming pool, private beach, hot tubs, library, gym, sauna, a Temazeal (Mexican sweat lodge); meditation areas, meeting rooms, health store; boutique, and tennis courts

Disability Access: No access

Special Notes: Punta Senena is an adults-only retreat. Swimsuits are optional in the hot tubs, massage area, swimming pool, and beach. Tenacatita Bay is a good place to spot dolphins in the waters offshore.

Nearest Airports: Manzanillo and Puerto Vallarta, Mexico

Getting There: Contact spa for details on airport transportation. Punta Senena is north of Tenacatita Bay on Mexico's western coastline 45 minutes from the Manzanillo airport and 2.5 hours from Puerto Vallarta.

Rancho La Puerta

U.S. Contact: P.O. Box 463057
Escondido, CA 92046
800/443-7565 or 760/744-4222; fax: 760/744-5007
Email: reservations@rancholapuerta.com
Website: www.rancholapuerta.com

Ranch La Puerta is known as the world's first fitness spa. The resort was built on 300 acres of unspoiled rolling countryside at 1,800 feet altitude and offers an ideal year-round climate, with beautiful sunny days accompanied by a pleasant prevailing breeze. With beautifully landscaped gardens in a valley set at the foot of the sacred Mount Kuchumaa, the ranch is designed in the style of a Mexican village with brick and tile villas that can accommodate up to 150 guests.

This spacious resort offers weekly programs, which include morning hikes, spa treatments, aerobics, weight training, yoga, and other mind-body activities. In addition to a fully equipped yoga room, the ranch has three outdoor swimming pools, five whirlpool-jet therapy pools, three saunas, six lighted tennis courts, six aerobic gyms, weight training equipment, and a volleyball court. Separate women's and men's health centers are used for massages, herbal wraps, and other spa services, including private hot tubs and steam rooms.

Guests arrive on Saturday for a minimum seven-day stay, which permits them to follow a progressive program, with each day's classes increasing in intensity. During the summer months (June to September), the ranch offers unique focus weeks on mind-body-spirit fitness, with the added bonus of guest instructors who offer their teaching expertise for that week. Each week offers a different teacher and focus, such as yoga and meditation, African dance, soul motion movement, Feldenkrais, Pilates, and water exercise, to name a few. All regular ranch classes and programs are also underway during these special sessions, so guests get to choose whether to delve into the week's specialty activities.

Accommodations: Single-level studio ranchera rooms, one-bedroom haciendas and villa studios, and two-bedroom villa suites are available, all with private baths.

Rates: $1,500–2,500 per person per week depending on the season and type of accommodations chosen

Credit Cards: V only

Meal Plans: The diet at Rancho La Puerta is lacto-ovo vegetarian, with fresh fish served twice weekly, plenty of greens, legumes, whole grains, and other fiber. Food is raised in organic gardens on the property.

Services: Facials, herbal wraps, massages, and other spa services; a full-scale salon for hair-styling, manicures, pedicures, and so forth; 60 classes offered each week, including aerobics, step, weight room exercise, water exercise, walking clinics, nutrition talks, African dance, tai chi, yoga, and more

Recreational Activities: Wonderful hiking in the mountains and lowlands

Facilities: Three swimming pools, six tennis courts, hot tubs, saunas, and steam baths, six aerobic gyms, a weight training gym, a volleyball court, men's and women's health centers for spa services, and a library

Disability Access: Yes; full access is provided for people with disabilities.

Special Notes: Complimentary transportation is provided from the San Diego airport.

Nearby Attractions: A 300-acre paradise of land for nature lovers and hikers.

Nearest Airport: San Diego, CA

Getting There: Complimentary airport transportation is provided on Saturdays only, departing the airport at 8 A.M., 10 A.M., 12:15 P.M., and 2:45 P.M. Car rental is also available; additional insurance and/or restrictions may apply for crossing U.S. border. Driving from San Diego, take I-5 south to the Highway 94 exit. Drive east on Highway 94 for 40 miles to Tecate turnoff (Country Route 188); right onto Route 188; drive 2 miles to Tecate International Border (open daily from 6 A.M. to midnight); cross border and proceed to 2nd stop light, opposite town plaza; turn right and drive west 3 miles to spa entrance on your right. (1 hour)

Rio Caliente Hot Springs Spa

U.S. Contact: **Marion Lewis**
Spa Vacations, Ltd.
P.O. Box 897
Millbrae, CA 94030
800/200-2927 or 650/615-9543; fax: 650/615-0601
Email: RioCal@aol.com
Website: www.riocaliente.com

Beyond the tiny village called La Primavera, in the subtropical forest of a Sierra Madre mountain valley, flows a hot mineral-water river that is channeled into the warm mineral pools of Rio Caliente Spa. The steam rising from the natural river—whose volcanic water has been used for thousands of years for curative purposes—is easily visible. Situated on 24 acres, Rio Caliente Spa provides four mineral pools and an Aztec steam room fed by volcanically heated water. The land was once a spiritual center for the Huichol Indians (the healing people) and now is the home of this spa, which offers overnight accommodations, spa treatments, yoga, hiking, and wonderful vegetarian food.

Guests sleep in brick and adobe *casitas* (cottages), which are scattered around the 24-acre spa. The atmosphere is casual and unpretentious. At 5,000 feet altitude, temperatures stay moderate year-round, ranging between 70–85 degrees Fahrenheit during the day, and dropping a bit cooler at night. The property has a sprawling, spacious feel, with tall trees, free-ranging horses, and a vegetable garden. The long, narrow valley and surrounding forest provide opportunities for many different levels of hiking, from virtually flat walking to gradual climbing to vigorous hiking trails, which connect ridges and canyons. The spa also offers horseback riding, swimming, a sauna, mineral baths, massages, facials, muds packs, and plenty of relaxation in the sun or shade.

Accommodations: Fifty guest rooms occupy both an upper level where the dining room is and a lower level by the pools and steam room. Each cottage has a private bath/shower, single and double beds, and a fireplace. The rooms are simple, clean, and decorated with native crafts. Windows look onto the spa and surrounding valley.

Rates: Nightly rates begin at $92 (plus tax) per person for double occupancy, which includes accommodations, meals, mineral baths, yoga, and hiking. A seven-day package is available between April and December for $675 (plus tax) per person for double occupancy, which includes accommodations, meals, mineral baths, yoga, hiking, one mud bath, two massages, and a shopping trip to Guadalajara.

Credit Cards: Not accepted

Meal Plans: Three vegetarian meals are served daily in an "all-you-can-eat" buffet style. Meals are grain-based, complex carbohydrates; low-fat cuisine that includes fresh fruits and vegetables; optional dairy products; and fresh homemade baked bread and muffins. Drinking water is purified.

Services: Massages, facials, mud wraps, water aerobics, and yoga

Recreational Activities: Hiking, swimming, horseback riding,

Facilities: A 24-acre resort including 49 guest rooms and two suites, a dining room, pools, massage therapy rooms, a gym, and a yoga room

Disability Access: No access

Special Notes: Smoking is allowed outside only.

Nearby Attractions: Transportation is provided to nearby sightseeing opportunities, including shopping tours to Guadalajara, Talquepaque, Tonala, Chapala, and Tequila.

Nearest Airport: Guadalajara, Mexico

Getting There: Taxi service is available at airport. Contact spa for additional details on airport transportation. Located in a national forest in the Primavera Valley 25 miles outside of Guadalajara. (.5 hour)

Sanoviv Health Retreat

Km. 39, Carretera Libre
Rosarito Beach, Baja California, Mexico
800/SANOVIV (726-6848); fax: 801/954-7666
Website: www.sanoviv.com

Gracing a bluff at the edge of Bahia del Descanso (The Bay of Rest) in Baja California, Sanoviv (meaning "healthy life") combines alternative healing therapies with world-class spa amenities, luxurious guest suites, and a professional medical staff. After a fitness assessment, a personalized treatment plan is developed for each guest. In addition, a European-style spa offers a range of hydrotherapies and massage techniques, as well as toxin-free salon amenities.

Nutrition for detoxification and healing is a core concept at Sanoviv. Central to the Sanoviv philosophy is the belief that the body has the power to heal itself when relieved of its accumulated toxic influences and provided with the proper environment. From the triple-filtered water system, providing cell culture–grade water, to the specially made, untreated fibers in the carpeting and fabrics, every effort has been made to create surroundings that support good health, and no expense has been spared to create a toxin-free environment.

Seven residential health programs are offered, which focus on cleansing and detoxification, diagnostics, medical, oral healthcare, and spa treatments. All guests receive individualized, compassionate care from physicians, counselors, massage therapists, detoxification specialists, and others, regardless of which program they choose. Education is a strong component at Sanoviv, with classes and lectures offered in each program. Guests leave with the information and inspiration needed for making positive, health-enhancing life choices.

Accommodations: 47 luxurious oceanfront suites with private balconies

Rates: Programs vary in cost. The Sanoviv Getaway for three nights and two days is $995. The Cleansing and Spa Detoxification program for two weeks is $5,100. The Medical and Spa program is $9,500 for two weeks or $13,500 for three weeks. Rates include accommodations, meals, therapies.

Credit Cards: MC, V

Meal Plans: The standard diet consists of 90 percent raw and 10 percent cooked vegetables, fruits, nuts, sprouts, gluten-free grains, and sea vegetables.

Services: Various massage techniques; reflexology; shiatsu; watsu; herbal wraps; seaweed therapy, colon hydrotherapy, infrared sauna, facials, Kneippe hydrotherapy, meditation classes, and health and nutrition education classes

Recreational Activities: Swimming, water aerobics, walking, jogging, fitness center, movies

Facilities: Meditation rooms, training kitchen, and a library. house 47 oceanfront guest suites, a dining room, 20 health assessment, diagnostic, and therapy rooms, a licensed hospital facility, a laboratory, biological dentistry, a 120-seat conference center, a fitness center, thermal seawater therapy pools, and a world-class spa.

Disability Access: Yes; full access is available.

Special Notes: Please call for a detailed description of the programs offered or review "Programs" online.

Nearby Attractions: Fox Studios; shopping; golf courses

Nearest Airport: San Diego, CA

Getting There: Spa provides complimentary transportation from San Diego airport, the Amtrak station, or a hotel in the San Diego area. Reservations recommended. (.5 hour)

Sanoviv Health Retreat **225**

Glossary

acupressure—An ancient Chinese system of healing that involves applying pressure to various meridians, or energy points, located throughout the body. Older than acupuncture, the technique is similar to the natural response to hold a place in the body that may be aching, wounded, or tense. Acupressure is used to relieve tension-related ailments in preventive health care.

acupuncture—An ancient Chinese system of healing, similar to acupressure, that involves pressing small needles into various meridians, or energy points, located throughout the body. These energy points can be compared to rivers that flow through the body to irrigate and nourish tissues. Obstructions in the flow of the "rivers" have the effect of a dam, restricting energy in one part of the body and causing backups in others. By stimulating the meridians with needles, the obstructions are dissolved. Consequently, acupuncture can help the body's internal organs correct imbalances in energy production, digestion, and nutrient absorption.

aikido—Japanese martial art of self-defense employing locks and holds and utilizing the principle of nonresistance to cause an opponent's momentum to work against him

Alexander technique—A system of bodywork developed in the late 1800s by Shakespearean actor F. M. Alexander, who discovered he could use his breath to change muscular responses. The technique is based on the practical study of the relationship between mind and body and is used to correct imbalances between the head and back. During sessions, a therapist uses gentle, noninvasive touch to increase the client's awareness, observation, and attention. Clients are also encouraged to observe the thought processes and tensions found within their daily lives.

applied kinesiology—The practice of determining health imbalances in organs and muscles by stimulating or relaxing specific muscle groups.

aromatherapy—Flower oil essences used to treat physical and emotional imbalances. The essences are either inhaled or used in massage oil, body wraps, and baths.

Ayurveda—An ancient Indian system of healing that involves determining the specific body type of an individual and eliminating toxins and prescribing a balanced health regimen. *Ayurveda* means "science of life."

Bach flower essences—A system of healing developed by Dr. Edward Bach, a homeopath and physician. Dr. Bach created a system of 38 flower remedies designed to treat the person, not the ailment. The remedies address emotional imbalances that may block a positive state of mind, which is considered essential by Dr. Bach for healing.

balneotherapy—Any healing treatment that specifically involves immersion in baths, whether in ozonated whirlpools, geothermal and mineral springs, or ocean water.

bioenergetics—A form of psychotherapy developed by psychologist Alexander Lowen, author of *Language of the Body*. The technique places emphasis on grounding oneself, breathing properly, and understanding individual character structure. Deep breathing, massage, and bioenergetic (life energy) movements are used to help the patient develop self-awareness and restore vibrancy in body and life.

biofeedback—A system of healing that trains a person to change and control physical reactions to pain and stress. The technique involves using a computer monitor to display tension levels, through which patients learn muscle awareness and control. During sessions, clients learn postural training and techniques for muscle control. Biofeedback is used to treat a variety of chronic ailments, including stress, headaches, and asthma.

body wraps—A treatment that involves lathering the body with algae, clay, mud, or a botanical mixture and sealing in the mixture with heated towels or plastic sheets. The relaxing treatment is used to pull toxins from the body. In the case of herbal wraps, herb-soaked heated linens may be used.

Breema massage—A method of body-work imported from the small Kurdish village of Breemava, used to restore vitality through a standardized set of movements that express a connection with the Earth. During a Breema massage, the client lies fully clothed on a padded floor while a therapist performs a series of rhythmic movements. The technique is also used to increase physical health, balance energy, and release tension.

Californian massage—Very soft brushing and kneading movements used to activate the blood circulation.

centropic integration (CI)—A body-focused approach to psychotherapy. The technique is based on the theory that unhealthy life experiences are stored in the body's tissues, often contributing to dysfunctional life patterns and disease. Each CI ses-

sion lasts two hours and is broken into two phases. Phase 1 can include reviewing the patient's medical history, taking personal histories and histories of how the patient is facing current life situations, examining aspects of the individual's life that have the most meaning and depth of feeling, choosing a desired outcome of current situations, and understanding what the body is "telling" the mind. Phase 2 can involve sustained acupressure, listening to evocative music, breathwork, and verbal emotional facilitation.

chakras—Seven major energy points throughout the human body. The Root Chakra found at the base of the spine is white and represents the highest spiritual level. The Sex or Hara Chakra is purple and based in emotions and sexuality. The Solar Plexus Chakra is blue-violet or gold and based in personal power and metabolic energy. The Heart Chakra, considered to be the most important, is rose-pink and based in love, associations, relations, and compassion. The Throat Chakra is blue and based in communication and creativity. The Third Eye, or Brow Chakra, is green and based in intuition and imagination. The Crown Chakra is yellow and based in knowledge, information, and understanding.

chelation therapy—The injection of a solution containing ethylenediaminetetraacetic acid (EDTA), vitamins, and minerals to relieve the body of heavy metals picked up through the normal course of everyday living. EDTA is approved by the Food and Drug Administration (FDA) to treat lead and heavy-metal toxicity, as evidenced by the U.S. Navy's use of chelation to treat lead poisoning.

chi nei tsang—A holistic approach to massage therapy developed by Chinese

Taoist monks, who used it to detoxify, strengthen, and refine their bodies. The technique integrates physical, mental, spiritual, and emotional aspects and addresses all of the main vital systems—digestion, respiration, lymphatic, nervous, endocrine, urinary, reproductive, integumentary, muscular, and the acupuncture meridian system. Today the practice is used to stimulate the immune system, provide deep detoxification of the body, and help overcome addictions. Practitioners focus mainly on the abdomen with deep and gentle touch to train internal organs to work more efficiently.

Chinese auriculotherapy—An acupuncture-related system of diagnosis and treatment that utilizes the outer ear, also known as the auricle. This modern technique was renewed in France in the 1950s, when Dr. Paul Nogier founded the French method. The Chinese then studied the French system and greatly expanded the technique. Auriculotherapy is used to determine food, drug, and other sensitivities, as well as to treat addiction. It is also used to determine the need for vitamins, supplements, herbs, and medications.

Chinese medicine—An ancient system of healing dating back approximately 4,000 years that combines the use of herbs, diet, massage, therapeutic exercise, meditation, and acupuncture. The practitioner looks for patterns to indicate the source of an imbalance and considers the effects of personal and environmental factors on the individual's health. The Chinese system emphasizes prevention and maintaining optimal health, which is defined as the proper flow of chi, or qi, along the body's internal energy meridians.

chiropractic—A system of bodywork based on the idea that disease results from a lack of normal nerve function. The chiropractor tries to relieve stress and pressure on the nervous system by manually manipulating the spinal segments or individual vertebra. The technique is used to treat back pain, headaches, and general pain caused by injury or chronic disorders.

colonic therapy—An ancient method of healing based on the theory that a congested colon contains stagnant wastes that pollute the entire body. In most cases, a diet of whole foods is combined with a series of warm-water or herbal enemas to remove fecal waste.

complementary medicine—Complements to traditional Western medicine, incorporating the ancient arts of acupuncture, Chinese herbal medicine, and other non-Western approaches to healing.

craniosacral therapy—A system of bodywork used to treat mental and physical imbalances that is based on the idea that the body "remembers" emotional or physical trauma. Breathing exercises are combined with the gentle manipulation of skull and pelvic bones. The technique is ideal for injuries, traumas, and chronic pain but may also be used to enhance the body's general state of health.

cupping—Also known as "the horn method" in ancient China. The technique is used to draw blood to the surface to produce a counterirritant and stimulate chi. One or more small cups made of glass, metal, or wood are placed on a relatively flat body surface after a partial vacuum has been created in them through heat. The cups are left on the body for 5-10 minutes.

Do-In—A self-help method of healing, otherwise known as self-acupressure massage, that incorporates body awareness, stretching, and breathing. Do-In focuses on vigorous techniques that stimulate the body's energy channels, or meridians.

electroacuscope—A computer-controlled device designed to operate either as an independent unit or in conjunction with a personal computer. The machine, which has both diagnostic and treatment capabilities, is used in physical therapy, rehabilitation, and preventive medicine.

energy medicine—A diagnostic system of healing that employs a screening device to determine imbalances in the body's energy levels.

Enneagram—A nine-pointed, starlike figure believed to have originated with the ancient Sarmoun Brotherhood of Sufis, who used it as part of their mystical training. The figure represents the relationships among interacting elements of various personality patterns. Each pattern possesses a character that perceives the world and self in a fundamentally unique way and that has both a positive and a negative side. The points are (1) serenity or anger, (2) humility or pride, (3) truth or deceit, (4) equanimity or envy, (5) detachment or avarice, (6) courage or fear, (7) temperance or gluttony, (8) forbearance or lust, and (9) action or sloth.

ethnoherbology—A term coined by Lynne Ihlstrom, a holistic psychotherapist and founder of Peaceways. Ethnoherbology involves the study of the edible and medicinal plants of a specific region, combined with a study of the cultures that used them and in which ways.

4-hand massage—Choreography of massage maneuvers performed by two therapists. Their synchronicity will take you to a deeper level of relaxation.

fango—A type of clay mud from the hot springs at Battaglio, Italy, used in body wraps and other external therapeutic applications.

fasting—Allows the body to rest from the digestion process and eliminate toxins. Fasting is recommended for a variety of symptoms, including colds and headaches. Anyone considering a fast should conduct extensive research or consult a physician.

Feldenkrais—A system of bodywork developed by Russian physicist Moshe Feldenkrais in the 1940s. The technique is based on the theory that the way an individual perceives him or herself is central to the way he or she physically carries him or herself. Through gentle movement and directed attention, the client improves movement and enhances the overall function of body, spirit, and mind. Clients are encouraged to expand their self-image through movement sequences that bring attention to parts of the self that may ordinarily be left unnoticed.

fomentation (sometimes spelled "foomentation")—Involves applying hot, moist substances, such as an herb-soaked linen cloth, to specific areas of the body to ease pain.

Gestalt—A therapy used by psychologists and counselors that emphasizes the inner experience of being and heightened sensory awareness through stimulus, perception, and response. "Now" is emphasized in Gestalt therapy, as evidenced by the fact that therapists do not focus on the client's past. Rather, the therapist deals directly with elements that comprise the "here and now." The client is encouraged to develop a more focused awareness and to fully experience and appreciate his or her complete self.

guided imagery—A process that involves relaxing the body muscle by muscle, concentrating on breathing, and visualizing positive scenarios. Guided imagery is particularly useful for people who are prone to stress and anxiety.

harmonics—The study of the physical properties and characteristics of musical sound. Also, a curative method of chanting, developed and practiced by Tibetan monks, in which particular sounds are associated with specific physical energy centers.

hatha yoga—A system of yoga that focuses on health through practice of asanas (postures), breath work, diet, positive thinking, relaxation, and meditation.

Hellerwork—A system of bodywork developed by Joseph Heller, a student of the late Ida Rolf. The technique is designed to realign the body and release chronic tension and stress. It consists of a series of one-hour sessions of deep-tissue bodywork and movement reeducation. Verbal dialogue is used in addition to hands-on therapy to help the client become more aware of emotional stress and how it relates to physical tension. For example, a physical manifestation of depression may be a sunken chest.

herbal wrap—A treatment in which moisture, heat, and herbs penetrate the skin while the body is wrapped in hot linens, plastic sheets, and blankets; the wrap is intended to promote muscle relaxation and eliminate toxins.

holoenergetics—A psychotherapeutic form of energy healing that, literally translated, means "to heal with energy of the whole." The technique, developed by Dr. Leonard Laskow, author of *Healing with Love,* is based on five premises: (1) separation is an illusion; (2) to maintain this illusion requires energy; (3) physical or mental illness can result from consuming this energy; (4) release from illusion liberates energy; and (5) healing is the gradual result of eliminating the illusion of separation. Throughout the session, clients are encouraged to recognize the source of their illness, come to terms with the truth of this source, release it, replace dysfunctional patterns with healthy ones, and align their bodies with the positive life force within the universe.

holotropic breathwork—A self-exploration and healing technique developed by psychiatrist Dr. Stanislov Grof and his wife, Christina Grof, a transpersonal teacher. *Holotropic* literally means "moving toward wholeness." The method is intended to activate a "nonordinary" state of consciousness in order to activate the psyche's innate healing potential. The technique involves sustained breathing and relaxation exercises, evocative music, focused energy work, and mandala drawing.

hydrotherapy—A system of bodywork that involves the external use of water, such as showers or mineral soaks. Treatments typically take place in a specially designed hydrotherapy tub equipped with 16 or more jets aimed at targeting the body's pressure points. It can also involve an underwater massage with a therapist manipulating a high-pressure hose. The treatment is particularly beneficial for people experiencing arthritis.

iridology—A diagnostic tool that involves close scrutiny of the iris to determine the patient's health, either through a special camera or through face-to-face examination.

jin shin jyutsu—A system of bodywork developed in Japan by Jiro Murai and based on the flow of qi, or life energy, throughout the body. Combinations of energy points are held for one minute or longer. Jin shin do and jin shin acupressure are slight variations of the original jin shin jyutsu.

journaling—The habit of regularly maintaining a journal, which is often recommended by counselors as a therapeutic tool. The benefits of journaling include increased creativity and the clarity to reflect on and grow from experiences.

kiatsu massage—An acupressure massage that utilizes life energy, or ki, also known as chi or qi.

Kneipp—Developed in Austria during the 1800s by Father Sebastian Kneipp, whose remedies recognize a natural lifestyle and emphasize the five basic elements of hydrotherapy, medicinal plants, diet, exercise, and lifestyle as a means to health. Father Kneipp's healing methods have evolved into the term "kneippism," which also indicates cold-warm-cold water stimulation.

kur—A series of spa treatments involving the use of natural ingredients and thermal baths received in combination with regenerating activities, which can include cultural history and the fine arts as well as health and wellness lectures.

lap pool—A pool with lanes for swimming laps.

LomiLomi—A system of bodywork based on ancient Hawaiian healing traditions. The therapist uses long, broad strokes and rhythmical rocking techniques.

macrobiotics—The study of the natural laws of change for the purpose of life extension. Macrobiotic principles are thousands of years old, but George Ohsawa is the father of the modern-day practice. Ohsawa's teachings promote nutrition and healing based on the fundamental belief that humans are designed to be healthy. Through eating and living in as natural a way as possible, one becomes and remains well. "Natural" includes a diet based on grains and fresh vegetables and limiting overprocessed foods.

marma point therapy—An Ayurvedic healing technique that involves applying medicated warm oil to specific points on the face that are key areas of circulation, otherwise known as marma points. The points are similar to the acupuncture points described in Chinese traditional medicine, but they are juncture points rather than points along a meridian. The facial points are massaged, then oil is spread across the entire face in broad strokes. Afterward, a heated towel is placed over the face. The technique is intended to release bodily toxins.

meditation—Literally hundreds of forms of meditation exist that cross all religious boundaries. In general, meditation involves focusing on a specific spoken or written idea to bring the mind's attention acutely into the present.

Moor mud—Mud taken from a 2,000-year-old Neydhardting Moor in Austria that contains more than 700 herbs and plants. The mud is used in baths, masks, soaps, and even in special mud drinks. The health spa adjacent to the Moor has a three-year waiting list.

moxabustion—A technique used to stimulate chi and characterized by the burning of a counterirritant, usually from dried leaves of the common mugwort or the wormwood tree.

Moxas are attached to an acupuncture needle, then placed directly on the skin in the form of small cones. The cones can also be placed on a thin layer of ginger.

mud wrap—A body treatment using warm mud to cleanse pores and lift impurities.

myotherapy—A technique used to relax muscle spasms, improve circulation, and alleviate pain. The method was developed by Bonnie Prudden, an internationally recognized fitness and health pioneer and author of *Pain Erasure the Bonnie Prudden Way*. In myotherapy, pain is viewed as a valuable warning tool, particularly acute and chronic pain that is closely tied to emotional stress. Clients learn to seek out and diffuse trigger points within the muscles that are responsible for a variety of aches, pains, and disabilities. Exercises designed to reeducate the muscles are also a part of the therapy.

nature therapy—Relaxing activities in nature, including walking, swimming, mineral soaks, viewing wildlife, and gardening.

naturopathic medicine—A system of healing disease that emphasizes natural remedies and treating the whole person—physical, emotional, spiritual, and social. Naturopathic physicians look for the root cause of disease rather than treating symptoms. Nontoxic remedies are prescribed on the basis of the theory that "like treats like."

neural therapy—A system of healing that involves the injection of anesthetics to relieve short-circuits in the body's electrical network. Neural therapy is used to treat a wide variety of chronic ailments.

neurolinguistic programming (NLP)—A system of healing that helps people recognize and change unconscious thought patterns and behavior to aid the overall healing process. It has been successful with a variety of chronic illnesses, including AIDS, cancer, migraines, and arthritis.

neuromuscular therapy—See trigger-point therapy.

Ohashiatsu—A method of centering touch developed by Ohashi, founder of the Ohashi Institute and author of several books, including *The Ohashi Bodywork Book*. The technique involves touch, exercise, meditation, and Eastern methods of healing that integrate mind, body, and spirit. Rather than focusing on specific acupuncture points, the therapist tries to sense and work with the overall flow of energy throughout the body and consequently balance it to activate the body's natural impulse to heal itself.

osteopathy—A system of healing based on the idea that disease results from structural imbalances in the tissues and that balance can be restored by manipulating specific areas of the body. Osteopathy treatments are supported by medicine, proper diet, and other therapies, which may include surgery.

panchakarma—A type of Ayurvedic massage therapy that uses warm, herbalized oils and aims to restore balance to the body.

par course—A walking trail equipped with several stations for exercise at various points.

permaculture—The term combines the words "permanent" and "agriculture." Tasmanian Bill Mollison coined the phrase in 1972 as a result of having no other word to describe a system of agriculture that does not deplete the land or endure without constant human interaction. The goal of permaculture is to create sustainable human settlements. Its principles are explained in Mollison's book *An Introduction to Permaculture.*

Pilates method—A series of controlled movements that engage both body and mind, developed by physical trainer Joseph Pilates in the 1920s. The method focuses on improved flexibility and strength without building bulk.

polarity therapy—A system of bodywork develop by Dr. Randolph Stone, who believed that illness resulted from energy blockages. Polarity combines the manipulations of pressure points, massage, hydrotherapy, breathing exercises, and reflexology.

prenatal and perinatal psychology—Counseling that involves the examination of time spent in the womb, during labor, in delivery, and up to a few days afterward. Regressive techniques, such as hypnosis or breathwork, are used to look at the emotions, behavior, defense mechanisms, and attitudes—both positive and negative—that may result from these experiences.

pressotherapy—A system of bodywork generally used in rehabilitation therapy designed to gradually and progressively drain metabolic waste and facilitate cell regeneration. The technique involves hand massage and applying varying degrees of pressure.

psychosynthesis—Developed by Italian psychiatrist Roberto Assagioli in 1910. The term implies the process of growth and the integration of previously separate elements into a more unified whole. The technique is based on the belief that every human being has an enormous potential that largely goes unrecognized or unused. Psychosynthesis also maintains that the individual possesses the inner wisdom and knowledge of what is necessary for life processes at any given time. During sessions, a guide helps the individual identify inner resources, supports the process, and is attentive to what is happening.

qigong—An ancient Chinese system of healing that combines the use of breathing, meditation, and movement exercises to increase vital energy, boost immune functions, and improve circulation. Qigong has a variety of spellings, including chi kung.

rebirthing—Through a combination of breath exercises, meditation, and in some cases therapeutic bodywork, a counselor guides the patient back to a deep unconscious level to relive the birth experience. During a rebirthing session, many people remember details about their birth. From these details, they learn how decisions made at birth and in early childhood have affected their life and relationships. The technique is intended to dissolve tension and stress in the body while integrating the body and mind into a rejuvenated sense of awareness.

reflexology—A system of bodywork based on the idea that the feet and hands are maps of the entire body. Pressure is applied to nerve endings in the feet and hands to relieve chronic pain and stress.

reiki—Translated from the Japanese, *reiki* means "universal life energy," which is similar to that of the Chinese chi and the Indian prana or kundalini. Reiki is a hands-on method of healing that involves a practitioner touching the body to realign energies.

Rolfing—A system of bodywork, also known as structural integration, developed by the late Ida Rolf. Rolf was inspired by the method her osteopathic doctor used to successfully treat her for a kick from a horse. Rolf was also heavily influenced by hatha yoga and developed the Rolfing technique based on the idea that the body structure influences mental and physical processes. The method is a process of reeducating the body through movement and touch. It is intended to release patterns of stress and impaired function through lengthening and opening the patterns in the body's connective tissue, otherwise known as the myofascial system.

Roman pool—A stepdown whirlpool bath, for one or two persons.

Rubenfeld synergy—A method of healing designed to integrate body, mind, emotions, and spirit, developed by Ilana Rubenfeld, eminent healer and pioneer in the field of mind-body medicine. The technique is based on the theory that memories, emotions, and deep yearnings are stored in the body and can result in psychospiritual imbalances. Rubenfeld integrated the techniques of F. M. Alexander and Moshe Feldenkrais with Gestalt practice and Ericksonian hypnotherapy to create a method of compassionate and "listening" touch that opens doors to recognizing and expressing feelings. The method includes body-mind exercises to relax, stretch, and enhance awareness.

Russian bath—Steam bath used to flush toxins from the body.

salt glow—An exfoliation and cleansing treatment that involves lathering the body with moist salt grains.

seaweed wrap—A wrap using concentrated seawater and nutrient-packed seaweed; minerals, proteins, and vitamins are absorbed into the bloodstream to revitalize the skin and body.

shamanism—A religious practice found in many indigenous cultures that can involve attributing conscious life to natural objects, a belief in spirits separate from our bodies, and the idea that immaterial forces inhabit the universe. A shaman mediates between the visible and spirit worlds for divination, healing, and controlling events.

shiatsu—A Japanese system of bodywork that involves applying finger pressure to specific points throughout the body for a period of 3-10 seconds. The technique is used to "awaken" energy meridians throughout the body to relieve pain and prevent illness.

Shirodhara—Ayurvedic massage in which warm herbal oil is dropped onto the forehead and rubbed gently into the scalp and hair.

somatoemotional release—Physical, energetic, and verbal support used in conjunction with craniosacral therapy to help empower the client to identify emotional or physical trauma and find a positive solution.

Spa cuisine—Fresh, natural foods low in saturated fats and cholesterol, with an emphasis on whole grains, low-fat dairy products, lean protein, fresh fruit, fish, and vegetables, and an avoidance of added salt and products containing sodium, artificial colorings, flavoring, and preservatives.

sweat lodge—Native American body purification ceremonies.

Swedana—Herbal steam treatment used to reduce tension and release impurities through the skin.

Swiss shower—A multijet bath that alternates hot and cold water, often used after mud wraps and other body treatments.

tai chi—An ancient Chinese method of movement, sometimes described as the physical expression of the principles of Taoism. Movements are intended to connect body and mind.

Thai massage—A 2,500-year-old system of

bodywork that implements the techniques of stimulating pressure points, joint movement, and muscle stretching. The client lies fully clothed on a floor mat as a therapist increases the client's range of motion and flexibility by gently rocking the body and applying rhythmic acupressure combined with yogalike stretching.

thalassotherapy—Developed in the late 1800s by French biologist René Quinton, who initially demonstrated its therapeutic curative and preventive qualities. Authentic thalassotherapy treatments use water pumped directly from the ocean. Algae, mud, and sand used in treatments are also gathered from the shore at low tide. Fresh sea air is also a part of the cure.

therapeutic massage—A system of bodywork useful in controlling pain that targets specific areas of the body to correct posture, release toxins, and eliminate headaches and stress.

therapeutic touch—A system of bodywork developed in 1972 by Dora Kunz, past president of the Theosophical Society in America. Hands rarely touch the body during the treatment, with practitioners using slow, rhythmic hand movements between 2–6 inches away from the body to locate and release energy blockages.

Trager—A system of bodywork developed in the late 1920s by a medical doctor. Trager involves gentle and rhythmic manipulation, movement exercises, and movement reeducation.

trigger-point therapy—Also known as neuromuscular therapy. A method of deep-tissue massage therapy developed by Togi Kinnaman, president and founder of the Colorado Institute of Massage Therapy. The technique is intended to release stress through specific and sensitive hand movements and relaxation and self-care techniques. Through the use of a charting system, the therapist recognizes and locates stress/trigger points in the muscular system. The points are tender spots or bands of excess muscle tension within muscle groups.

tui na Chinese bodywork therapy—A 2,000-year-old system of bodywork that uses traditional Chinese medical theory concerning the flow of qi through the body's meridians as its basic therapeutic orientation. The method includes hand techniques to massage the muscles and tendons, acupressure techniques to directly affect the flow of qi, and manipulation techniques to realign the musculoskeletal and ligament relationships. Herbal poultices, compresses, liniments, and salves are also used to enhance the therapeutic effects.

vibrational healing—Also known as energy healing. A healing technique that utilizes the vibrations of gemstones and crystals to heal injuries or wounds, improve stress, and balance the body's natural energy systems (meridians and chakras). Gems and minerals can be taken orally or applied externally. Flower essences, color healing, and affirmations may also be used in vibrational healing.

Vichy shower—A large, rectangular showerhead situated above a cushioned, waterproof mat, equipped with several jets aimed at specific areas of the body for hydrotherapy treatments.

Watsu—An in-water form of massage developed by Harold Dull, director of Harbin Hot Springs in Middletown, California. The treatment involves cradling, pulling, stretching, and applying pressure to "energy centers," described in the Taoist creation myth.

yoga—A system of exercises based on Hindu philosophy rooted in the idea that the progressive discipline of the body leads to a connection with the universal spirit, self-liberation, and well-being. A discipline of stretching and toning the body through asana (postures), controlled deep breathing, relaxation techniques, and diet. A philosophy that advocates unity for mind, body, and spirit.

zero balancing—A form of bodywork developed by Dr. Fritz Frederick Smith that includes both structural and energetic balancing. Gentle holding and applied traction are used to stimulate energy flow through the body's structure to balance and relax the client and to make him or her feel more alert, open, and centered.

zero-point process—A psychospiritual development course offered through the Tree of Life Rejuvenation Center that examines methods for dissolving dysfunctional habits, beliefs, and identities. The process blends ancient and modern Eastern and Western philosophies of mind and spirit.

Spa Index
(Spas are listed by name)

Activity Index

Beauty/Relaxation Spas

AB
Alamo Plaza Spa at the Menger Hotel (TX), 174, 175
Birdwing Spa (MN), 84, 85

C
Canyon Ranch Health Resort (AZ), 152, 153
Canyon Ranch in the Berkshires Health Resort (MA), 8, 9
Centre de Santé d'Eastman (Canada), 190, 191
Centre for Well-Being at the Phoenician (AZ), 154, 155
Christine Center, The (WI), 96, 97
Coolfont Resort, Conference Center, and Health Spa (WV), 56, 57

DE
Deerfield Manor Spa (PA), 20, 21
Equinox, The (VT), 24, 25

FG
Foxhollow Life Enrichment and Healing Center (KY), 46, 47
Gold Lake Mountain Resort and Spa (CO), 64, 65
Golden Door Fitness Resort, The (CA), 108, 109
Grand Wailea Resort Hotel and Spa (HI), 134, 135
Greenbrier, The (WV), 58, 59

H–K
Harbin Hot Springs (CA), 110, 111
Heartland Health Spa (IL), 76, 77
Hills Health Ranch, The (Canada), 192, 193
Hollyhock (Canada), 194, 195
Hostería Las Quintas Resort Spa (Mexico), 210, 211
Hotel Qualton Club and Spa Vallarta (Mexico), 212, 213
Indian Springs Resort and Spa (CA), 114, 115
JW Marriott Ihilani Resort and Spa at Ko Olina (HI), 142, 143

Kenwood Inn and Spa, The (CA), 116, 117
Kerr House (OH), 92, 93

L
Lake Austin Spa Resort (TX), 178, 179
Lodge and Spa at Cordillera, The (CO), 70, 71
Lodge at Skylonda, The (CA), 118, 119

M
Marsh, The, A Center for Balance and Fitness (MN), 86, 87
Miraval, Life in Balance Resort and Spa (AZ), 158, 159
Mountain Trek Fitness Retreat and Health Spa (Canada), 198, 199

NOP
New Age Health Spa (NY), 14, 15
PGA National Resort and Spa (FL), 36, 37

R
Rancho La Puerta (Mexico), 218, 219
Red Mountain Resort and Spa (UT), 184, 185
Regency House Natural Health Spa (FL), 38, 39
Rio Caliente Hot Springs Spa (Mexico), 220, 221

S
Spa Atlantis Health and Fitness (FL), 40, 41
Spa Concept Bromont (Canada), 208, 209
Spa at Camelback Inn, Marriott, The (AZ), 160, 161
Spa at Chateau Elan, The (GA), 42, 43
Spa at Norwich Inn, The (CT), 2, 3

TU
Ten Thousand Waves (NM), 170, 171
Tennessee Fitness Spa (TN), 50, 51

V
Vatra Natural Weight Loss Spa (NY), 18, 19
Vista Clara Ranch Resort and Spa (NM), 172, 173

Acknowledgments

There are many people who contributed to the formation of this book. I wish to thank the staff at Avalon Travel Publishing for their participation with the project. In particular I would like to thank my editor Angelique Clarke who was committed to making positive changes that spoke of quality for the book. I'd also like to acknowledge Jennifer Miller for creating a strong foundation for this book, and the folks formerly at John Muir Publications for inviting me to author this guide.

The nature of writing this type of book requires assistance from many people. I'd like to thank all the owners, directors, employees and guests I communicated with at the various spas and healing retreats for their information, cooperation and support. I especially want to thank those people who invited me to be a guest at their spa or retreat. Traveling to various spas and healing centers was by far, the most rewarding part of my research.

I appreciate all my yoga students who eagerly awaited news about which new place I had visited. Your enthusiasm helped feed the project. I am forever grateful to the various teachers and healers who have touched my life and helped me to grow. Writing this book has reminded me of how wonderful it is to have people who heal in the world.

Finally, I am grateful to my family and friends who continually support my writing endeavors with such curiosity, enthusiasm and respect. Without mentioning names, I will simply say, you grace my life with your love.

About the Author

Annalisa Cunningham, MA Counseling, has been a certified hatha yoga instructor and massage therapist for more than 20 years. She specializes in gentle hatha yoga for mind/body healing, and stress-reduction lifestyle training. She is the author of *Yoga Vacations: A Guide to International Yoga Retreats*; and her first book: *Stretch & Surrender: A Guide to Yoga, Health and Relaxation for People in Recovery*. Combining her love of yoga, health, and travel, Annalisa offers annual yoga vacations in Mexico, Costa Rica, Hawaii, and Northern California.

For more information visit **www.opening-heartjourneys.com**

AVALON
TRAVEL
p u b l i s h i n g

How far will our travel guides take you? As far as you want.

Discover a rhumba-fueled nightspot in Old Havana, explore prehistoric tombs in Ireland, hike beneath California's centuries-old redwoods, or embark on a classic road trip along Route 66. Our guidebooks deliver solidly researched, trip-tested information—minus any generic froth—to help globetrotters or weekend warriors create an adventure uniquely their own.

And we're not just about the printed page. Public television viewers are tuning in to Rick Steves' new travel series, *Rick Steves' Europe*. On the Web, readers can cruise the virtual black top with *Road Trip USA* author Jamie Jensen and learn travel industry secrets from Edward Hasbrouck of *The Practical Nomad*.

In print. On TV. On the Internet.

We supply the information. The rest is up to you.

Avalon Travel Publishing

Something for everyone

www.travelmatters.com

Avalon Travel Publishing guides are available at your favorite book or travel store.

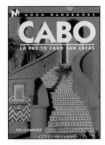